lonely

Bulgarian

Phrasebook & Dictionary

Alexander

...rcher Naomi Parker

Thanks

James Hardy, Wayne Murphy, Mazzy Prinsep, Angela Tinson,
Saralinda Turner, Maja Vatrić, Branislava Vladisavljevic

Published by Lonely Planet Global Limited
CRN 554153

3rd Edition – June 2024
ISBN 978 1 78657 590 6
Text © Lonely Planet 2024
Cover Image Plovdiv, Bulgaria, Andrea Armellin/4Corners Images ©

Printed in Malaysia   10 9 8 7 6 5 4 3 2 1

Contact lonelyplanet.com/contact

MIX
Paper from
responsible sources
FSC™ C021741

acknowledgments

Lonely Planet would like to acknowledge the following people for their contributions to this phrasebook:

Ronelle Alexander for the comprehensive translations, cultural information and extensive notes on Bulgarian grammar and pronunciation. Ronelle teaches at the University of California in Berkeley, California. She travels frequently to Bulgaria, both its cities and villages, and has grown to love the country and its culture over the years.

Among Ronelle's many Bulgarian-connected friends, those who have given input on this book, and whom she wishes to acknowledge, include Lauren Brody, Olga Mladenova, Malvina Rousseva, Milena Savova, Roumen Starkovski, Vladimir and Kiril Zhobov, and Aglaia and Kremena Zhobova.

make the most of this phrasebook ...

Anyone can speak another language! It's all about confidence. Don't worry if you can't remember your school language lessons or if you've never learnt a language before. Even if you learn the very basics (on the inside covers of this book), your travel experience will be the better for it. You have nothing to lose and everything to gain when the locals hear you making an effort.

finding things in this book

For easy navigation, this book is in sections. The Basics chapters are the ones you'll thumb through time and again. The Practical section covers basic travel situations like catching transport and finding a bed. The Social section gives you conversational phrases, pick-up lines, the ability to express opinions – so you can get to know people. Food has a section all of its own: gourmets and vegetarians are covered and local dishes feature. Safe Travel equips you with health and police phrases, just in case. Remember the colours of each section and you'll find everything easily; or use the comprehensive Index. Otherwise, check the two-way traveller's Dictionary for the word you need.

being understood

Throughout this book you'll see coloured phrases on each page. They're phonetic guides to help you pronounce the language. Start with them to get a feel for how the language sounds. The pronunciation chapter in Basics will explain more, but you can be confident that if you read the coloured phrase, you'll be understood.

communication tips

Body language, ways of doing things, sense of humour – all have a role to play in every culture. 'Local talk' boxes show you common ways of saying things, or everyday language to drop into conversation. 'Listen for ...' boxes supply the phrases you may hear. They start with the foreign language and then lead in to the phonetic guide and the English translation.

about bulgarian 8

map 8   introduction 9

basics 11

pronunciation 11
vowel sounds 11
consonant sounds 11
word stress & intonation 12
reading & writing 13

a–z phrasebuilder 15
contents 15
adjectives & adverbs 17
articles 18
be 19
demonstratives 19
gender 20
have 20
negatives 21
nouns 22
personal pronouns 22
plurals 25
possessives 25
prepositions 27

questions 27
verbs 28
word order 32
glossary 33

language difficulties 35

numbers & amounts 37
cardinal numbers 37
ordinal numbers 38
fractions & decimals 39
useful amounts 40

time & dates 41
telling the time 41
the calendar 42
present 43
past 44
future 45
during the day 45

money 47

practical 49

transport 49
getting around 49
tickets 51
luggage 52
plane 53
bus & coach 54
train 55
boat 56
taxi 57
car & motorbike 58
bicycle 62

border crossing 63
border crossing 63
at customs 64

directions 65

accommodation 69
finding accommodation 69
booking ahead &
checking in 70
requests & queries 73
complaints 74
checking out 75
camping 76
renting 77
staying with locals 78

shopping 79
looking for 79
making a purchase 80
bargaining 82

CONTENTS

5

books & reading........................83
clothes..................................84
hairdressing............................84
music & DVD..............................85
video & photography.....................86
repairs...................................88
communications **89**
the internet.............................89
mobile/cell phone.......................90
phone.....................................91
post office...............................94
banking **95**
sightseeing **97**
getting in................................98

tours.....................................99
business **101**
doing business.........................101
looking for
a job....................................103
senior & disabled
travellers **105**
children **107**
travelling with children.......107
talking with children...........109
talking about children.........110

social 111

meeting people..................**111**
basics.................................. 111
greetings & goodbyes........112
addressing people..............113
making conversation.........114
nationalities......................116
age.....................................116
occupations & studies........117
family.................................118
farewells............................120
interests...........................**121**
common interests...............121
music..................................122
cinema & theatre................124
feelings & opinions............**127**
feelings..............................127
opinions.............................128
politics & social issues.........129
the environment.................131
going out..........................**133**
where to go........................133
invitations.........................134
responding to
invitations.........................136
arranging to meet..............137
drugs..................................138

romance...........................**139**
asking someone out...........139
pick-up lines......................140
rejections...........................140
getting closer....................141
sex.....................................142
love....................................143
problems............................144
leaving...............................144
beliefs & cultural
differences **145**
religion..............................145
cultural differences............146
art...................................**147**
sport...............................**149**
sporting interests..............149
going to a game.................150
playing sport......................151
fishing................................153
skiing.................................154
soccer/football...................155
water sports.......................156
outdoors..........................**157**
hiking.................................157
beach..................................159
weather..............................160
flora & fauna......................161

food 163

eating out **163**
  basics.................................... 163
  finding a place to eat 164
  at the restaurant 165
  at the table........................... 168
  talking food 168
  methods of preparation.... 170
  nonalcoholic drinks 171
  alcoholic drinks 171
  in the bar 172

  drinking up 174
self-catering **175**
  buying food........................... 175
  cooking utensils.................. 178
vegetarian &
special meals **179**
  ordering food........................ 179
  special diets & allergies 180
menu decoder **181**

safe travel...189

essentials **189**
  emergencies.......................... 189
  police 190
health................................... **193**
  doctor 193
  symptoms & conditions 196

  women's health.................... 198
  allergies.................................. 200
  parts of the body 201
  alternative treatments....... 202
  pharmacist............................ 202
  dentist.................................... 204

dictionaries 205

english–bulgarian
  dictionary 205

bulgarian–english
  dictionary 237

index 251

finder..255

bulgarian

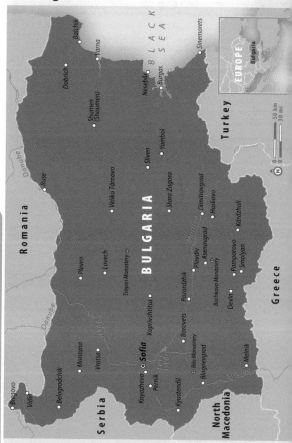

official language

For more details, see **About Bulgarian**

ABOUT BULGARIAN

Surprisingly, the name of the oldest South Slavic literary language, Bulgarian, isn't of Slavic origin at all. It's one of a handful of words remaining in Bulgarian from the language of the Bulgars, a Turkic people who invaded the eastern Balkans in the late 7th century. Along with their language, they assimilated with the local Slavs who had crossed the Danube and settled in the Balkan peninsula at the dawn of the 6th century.

As a member of the South Slavic group of languages, Bulgarian has Macedonian and Serbian as its closest relatives. However, it also shares similarities with the non-Slavic languages in the so-called Balkan linguistic union (Romanian, Albanian and Greek), as a result of multilingualism and prolonged contact between the Balkan peoples. These foreign influences explain many of its grammatical features – for example, its simplified noun system, which sets Bulgarian (and Macedonian) apart from other Slavic languages. In addition, numerous Turkish words entered Bulgarian over five centuries of Ottoman rule. In the 19th century, many of these Turkish loanwords were eliminated from the language. Their place was partially filled by Russian words, as Russian has influenced Bulgarian through both Bulgaria's ties with the Orthodox Church and long-standing cultural links with Russia.

Old Bulgarian (which is very similar to Old Church Slavonic) was the first Slavic language recorded in

at a glance ...

language name:
Bulgarian

name in language:
български
buhl·gar·skee

language family:
South Slavic

approximate number of speakers: 9 million

key country: Bulgaria

close relatives:
Macedonian, Serbian, Russian

about bulgarian

written form in religious literature from the 9th century. The central figures in the development of the Slavic literary language were Saints Cyril and Methodius, missionaries of the Byzantine emperor who invented the Glagolitic alphabet around AD 863 and used it to translate Greek liturgical texts into Old Church Slavonic. Their disciples devised the Cyrillic alphabet (based on Greek and Glagolitic) in which Bulgarian has been written ever since.

In its modern version, standardised after the last spelling reform in 1945, the Bulgarian alphabet is very similar to the Russian Cyrillic alphabet. Today, Bulgarians celebrate St Cyril and Methodius Day as a national holiday on the 24th of May (also known as the Day of Bulgarian Culture or the Cyrillic Alphabet Day). On joining the European Union in January 2007, Bulgaria also had the honour of introducing the Cyrillic alphabet to the EU as its third official writing system, alongside the Roman and Greek alphabets.

Modern Bulgarian has about 10 million speakers and is the official language of Bulgaria, with Bulgarian-speaking minorities in Ukraine, Moldova, Romania, Serbia, Hungary, Greece and Turkey. The literary standard is based on the northeastern dialects. The transitional dialects spoken around the borders between Bulgaria, Serbia and North Macedonia are very similar to one another and this has provoked sensitive political issues over the centuries.

This book gives you the practical phrases you need to get by as well as all the fun, spontaneous phrases that lead to a more successful interaction with Bulgarian people and a deeper understanding of their culture. Local knowledge, new relationships and a sense of satisfaction are on the tip of your tongue. So don't just stand there, say something!

abbreviations used in this book

a	adjective	n	(after English) noun
adv	adverb	n	(after Bulgarian) neuter
f	feminine	pl	plural
inf	informal	pol	polite
lit	literally	sg	singular
m	masculine	v	verb

Even if you're not familiar with the Cyrillic alphabet, you'll soon realise that Bulgarian is easy to read. There's generally a one-to-one correspondence between the written form and pronunciation, and the sounds found in Bulgarian are familiar to English speakers. Read the coloured pronunciation guides as if you were reading English, and then move on to the Cyrillic script as you gain confidence.

vowel sounds

Bulgarian vowel sounds all have equivalents in English. To make yourself sound more like a native, just remember that in Bulgarian vowels in unstressed syllables are generally pronounced shorter and weaker than in stressed syllables.

symbol	english equivalent	bulgarian example	transliteration
a	father	дата	*da*·ta
ai	aisle	май	mai
e	ten	лек	lek
ee	feet	бира	*bee*·ra
o	lot	вода	vo·*da*
oo	boot	тук	took
uh	ago	къде, часа	kuh·*de*, cha·*suh*

consonant sounds

Bulgarian consonant sounds are pretty straightforward, as they all have equivalents in English. The only sound you might trip over is ts, which can occur at the start of words. Try saying 'cats', then 'ats', then 'ts' to get the idea.

symbol	english equivalent	bulgarian example	transliteration
b	bit	брат	brat
ch	chop	чист	cheest
d	day	душ	doosh
f	fun	фенерче	fe·ner·che
g	goat	гума	goo·ma
h	hard	хотел	ho·tel
k	king	карта	kar·ta
l	lump	билет	bee·let
m	my	масло	mas·lo
n	not	нула	noo·la
p	put	грип	greep
r	rib	утро	oot·ro
s	sit	син	seen
sh	ship	шест	shest
t	ton	сто	sto
ts	cats	крадец	kra·dets
v	vet	вчера	vche·ra
y	yes	брой	broy
z	zoo	зад	zad
zh	pleasure	плаж	plazh

word stress & intonation

There's no general rule regarding word stress in Bulgarian – stress can fall on any syllable and sometimes changes in different grammatical forms of the same word. Just follow our coloured pronunciation guides, in which the stressed syllable is in italics.

An important aspect of Bulgarian pronunciation is stress on certain single-syllable words following negation. Several commonly used single-syllable words (given in the list on the opposite page) are not stressed, but lean upon the following word and are pronounced together with it. However, when one of these words comes in between не ne (not) and a verb, it carries a very strong stress, as shown in the example phrases.

ви	vee	са	suh
ги	gee	се	se
го	go	си	see
е	e	сме	sme
им	eem	сте	ste
й	ee	съм	suhm
ме	me	те	te
ми	mee	ти	tee
ни	nee	я	ya

I feel well.	Добре ми е.	do·*bre* mee e
I don't feel well.	Не ми е добре.	ne *mee* e do·*bre*
My name is …	Аз се казвам …	*az* se *kaz*·vam …
My name isn't …	Аз не се казвам …	*az* ne se *kaz*·vam …

For reasons of consistency, in our coloured pronunciation guides word stress is only marked (with italics) in words with more than one syllable, but if you keep this general rule in mind you can easily apply it to relevant phrases in this book.

reading & writing

Bulgarian spelling is almost entirely phonetic, meaning that there's generally a one-to-one correspondence between the letters and the sounds they represent. There are some exceptions, however. For example, there are a few instances when the letter 'a' is pronounced uh (not a), even (and in fact most noticeably) when accented. You don't have to worry about these rules, though, as our coloured pronunciation guides show the correct pronunciation of sounds in the context of any given phrase.

Bulgarian uses the Cyrillic alphabet, which was developed in the 9th century on the basis of the Greek alphabet. In its modern version, it's very similar to the Russian Cyrillic alphabet. Note that the letter 'ь' (er ma·luhk) has no sound of its own – it appears only before the vowel 'о' to indicate that the preceding consonant is pronounced 'soft' (ie followed by a slight 'y' sound), eg шофьор sho·*fyor* (driver). There's no upper-case form of this letter as it never occurs at the beginning of a word. Be careful not to confuse it with the letter 'ъ' (er gol·*yam*), pronounced uh (as in '**a**go'), which has both upper- and lower-case forms and is a fully fledged vowel in Bulgarian.

For spelling purposes (eg when you spell your name to book into a hotel), the pronunciation of each letter is provided in the first box below. The letters are presented in alphabetical order (reading down the page) and words in the **menu decoder** and **bulgarian–english dictionary** are also listed in this order.

alphabet

А а	a	К к	kuh	Ф ф	fuh
Б б	buh	Л л	luh	Х х	huh
В в	vuh	М м	muh	Ц ц	tsuh
Г г	guh	Н н	nuh	Ч ч	chuh
Д д	duh	О о	o	Ш ш	shuh
Е е	e	П п	puh	Щ щ	shtuh
Ж ж	zhuh	Р р	ruh	Ъ ъ	er gol·*yam*
З з	zuh	С с	suh	ь	er *ma*·luhk
И и	ee	Т т	tuh	Ю ю	yoo
Й й	ee *krat*·ko	У у	oo	Я я	ya

Just as letters in the Latin alphabet look different when they're in roman font (like 'a') as opposed to italics (like '*a*'), so do some Cyrillic letters. To eyes accustomed to the English alphabet, understanding that 'дата' and '*дата*' are both forms of *da*·ta (date) can be a challenge. Here's the Bulgarian Cyrillic alphabet in both roman and italic font to help you with menus, schedules and signs.

italic cyrillic

Аа	Бб	Вв	Гг	Дд	Ее	Жж	Зз	Ии	Йй
Аа	*Бб*	*Вв*	*Гг*	*Дд*	*Ее*	*Жж*	*Зз*	*Ии*	*Йй*
Кк	Лл	Мм	Нн	Оо	Пп	Рр	Сс	Тт	Уу
Кк	*Лл*	*Мм*	*Нн*	*Оо*	*Пп*	*Рр*	*Сс*	*Тт*	*Уу*
Фф	Хх	Цц	Чч	Шш	Щщ	Ъъ	ь	Юю	Яя
Фф	*Хх*	*Цц*	*Чч*	*Шш*	*Щщ*	*Ъъ*	*ь*	*Юю*	*Яя*

contents

The list below shows which grammatical structures you can use to say what you want. Look under each function – in alphabetical order – for information on how to build your own phrases. For example, to tell the taxi driver where your hotel is, look for **giving instructions** and you'll be directed to information on **demonstratives** and **prepositions**. A **glossary** of grammatical terms is included at the end of this chapter to help you.

asking questions
questions   27

describing people/things
adjectives & adverbs   17   be   19

doing things
personal pronouns   22   verbs   28

giving instructions
demonstratives   19   prepositions   27

indicating location
demonstratives   19   prepositions   27

making statements
be   19   personal pronouns   22
verbs   28   word order   32

naming people/things

articles	18	gender	20
nouns	22	plurals	25

negating

negatives	21

pointing things out

demonstratives	19	prepositions	27

possessing

have	20	personal pronouns	22
possessives	25		

adjectives & adverbs

Adjectives in Bulgarian come before the noun they modify. They change form to agree with the noun in gender and number, and can have the definite article ('the' in English) attached to them (see **articles**, **gender** and **plurals**). In the singular, masculine adjectives usually end in a consonant or in -и -i, feminine adjectives in -a -a and neuter ones in -o -o. Plural adjectives of all genders end in -и -i. In the **dictionaries** and word lists in this book, adjectives are given in the masculine form only.

singular		
nice city	хубав град m	*hoo*·bav grad
nice picture	хубава картина f	*hoo*·ba·va kar·*tee*·na
nice village	хубаво село n	*hoo*·ba·vo *se*·lo
plural		
nice cities	хубави градове m	*hoo*·ba·vee gra·do·*ve*
nice pictures	хубави картини f	*hoo*·ba·vee kar·*tee*·ne
nice villages	хубави села n	*hoo*·ba·vee se·*la*

Adverbs don't change their form and can be placed before or after the verb they refer to (see also **verbs**). Adverbs often have the neuter singular form of adjectives (ending in -o -o). Less frequently they end in -e -e or -и -i.

fast train	бърз влак	buhrz vlak
	(lit: fast train)	
Drive fast.	Карай бързо.	*ka*·rai *buhr*·zo
	(lit: drive-you fast)	

articles

Bulgarian has only a definite article (like 'the' in English) – so 'a room' is стая *sta·ya* (lit: room) and 'the room' is стаята *sta·ya·ta* (lit: room-the). As shown by this example, the definite article in Bulgarian is an ending attached to the noun. The table below shows different forms of the definite article in the singular depending on the noun's gender. In the plural, nouns which end in -a -a (in their plural form) add the article -та -ta, and all other nouns add the article -те -te (see **gender** and **plurals**).

a city	град m	grad
a picture	картина f	kar·*tee*·na
a village	село n	*se*·lo

singular		
the city	градът m	gra·*duht*
the picture	картината f	kar·*tee*·na·ta
the village	селото n	*se*·lo·to
plural		
the cities	градовете m	gra·do·*ve*·te
the pictures	картините f	kar·*tee*·nee·te
the villages	селата n	se·*la*·ta

When the definite article is added to masculine nouns, they have a subject form (ending in -ът -uht) and an object form (ending in -a, but pronounced as if it were spelled -ъ -uh).

The city is big.	Градът е голям.	gra·*duht* e go·*lyam*
	(lit: city-the is big)	
We live in the city.	Живеем в града.	zhee·*ve*·em v gra·*duh*
	(lit: live-we in city-the)	

If the noun is accompanied by an adjective, the definite article is attached to the adjective instead of the noun. For masculine nouns the article on the adjective takes the form -ият -ee·yuht.

the big suitcase	големият куфар m (lit: big-the suitcase)	go·le·mee·yuht koo·far
the small bag	малката чанта f (lit: small-the bag)	mal·ka·ta chan·ta
the nice village	хубавото село n (lit: nice-the village)	hoo·ba·vo·to se·lo

be

describing people/things • making statements

In Bulgarian, the verb съм suhm (be) changes in person and number to match the subject of the sentence. The present tense forms of the verb 'be' are given in the table below. See also **negatives** and **verbs**.

be – present tense			
I	am	съм	suhm
you sg inf	are	си	see
you sg pol		сте	ste
he/she/it	is	е	e
we		сме	sme
you pl	are	сте	ste
they		са	suh

demonstratives

giving instructions • indicating location • pointing things out

Words for 'this' and 'that' in Bulgarian change form for number, and in the singular for gender as well, to agree with the noun they refer to. They're placed before the noun. See also **gender** and **plurals**.

demonstratives					
	m sg	f sg	n sg	pl	
this	този *to·zee*	тази *ta·zee*	това *to·va*	these	тези *te·zee*
that	онзи *on·zee*	онази *o·na·zee*	онова *o·no·va*	those	онези *o·ne·zee*

gender

naming people/things

Bulgarian nouns have grammatical gender – masculine (m), feminine (f) or neuter (n). It's important to know a noun's gender, as it dictates the form of the adjective, definite article or demonstrative accompanying the noun, as well as the form of the pronoun used to refer to the noun.

The rules for determining the gender of nouns are fairly regular: most masculine nouns end in a consonant, feminine nouns generally end in -a -a or -я -ya (although there are a number of feminine nouns which end in a consonant), and neuter nouns usually end in -e -e or -o -o. All the nouns in this book's word lists, **dictionaries** and **menu decoder** have gender marked. See also **plurals**.

град m	grad	**city**
картина f	kar·*tee*·na	**picture**
село n	*se*·lo	**village**

have

possessing

An easy way of expressing possession in Bulgarian is by using the verb имам *ee*·mam (have). The present tense forms of this verb, both affirmative and negative, are shown in the tables below. See also **possessives**.

have – present tense (affirmative)			
I		имам	*ee*·mam
you sg inf	have	имаш	*ee*·mash
you sg pol		имате	ee·ma·te
he/she/it	has	има	*ee*·ma
we		имаме	ee·ma·me
you pl	have	имате	ee·ma·te
they		имат	*ee*·mat

have – present tense (negative)			
I		нямам	*nya*·mam
you sg inf	don't have	нямаш	*nya*·mash
you sg pol		нямате	nya·ma·te
he/she/it	doesn't have	няма	*nya*·ma
we		нямаме	nya·ma·me
you pl	don't have	нямате	nya·ma·te
they		нямат	*nya*·mat

negatives

negating

To form negatives in Bulgarian, simply put the word не ne (not) before the verb. Bulgarian also uses double negatives, as shown below. For the negative forms of 'have', see above.

I eat fish.	Ям риба. (lit: eat-I fish)	yam *ree*·ba
I don't eat eggs.	Не ям яйца. (lit: not eat-I eggs)	ne yam yai·*tsa*
I don't eat any meat.	Не ям никакво месо. (lit: not eat-I no-sort meat)	ne yam *nee*·kak·vo me·*so*

nouns

Bulgarian nouns take different endings in plural and when they are used with a definite article. For more information, see **articles**, **gender** and **plurals**.

personal pronouns

doing things • making statements • possessing

Personal pronouns ('I', 'you' etc) are frequently omitted in Bulgarian as the subject of a sentence, if the verb endings make it clear who is referred to (see **verbs**). Their main use in the subject role is for emphasis.

Do you eat meat?

Ядеш ли месо?　　　　　　　　ya·*desh* lee me·*so*
(lit: eat-you *question particle* meat)

I don't eat meat.

Не ям месо.　　　　　　　　　ne yam me·*so*
(lit: no eat-I meat)

I'm from Australia, and he's from America.

Аз съм от Австралия,　　　　　az suhm ot av·*stra*·lee·ya
а той е от Америка.　　　　　　a toy e ot a·*me*·ree·ka
(lit: I am from Australia
and he is from America)

subject pronouns					
I	аз	az	we	ние	*nee*·e
you sg inf	ти	tee	you pl	вие	*vee*·e
you sg pol	вие	*vee*·e			
he	той	toy			
she	тя	tya	they	те	te
it	то	to			

BASICS

22

Bulgarian has both an informal and a polite word for 'you' – basically, unless you know the person well, use the polite form, **вие** *vee·e*, and the matching second-person plural form of the verb. See the box **all about you** on page 138 for more information. Note also that 'it' is expressed by pronouns meaning 'he/him' or 'she/her' if the noun it refers to is of masculine or feminine gender.

The direct and indirect object pronouns ('me', 'us' etc) have both a short and a long version (separated in the tables below with a slash). Note that the long forms of the indirect object pronouns correspond to those of the direct object pronouns preceded by the preposition **на** na (to) (eg like 'me' and 'to me' in English).

direct object pronouns (short/long)

me	ме/мене	me/*me·ne*	us	ни/нас	nee/nas
you sg inf	те/тебе	te/*te·*be	you pl	ви/вас	vee/vas
you sg pol	ви/вас	vee/vas			
him	го/него	go/*ne·*go			
her	я/нея	ya/*ne·*ya	them	ги/тях	gee/tyah
it	го/него	go/*ne·*go			

indirect object pronouns (short/long)

me	ми/ на мене	mee/ na *me·*ne	us	ни/ на нас	nee/ na nas
you sg inf	ти/ на тебе	tee/ na *te·*be	you pl	ви/ на вас	vee/ na vas
you sg pol	ви/ на вас	vee/ na vas			
him	му/ на него	moo/ na *ne·*go			
her	й/ на нея	ee/ na *ne·*ya	them	им/ на тях	eem/ na tyah
it	го/ на него	go/ na *ne·*go			

The long forms are used for contrast or after prepositions, while the short forms are used elsewhere. With verbs, the short forms of direct object pronouns are more frequently used than the long ones, but with prepositions, only the long forms are used.

I gave it to him.

Дадох му га.   *da*·doh moo ga
(lit: gave-I to-him it)

I gave it to her, but not to him.

Дадох га на нея,   *da*·doh ga na *ne*·ya
а не на него.   a ne na *ne*·go
(lit: gave-I it to her but not to him)

The short forms of the direct object pronouns are normally placed before the verb (unless the verb is first in the sentence, in which case they come after the verb), while the long forms are placed after the verb.

He knows me.

Той ме познава.   toy me poz·*na*·va
(lit: he me knows-he)

He knows me, but not you.

Той познава мене,   toy poz·*na*·va *me*·ne
а не тебе.   a ne *te*·be
(lit: he knows-he me but not you)

Sometimes the short form is used together with the long form in the sentence to refer to the same object.

I'm cold.

На мене ми е студено.   na *me*·ne mee e stoo·*de*·no
(lit: to me to-me is cold)

The short form can also be used to refer to a noun object in the same sentence when it's necessary to make clear that the noun is acting as an object rather than a subject.

Mara doesn't know that person.

Мара този човек   *ma*·ra *to*·zee cho·*vek*
не го познава.   ne go poz·*na*·va
(lit: Mara that person not him knows-she)

See also **gender** and **plurals**.

plurals

Plurals of nouns are formed by using a variety of endings – the most common endings are shown in the table below. Note that masculine nouns which denote objects have separate forms when they're used with cardinal numbers and words expressing quantity, eg 'several'. For more on these forms, see the **numbers & amounts** chapter. See also **gender**.

singular & plural nouns				
pencil	молив m	mo·leev	моливи m pl	mo·lee·vee
city	град m	grad	градове m pl	gra·do·ve
picture	картина f	kar·tee·na	картини f pl	kar·tee·nee
candle	свещ f	svesht	свещи f pl	svesh·tee
village	село n	se·lo	села n pl	se·la
piece	парче n	par·che	парчета n pl	par·che·ta

possessives

As in English, possession can be expressed in Bulgarian by using the verb 'have' (see **have**) or by using possessive adjectives (eg 'my' and 'your') before the noun. Just like other adjectives, Bulgarian possessive adjectives can have the definite article attached to them, and they change to match the number and gender of the noun they go with (see **articles**, **gender** and **plurals**).

possessive adjectives				
	m sg	f sg	n sg	pl
my	мой moy	моя *mo·ya*	мое *mo·ye*	мои *mo·yee*
your sg inf	твой tvoy	твоя *tvo·ya*	твое *tvo·ye*	твои *tvo·yee*
your sg pol	ваш vash	ваша *va·sha*	ваше *va·she*	ваши *va·shee*
his	негов *ne·gov*	негова *ne·go·va*	негово *ne·go·vo*	негови *ne·go·vee*
her	неин *ne·een*	нейна *ney·na*	нейно *ney·no*	нейни *ney·nee*
our	наш nash	наша *na·sha*	наше *na·she*	наши *na·shee*
your pl	ваш vash	ваша *va·sha*	ваше *va·she*	ваши *va·shee*
their	техен *te·hen*	тяхна *tyah·na*	тяхно *tyah·no*	техни *teh·nee*

Another way of expressing possession is by placing the short form of the indirect pronoun after the thing possessed.

my handbag
    чантата ми   *chan·ta·ta mee*
    (lit: handbag-the to-me)

If the possessor is indicated with a noun, it must be expressed using the construction 'на na (of) + noun' after the object possessed:

the girl's handbag
    чантата на момичето   *chan·ta·ta na mo·mee·che·to*
    (lit: handbag-the of girl-the)

prepositions

giving instructions • indicating location •
pointing things out

In Bulgarian, prepositions are used to show relationships
between words in a sentence, just like in English.

prepositions					
about	за	za	on	на	na
at	на	na	to (place)	в	v
from (place)	от	ot	to (time)	до	do
from (time)	от	ot	with	с	s
in	в	v	without	без	bez

For the use of the preposition 'to' with indirect objects, see
personal pronouns. For the use of the preposition 'of' with
direct objects to indicate possession, see **possessives**.

questions

asking questions

To form a yes/no question in Bulgarian, place the verb at the
start of the sentence and insert the particle ли lee (indicating a
question) immediately after the main verb.

I speak English.
Говоря английски.   go·*vor*·yuh ang·*leey*·skee
(lit: speak-I English)

Do you speak English?
Говорите ли английски?   go·*vo*·ree·te lee ang·*leey*·skee
(lit: speak-you *question particle* English)

To ask for specific information, just add one of the question
words (shown on the next page) to the start of a sentence:

question words		
How?	Как?	kak
How many/much?	Колко?	*kol·ko*
What?	Какво?	*kak·vo*
When?	Кога?	ko·*ga*
Where?	Къде?	kuh·*de*
Who?	Кой? m sg Коя? f sg Кое? n sg Кои? pl	koy ko·*ya* ko·*e* ko·*ee*
Why?	Защо?	zash·*to*

verbs

doing things • making statements

There's no infinitive in Bulgarian. In dictionaries, Bulgarian verbs are given in the first person singular present tense form. The present tense form is used after the conjunction да da (that) in a meaning similar to the English infinitive.

I want to learn Bulgarian.

Искам да уча   *ees*·kam da *oo*·chuh
български   *buhl*·gar·skee
(lit: want-I that learn-I Bulgarian)

Verbs in Bulgarian change form to match the person and number of the subject in a sentence. There are three different classes of verbs, depending on the verb stem. The verb stem is the basic form of the verb left after taking off the ending -ш -sh from the present tense second person singular form of the verb. The three classes are: the -e -e stem (eg пишеш *pee*·shesh 'write'), the -и -i stem (eg говориш go·*vo*·reesh 'speak') and the -a -a stem (eg искаш *ees*·kash 'want').

verbal aspect

Most Bulgarian verbs have two 'aspects' – meaning that an English verb can usually be translated into Bulgarian in two different ways (eg 'answer' can be either отговоря ot·go·*vor*·yuh or отговарям ot·go·*var*·yam). The first form is called the 'perfective aspect' and refers to completed single actions in the present, past or future. The second form is called the 'imperfective aspect' and is used for habitual or continuing actions in the present, past or future. Note, however, that there are a number of very common verbs referring to basic actions which are not marked for aspect – their form simply designates the action (eg 'drink', 'eat', 'read', 'speak'). Where applicable, Bulgarian verbs in this book's **dictionaries** are given in both perfective and imperfective aspects.

I saw him yesterday.
Вчера го видях.   vche·ra go vee·*dyah*
(lit: yesterday him saw-I – *ie perfective aspect*)

I used to see him often.
Виждал съм го често.   veezh·dal suhm go *ches*·to
(lit: seen am-I him often – *ie imperfective aspect*)

present tense

The present tense is formed from the verb stem (the -е -e, -и -i or -a -a stem) and a set of endings. See also **negatives**.

'read' – present tense (-е stem)

I		чета	che·*tuh*
you sg inf	read	четеш	che·*tesh*
you sg pol		четете	che·*te*·te
he/she	reads	чете	che·*te*
we		четем	che·*tem*
you pl	read	четете	che·*te*·te
they		четат	che·*tuht*

a–z phrasebuilder

'speak' – present tense (-i stem)			
I		говоря	go·*vor*·yuh
you sg inf	speak	говориш	go·*vor*·eesh
you sg pol		говорите	go·*vor*·ee·te
he/she	speaks	говори	go·*vor*·ee
we		говорим	go·*vor*·eem
you pl	speak	говорите	go·*vor*·ee·te
they		говорят	go·*vor*·yuht

'want' – present tense (-a stem)			
I		искам	*ees*·kam
you sg inf	want	искаш	*ees*·kash
you sg pol		искате	*ees*·ka·te
he/she	wants	иска	*ees*·ka
we		искаме	*ees*·ka·me
you pl	want	искате	*ees*·ka·te
they		искат	*ees*·kat

past tense

There are two simple past tenses in Bulgarian (plus several compound ones). The two simple past tenses are the imperfect tense (used to describe an action in progress over a period of time), and the aorist tense (used to describe the fact of an action – usually completed, but not necessarily). The examples of these tenses are shown in the tables on the page opposite. Both tenses can be used in both the perfective and imperfective aspects. See also **negatives**.

'read' – imperfect tense			
I	was reading	четях	che·*tyah*
you sg inf	were reading	четеше	che·*te*·she
you sg pol		четяхте	che·*tyah*·te
he/she	was reading	четеше	che·*te*·she
we		четяхме	che·*tyah*·me
you pl	were reading	четяхте	che·*tyah*·te
they		четяха	che·*tya*·ha

'read' – aorist tense			
I		четох	che·*toh*
you sg inf		чете	che·*te*
you sg pol		четохте	che·*toh*·te
he/she	read	чете	che·*te*
we		четохме	che·*toh*·me
you pl		четохте	che·*toh*·te
they		четоха	che·*to*·ha

future tense

The future tense is formed from the present tense forms and the word ще shte. For the negative forms, the construction няма да *nya*·ma da is used instead of ще.

'read' – future tense (affirmative)			
I		ще чета	shte che·*tuh*
you sg inf		ще четеш	shte che·*tesh*
you sg pol		ще четете	shte che·*te*
he/she	will read	ще чете	shte che·*te*·te
we		ще четем	shte che·*tem*
you pl		ще четете	shte che·*te*·te
they		ще четат	shte che·*tuht*

'read' – future tense (negative)			
I		няма да чета	*nya·ma da che·tuh*
you sg inf		няма да четеш	*nya·ma da che·tesh*
you sg pol		няма да четете	*nya·ma da che·te·te*
he/she	will not read	няма да чете	*nya·ma da che·te*
we		няма да четем	*nya·ma da che·tem*
you pl		няма да четете	*nya·ma da che·te·te*
they		няма да четат	*nya·ma da che·tuht*

word order

making statements

In Bulgarian, there are strict rules regarding the position of single-syllable words relative to one another and to the verb when used in a sentence with negation. Generally, however, you can stick to the subject–verb–object order, just like in English.

Ivan doesn't eat meat.
Иван не яде месо.   ee·*van* ne ya·*de* me·*so*
(lit: Ivan not eats-he meat)

See also **negatives** and **questions**.

glossary

adjective	a word that describes something – 'The invention of the **Cyrillic** alphabet …'
adverb	a word that explains how an action is done – '… is **traditionally** linked with the Byzantine missionaries St Cyril and Methodius …'
article	the words 'a', 'an' and 'the'
aspect	most Bulgarian *verbs* express one of two aspects – *perfective* or *imperfective*
demonstrative	a word that means 'this' or 'that'
direct object	the thing or person in the sentence that's the direct recipient of the action – '… who invented **the Glagolitic alphabet** in the 9th century …'
gender	classification of *nouns* into classes (masculine, feminine and neuter), requiring other words (eg *adjectives*) to belong to the same class
imperfective	verbal *aspect* denoting a repeated action or an action in progress – '… while they **were translating** Greek texts into Old Church Slavonic.'
indirect object	the person or thing in the sentence that is the indirect recipient of the action – 'They contributed **to the development** of the Cyrillic alphabet …'
infinitive	the dictionary form of a verb – '… which has been used to **write** Bulgarian since the 10th century.'
noun	a thing, person or idea – 'The **author** of the Cyrillic **alphabet** is probably St Clement …'
number	whether a word is singular or plural – '… who was the **disciple** of the two **brothers**.'
object	see *direct object* and *indirect object*
perfective	verbal *aspect* denoting a completed action – 'He most likely **based** the Cyrillic alphabet on the Glagolitic script.'

personal pronoun	a word that means 'I', 'you' etc
possessive adjective	a word that means 'my', 'your' etc
preposition	a word like 'for' or 'before' in English
subject	the thing or person in the sentence that does the action – '**The alphabet** spread across Eastern Europe with the Orthodox Christianity …'
tense	form of a *verb* that shows the time of the action – 'eat' (present), 'ate' (past), 'will eat' (future)
verb	the word that shows what action happens – '… and it **developed** regional variations.'
verb stem	the part of a verb which does not change – '**write**' in '**writ**ing' and '**writ**ten'

language difficulties

Do you speak (English)?
Говорите/Говориш ли
(английски)? pol/inf
go·vo·ree·te/go·vo·reesh lee
(an·glee·skee)

Does anyone speak (English)?
Говори ли някой тук
(английски)?
go·vo·ree lee *nya·*koy took
(an·*glee·*skee)

Do you understand (me)?
Разбирате/Разбираш
ли (ме)? pol/inf
raz·*bee·*ra·te/raz·*bee·*rash
lee (me)

I (don't) understand.
(Не) Разбирам.
(ne) raz·*bee·*ram

I speak (English).
Говоря (английски).
go·*vor·*yuh (an·*glee·*skee)

I don't speak Bulgarian.
Не говоря български.
ne go·*vor·*yuh *buhl·*gar·skee

I speak a little.
Говоря малко.
go·*vor·*yuh *mal·*ko

---

false friends

магазин m   ma·ga·*zeen*   store/shop
   not 'magazine', which is *списание* n spee·*sa·*nee·e

митинг m   *mee·*teeng   political rally
   not 'appointment', which is *среща* f *sresh·*ta

паста f   *pas·*ta   pastry/paste
   not 'spaghetti', which is *макарони* m ma·ka·*ro·*nee

презерватив m   pre·zer·va·*teev*   condom
   not 'stabiliser', which is *стабилизатор* m sta·bee·lee·*za·*tor

хол m   hol   living room
   not 'hall' or 'entry area', which is *антре* n an·*tre*

I'd like to learn some Bulgarian.

Искам да науча малко   *ees*·kam da na·*oo*·chuh *mal*·ko
български.   *buhl*·gar·skee

Let's speak Bulgarian.

Хайде да говорим   *hai*·de da go·*vo*·reem
български.   *buhl*·gar·skee

What's this called in Bulgarian?

Как се казва това   kak se *kaz*·va to·*va*
на български?   na *buhl*·gar·skee

What does (влак) mean?

Какво значи (влак)?   kak·*vo zna*·chee (vlak)

Pardon?

Моля?   *mol*·yuh

How do you …?	Как се …?	kak se …
pronounce this	произнася	pro·eez·*nas*·ya
	това	to·*va*
write (*shtuhr*·kel)	пише (щъркел)	*pee*·she (*shtuhr*·kel)

Could you please …?	Моля да …	*mol*·yuh da …
repeat that	повторите/	pov·*to*·ree·te/
	повториш	pov·*to*·reesh
	това pol/inf	to·*va*
speak more slowly	говорите/	go·*vo*·ree·te/
	говориш	go·*vo*·reesh
	по-бавно pol/inf	*po*·bav·no
write it down	напишете/	na·*pee*·she·te/
	напишеш	na·*pee*·shesh
	това pol/inf	to·*va*

---

yes or no?

In Bulgaria, shaking your head from side to side means 'yes', while moving it up and down means 'no'. Although these gestures are the opposite of those used by English speakers, there are enough other cues (eg smiles or frowns) to ensure that there's less confusion than you might expect. Of course, it's always a good bet to verify the meaning by using the words *да* da (yes) or *не* ne (no).

numbers & amounts

cardinal numbers

бройни числа

After numbers or the words *колко* kol·ko (how much/many) and *няколко* nya·kol·ko (several), add the ending -*а* -a to masculine nouns – eg *молив* mo·leev (pencil), *два/няколко молива* dva/nya·kol·ko mo·lee·va (two/several pencils).

The numbers 'one' and 'two' (and higher numbers adding 'one' or 'two') change form depending on the gender of the noun following them. When counting in general, the neuter gender is used – *едно, две,* … ed·no, dve … (one, two, …).

0	нула	noo·la
1	един m	e·deen
	една f	ed·na
	едно n	ed·no
2	два/две m/f&n	dva/dve
3	три	tree
4	четири	che·tee·ree
5	пет	pet
6	шест	shest
7	седем	se·dem
8	осем	o·sem
9	девет	de·vet
10	десет	de·set
11	единайсет	e·dee·nai·set
12	дванайсет	dva·nai·set
13	тринайсет	tree·nai·set
14	четиринайсет	che·tee·ree·nai·set
15	петнайсет	pet·nai·set
16	шестнайсет	shest·nai·set
17	седемнайсет	se·dem·nai·set
18	осемнайсет	o·sem·nai·set
19	деветнайсет	de·vet·nai·set
20	двайсет	dvai·set

21	двайсет и един/	dvai·set ee e·deen/
	една/едно m/f/n	ed·na/ed·no
22	двайсет и	dvai·set ee
	два/две m/f&n	dva/dve
30	трийсет	tree·set
40	четирийсет	che·tee·ree·set
50	петдесет	pet·de·set
60	шестдесет	shest·de·set
70	седемдесет	se·dem·de·set
80	осемдесет	o·sem·de·set
90	деветдесет	de·vet·de·set
100	сто	sto
200	двеста	dve·sta
1000	хиляда	heel·ya·da
1,000,000	един милион	e·deen mee·lee·yon

ordinal numbers

Ordinal numbers are formed by adding -u -ee to the cardinal number. In some cases, though, the form of the cardinal number changes (most notably in 'first' and 'second', as shown below). Ordinal numbers are abbreviated in writing by adding the last two letters of the written form to the numeral, eg 18-mu for осемнайсети o·sem·nai·stee (18th/eighteenth). Dates are written with the number first and read as the ordinal number, eg 18 октомври o·sem·nai·stee ok·tom·vree (18 October).

1st	първи	puhr·vee
2nd	втори	vto·ree
3rd	трети	tre·tee
4th	четвърти	chet·vuhr·tee
5th	пети	pe·tee

Петър пет плета плете преплита;
преплети, Петре, петте плета.
pe·tuhr pet *ple*·ta ple·*te* pre·*plee*·ta
pre·ple·*tee pet*·re pet·*te ple*·ta
(Peter is weaving and interweaving five hedges;
weave, Peter, the five hedges.)

Шейсет и шест шишета от швепс се сушат
на шейсет и шест шосета.
shey·*set* ee shest shee·*she*·ta ot shveps se *soo*·shat
na shey·*set* ee shest sho·*se*·ta
(Sixty-six bottles of Schweppes are drying out
on sixty-six roads.)

fractions & decimals

Fractions are formed from a cardinal number followed by the
plural form of the ordinal number, eg *три четвърти* tree
chet·vuhr·tee (three-quarters).

a quarter	една четвърт	ed·na chet·vuhrt
a third	една трета	ed·na tre·ta
a half	половин	po·lo·veen
all	всичко	vseech·ko
none	нищо	neesh·to

Decimals are written as in English, except that a comma is used
instead of a dot. In speech, the phrase *цяло и* tsya·lo ee is used
for the English 'point'.

3.14	три цяло и четиринайсет	tree tsya·lo ee che·tee·ree·nai·set
4.2	четири цяло и две	che·tee·ree tsya·lo ee dve
5.1	пет цяло и едно	pet tsya·lo ee ed·no

numbers & amounts

39

useful amounts

How much/many?	Колко?	kol·ko
Please give me ...	Дайте ми,	dai·te mee
	моля ...	mol·yuh ...
(100) grams	(сто) грама	(sto) gra·ma
half a dozen	половин	po·lo·veen
	дузина	doo·zee·na
a dozen	дузина	doo·zee·na
half a kilo	половин	po·lo·veen
	килограм	kee·lo·gram
a kilo	един килограм	e·deen kee·lo·gram
a bottle	шише	shee·she
a jar	буркан	bur·kan
a packet	опаковка	o·pa·kov·ka
a slice	филия	fee·lee·ya
a tin	кутия	koo·tee·ya
a few	няколко	nya·kol·ko
less	по-малко	po·mal·ko
(just) a little	(само) малко	(sa·mo) mal·ko
a lot	много	mno·go
many	много	mno·go
more	повече	po·ve·che
some	няколко	nya·kol·ko

For more amounts, see **self-catering**, page 176.

handy hints

- Bulgarians finger-count by holding the palm face up and flat, and starting with the little finger.
- The entire hand is used for beckoning, and tilting the head in the intended direction equates to 'pointing'.
- Indicating height and length with the use of hands is done as in English; otherwise hand gestures are avoided.
- Using a single finger for any purpose (counting, pointing etc) is considered rude.

BASICS

telling the time

The 24-hour clock is the norm in formal contexts, but in most informal situations the 12-hour clock is used. Minutes up to half-past the hour are added, eg 10.20 is *десет и двайсет* de·set ee dvai·set (lit: ten and twenty). Minutes after half-past are subtracted from the next hour, so that 10.50 is *единайсет без десет* e·dee·nai·set bez de·set (lit: eleven without ten). Note also that the form *час* chas (o'clock) is used with 'one' and numbers adding 'one', but *часа* cha·suh is used with other numbers.

What time is it?	Колко е часът?	*kol·ko e cha·suht*
It's one o'clock.	Часът е един.	*cha·suht e e·deen*
It's (two) o'clock.	(Два) часа е.	*(dva) cha·suh e*
Five past (two).	(Два) и пет.	*(dva) ee pet*
Quarter past (two).	(Два) и петнайсет.	*(dva) ee pet·nai·set*
Half past (two).	(Два) и половина.	*(dva) ee po·lo·vee·na*
Quarter to (three).	(Три) без петнайсет.	*(tree) bez pet·nai·set*
Twenty to (three).	(Три) без двайсет.	*(tree) bez dvai·set*
am	сутрин	*soo·treen*
pm	следобед	*sle·do·bed*
At what time ...?	В колко часа ...?	*v kol·ko cha·suh ...*
At (five).	В (пет).	*v (pet)*
At (7.57pm).	В (деветнайсет и петдесет и седем).	*v (de·vet·nai·set ee pet·de·set ee se·dem)*

Times during the day are expressed in the following way:

сутринта	soo·treen·ta	**in the morning (4–10am)**
през деня	prez den·yuh	**during the day (10am–5pm)**
следобед	sle·do·bed	**in the afternoon (2–6pm)**
вечерта	ve·cher·ta	**in the evening (6–11pm)**
през нощта	prez nosht·ta	**during the night (11pm–4am)**

the calendar

календарът

days of the week

Monday	понеделник m	po·ne·del·neek
Tuesday	вторник m	vtor·neek
Wednesday	сряда f	srya·da
Thursday	четвъртък m	chet·vuhr·tuhk
Friday	петък m	pe·tuhk
Saturday	събота f	suh·bo·ta
Sunday	неделя f	ne·del·ya

months

January	януари m	ya·noo·a·ree
February	февруари m	fev·roo·a·ree
March	март m	mart
April	април m	ap·reel
May	май m	mai
June	юни m	yoo·nee
July	юли m	yoo·lee
August	август m	av·goost
September	септември m	sep·tem·vree
October	октомври m	ok·tom·vree
November	ноември m	no·em·vree
December	декември m	de·kem·vree

BASICS

dates

What date is it today?
  Коя дата е днес?   ko·*ya da*·ta e dnes

It's (18 October).
  (Осемнайсети октомври).   (o·sem·*nai*·stee ok·*tom*·vree)

seasons

spring	пролет f	*pro*·let
summer	лято n	*lya*·to
autumn/fall	есен f	*e*·sen
winter	зима f	*zee*·ma

spring symbols

During the first week of March, small decorations of red and white yarn are worn pinned to the lapel. They're called *мартеници mar*·te·nee·tsee and symbolise spring. The month of March is personified as an old woman or grandmother – *баба Марта ba*·ba *mar*·ta.

present

настоящето

now	сега	se·*ga*
today	днес	dnes
tonight	довечера	do·*ve*·che·ra
this ...	днес ...	dnes ...
morning	сутринта	soo·*treen·ta*
afternoon	следобед	sle·*do*·bed

this ...	този ... m	to·zee ...
	тази ... f	ta·zee ...
week	седмица f	sed·mee·tsa
month	месец m	me·sets
year	година f	go·dee·na

past

day before yesterday	онзи ден	on·zee den
(three days) ago	преди (три дена)	pre·dee (tree de·na)
since (May)	от (май)	ot (mai)
last ...	миналият ... m	mee·na·lee·yuht ...
	миналата ... f	mee·na·la·ta ...
night	нощ f	nosht
week	седмица f	sed·mee·tsa
month	месец m	me·sets
year	година f	go·dee·na
yesterday ...	вчера ...	vche·ra ...
morning	сутринта	soo·treen·ta
afternoon	следобед	sle·do·bed
evening	снощи	snosh·tee

reading through the ages

Bulgarian equivalents of the abbreviations BC and AD are
преди н.е. for преди нашата ера pre·dee na·sha·ta e·ra
(before our era), and от н.е. for от нашата ера ot na·sha·ta
e·ra (from our era). Since the fall of communism the older
forms – пр. Хр. for преди Христос pre·dee hrees·tos (before
Christ) and след Хр. for след Христос sled hrees·tos (after
Christ) – are returning into use.

In Bulgarian, Roman numerals are used for centuries,
and the abbreviation в. stands for век vek (century) – for
example IV в. пр. Хр. (4th century BC).

future

day after tomorrow	в други ден	v *droo*·gee den
in (six days)	след (шест дена)	sled (shest *de*·na)
until (June)	до (юни)	do (*yoo*·nee)
next ...	следващият ... m	sled·vash·tee·yuht ...
	следващата ... f	sled·vash·ta·ta ...
week	седмица f	*sed*·mee·tsa
month	месец m	*me*·sets
year	година f	go·*dee*·na
tomorrow ...	утре ...	*oo*·tre ...
morning	сутринта	soo·treen·*ta*
afternoon	следобед	sle·*do*·bed
evening	вечер	*ve*·cher

during the day

afternoon	следобед m	sle·*do*·bed
dawn	зора f	zo·*ra*
day	ден m	den
evening	вечер f	*ve*·cher
midday/noon	обяд m	ob·*yad*
midnight	полунощ f	po·loo·*nosht*
morning	утро n	*oot*·ro
night	нощ f	nosht
sunrise	изгрев слънце m	*eez*·grev *sluhn*·tse
sunset	залез слънце m	za·lez *sluhn*·tse

celebration time

Christmas	Коледа f	*ko*·le·da
New Year	Нова година f	*no*·va go·*dee*·na

The traditional greetings is *Честита Коледа!* ches·*tee*·ta *ko*·le·da (Merry Christmas!) and *Честита Нова година!* ches·*tee*·ta *no*·va go·*dee*·na (Happy New Year!). The abbreviation ЧНГ is seen everywhere and biscuits are even baked in the shape of the letters. A popular custom on New Year's morning is *сурвакане* soor·*va*·ka·ne. Using decorated branches of cornelwood, young children strike their elders lightly on the back, chanting *Сурва сурва година, весела година, живо здраво догодина, догодина до амина soor*·va *soor*·va go·*dee*·na ve·se·la go·*dee*·na *zhee*·vo *zdra*·vo do·go·*dee*·na do go·*dee*·na do a·*mee*·na (lit: happy happy year, joyous year, live healthily next year, next year to amen). The adults give them shiny new coins in return.

Easter	Великден m	ve·*leek*·den

The traditional Easter greeting is *Христос возкресе!* hris·*tos* voz·*kre*·se (Christ has risen!). The proper reply is *Во истина возкресе!* vo ees·*tee*·na voz·*kre*·se (Truly he has risen!).

St Cyril and	Ден на Св.	den na *sve*·tee
Methodius	Кирил и	*kee*·reel ee
Day	Методи m	me·*to*·dee

A holiday dear to Bulgarians, the 24th of May honours the founders of *кирилица* kee·ree·*lee*·tsa (the Cyrillic alphabet). Everything closes, and the whole country partakes in festivals and parades celebrating the alphabet named after St Cyril (for more information, see **About Bulgarian**, page 10).

3 March	3 март m	*tre*·tee mart

During the communist era the national holiday was *9 септември* de·ve·tee sep·*tem*·vree (9 September), the date of Bulgaria's liberation from fascism in WWII. Since the collapse of communism in 1989, the national holiday has reverted to the 3rd of March, the date of the 1878 San Stefano treaty and the creation of what Bulgarians consider to be the true Bulgarian state (whose borders were considerably reduced by the Congress of Berlin in July of the same year).

BASICS

46

The Bulgarian currency is the *лев* lev (almost always used in the counting form *лева* le·va), which comprises 100 *стотинки* sto·*teen*·kee. A common slang word for the lev is *кинт* keent. With Bulgaria's entry into the EU in 2007, it committed to replacing the lev with the *евро* ev·ro (euro), but recent economic instability has prompted a deceleration of this process. Check the situation before you travel.

How much is it?
Колко струва? *kol*·ko *stroo*·va

Can you write down the price?
Моля, напишете цената. *mol*·yuh na·pee·*she*·te tse·*na*·ta

Do I have to pay?
Трябва ли да платя? *tryab*·va lee da plat·*yuh*

There's a mistake in the bill.
Има грешка в сметката. *ee*·ma *gresh*·ka v *smet*·ka·ta

Do you accept …?	Приемате ли …?	pree·*e*·ma·te lee …
credit cards	кредитни	kre·*deet*·nee
	карти	*kar*·tee
debit cards	дебитни	de·*beet*·nee
	карти	*kar*·tee
travellers	пътнически	puht·*nee*·ches·kee
cheques	чекове	*che*·ko·ve
I'd like …, please.	Дайте ми моля …	*dai*·te mee *mol*·yuh …
my change	ресто	*res*·to
a receipt	квитанция	kvee·*tan*·tsee·ya
I'd like …	Искам …	*ees*·kam …
a refund	да ми се върнат парите	da mee se *vuhr*·nuht pa·*ree*·te
to return this	да върна това	da *vuhr*·nuh to·*va*

I'd like to …	Искам да …	*ees*·kam da …
cash a cheque	осребря чек	o·sreb·*ryuh* chek
change a	обменя	ob·men·*yuh*
travellers	пътнически	puht·*nee*·ches·kee
cheque	чек	chek
change money	сменя пари	smen·*yuh* pa·*ree*
get a cash	изтегля пари	eez·*teg*·lyuh pa·*ree*
advance	от кредитната	ot kre·*deet*·na·ta
	си карта	see *kar*·ta
get change for	разваля тази	raz·*val*·yuh *ta*·zee
this note	банкнота	bank·*no*·ta
withdraw	тегля пари	*teg*·lyuh pa·*ree*
money	в брой	v broy
Where's a/an …?	Къде има …?	kuh·*de* ee·ma …
ATM	банкомат	ban·ko·*mat*
foreign	бюро за	byoo·*ro* za
exchange	обмяна на	ob·*mya*·na na
office	валута	va·*loo*·ta
What's the …?	Какъв/Каква	ka·*kuhv*/kak·*va*
	е …? m/f	e …
charge	таксата f	*tak*·sa·ta
exchange	валутният	va·*loot*·nee·yuht
rate	курс m	koors
It's …	… е.	… e
(12) lev	(Дванайсет)	(dva·*nai*·set)
	лева	*le*·va
(5) euros	(Пет) евра	(pet) *ev*·ra
free	Безплатно	bez·*plat*·no
How much is	Колко	*kol*·ko
it per …?	струва …?	*stroo*·va …
day	на ден	na den
hour	на час	na chas
(five) minutes	за (пет)	za (pet)
	минути	mee·*noo*·tee
night	една нощ	ed·*na* nosht
person	на човек	na cho·*vek*
week	на седмица	na *sed*·mee·tsa

For more money-related phrases, see **banking**, page 95.

getting around

Which ... goes to (Knyazhevo)?	Кой/Коя е ... за (Княжево)? m/f	koy/ko·*ya* e ... za (*knya*·zhe·vo)
bus	автобусът m	av·to·*boo*·suht
minibus	маршрутката f	marsh·*root*·ka·ta
train	влакът m	*vla*·kuht
Is this the ... to (Varna)?	Това ли е ... за (Варна)?	to·*va* lee e ... za (*var*·na)
boat	корабът	*ko*·ra·buht
train	влакът	*vla*·kuht
When's the ... bus?	Кога тръгва ... автобус?	ko·*ga* truhg·va ... av·to·*boos*
first	първият	*puhr*·vee·yuht
last	последният	po·*sled*·nee·yuht
next	следващият	*sled*·vash·tee·yuht

What time does it leave?

В колко часа тръгва?   v *kol*·ko cha·*suh* truhg·va

What time does it get to (Kyustendil)?

В колко часа пристига   v *kol*·ko cha·*suh* prees·*tee*·ga
в (Кюстендил)?   v (kyoo·sten·*deel*)

How long will it be delayed?

Колко е закъснението?   *kol*·ko e za·kuhs·*ne*·nee·ye·to

Is this seat available?

Това място свободно ли е?   to·*va myas*·to svo·*bod*·no lee e

That's my seat.

Това е моето място.   to·*va* e mo·ye·to *myas*·to

Please tell me when we get to (Plovdiv).

Кажете ми моля когато   ka·*zhe*·te mee *mol*·yuh ko·*ga*·to
пристигнем в (Пловдив).   prees·*teeg*·nem v (*plov*·deev)

Please stop here.

Моля, спрете тук. *mol·yuh spre·te took*

How long do we stop here?

След колко време тръгваме оттук? *sled kol·ko vre·me truhg·va·me ot·took*

Let's take public transport.

Хайде да отидем с градския транспорт. *hai·de da o·tee·dem s grad·skee·yuh trans·port*

Can we get there by public transport?

Може ли да отидем там с градския транспорт? *mo·zhe lee da o·tee·dem tam s grad·skee·yuh trans·port*

Let's walk there.

Хайде да отидем пеша. *hai·de da o·tee·dem pe·sha*

Let's ride there by bike.

Хайде да отидем с колело. *hai·de da o·tee·dem s ko·le·lo*

Are you waiting for more people?

Чакате ли още хора? *cha·ka·te lee osh·te ho·ra*

Can you take us around the city, please?

Ще можете ли да ни разходите из града? *shte mo·zhe·te lee da nee raz·ho·dee·te eez gra·duh*

How many people can ride on this?

Колко души могат да се качат на това? *kol·ko doo·shee mo·guht da se ka·chuht na to·va*

---

sharing a ride

A popular form of transport in the Bulgarian capital Sofia is the *маршрутка* marsh·root·ka (shared minibus). These operate along fixed routes just like buses, except that you can hail them or ask to be let off at any point along the route. The route is identified by a placard on the dashboard bearing a large number and a few key points along the route. Fares for this mode of transport cost somewhat more than bus or tram fares. You pay a flat rate, whatever the distance, and the money is handed directly to the driver. In the countryside you might see the *каруца* ka·roo·tsa (horse-drawn carriage), used as the traditional way of getting around.

tickets

Where do I buy a ticket?
Къде мога да си
купя билет?

kuh·*de mo*·guh da see
koop·yuh bee·*let*

Do I need to book?
Трябва ли да направя
резервация?

tryab·va lee da na·*prav*·yuh
re·zer·*va*·tsee·ya

A … ticket	Един … билет	e·*deen* … bee·*let*
(to Rila).	(за Рила).	(za *ree*·la)
1st-class	първокласен	*purh*·vo·kla·sen
2nd-class	второкласен	*vto*·ro·kla·sen
child's	детски	*det*·skee
one-way	еднопосочен	ed·no·po·*so*·chen
return	двупосочен	dvoo·po·*so*·chen
student	студентски	stoo·*dent*·skee

I'd like a/an	Искам място	ees·kam *myas*·to
… seat.	…, моля.	… *mol*·yuh
aisle	до коридора	do ko·ree·*do*·ra
nonsmoking	за	za
	непушачи	ne·poo·*sha*·chee
smoking	за пушачи	za poo·*sha*·chee
window	до прозореца	do pro·*zo*·re·tsa

Is there (a) …?	Има ли …?	*ee*·ma lee …
air conditioning	климатик	klee·ma·*teek*
blanket	одеяло	o·de·*ya*·lo
sick bag	торбичка за	tor·*beech*·ka za
	повръщане	po·*vruhsh*·ta·ne
toilet	тоалетна	to·a·*let*·na

How much is it?
Колко струва?

kol·ko *stroo*·va

How long does the trip take?
Колко трае пътуването?

kol·ko *tra*·ye puh·*too*·va·ne·to

Is it a direct route?
Директен ли е?

dee·*rek*·ten lee e

Can I get a couchette/sleeper?
Има ли спален вагон? ee·ma lee *spa*·len va·*gon*

What time should I check in?
Кога е регистрацията? ko·*ga* e re·gees·*tra*·tsee·ya·ta

I'd like to … my ticket, please.	Искам да … своя билет, моля.	*ees*·kam da … *svo*·yuh bee·*let* *mol*·yuh
cancel	върна	*vuhr*·nuh
change	сменя	smen·*yuh*
collect	взема	*vze*·muh
confirm	потвърдя	pot·vuhr·*dyuh*

luggage

багаж

Where can I find a/the …?	Къде …?	kuh·*de* …
baggage claim	се получава багаж	se po·loo·*cha*·va ba·*gazh*
left-luggage office	има гардероб	*ee*·ma gar·de·*rob*
luggage locker	има гардероб	*ee*·ma gar·de·*rob*
trolley	има количка	*ee*·ma ko·*leech*·ka

PRACTICAL

My luggage has been ...	Багажът ми е ...	ba·ga·zhuht mee e ...
damaged	повреден	po·vre·den
lost	загубен	za·goo·ben
stolen	откраднат	ot·krad·nat

That's (not) mine.
Това (не) е мое.   to·va (ne) e mo·ye

Can I have some coins/tokens?
Дайте ми моля   dai·te mee mol·yuh
монети/жетони.   mo·ne·tee/zhe·to·nee

backpack/rucksack	раница f	ra·nee·tsa
bag	пътна чанта f	puht·na chan·ta
box	кутия f	koo·tee·ya
cosmetic bag	козметична чантичка f	koz·me·teech·na chan·teech·ka
suitcase	куфар m	koo·far

plane

самолет

Where does flight (357) arrive?
Къде пристига полет   kuh·de pree·stee·ga po·let
номер (три пет седем)?   no·mer (tree pet se·dem)

Where does flight (357) depart?
Откъде тръгва полет   ot·kuh·de truhg·va po·let
номер (три пет седем)?   no·mer (tree pet se·dem)

Where's (the) ...?	Къде се намира ...?	kuh·de se na·mee·ra ...
arrivals hall	терминал 'пристигащи'	ter·mee·nal pree·stee·gash·tee
departures hall	терминал 'заминаващи'	ter·mee·nal za·mee·na·vash·tee
duty-free shop	безмитен магазин	bez·mee·ten ma·ga·zeen
gate (12)	изход (дванайсет)	ees·hod (dva·nai·set)

бордна карта f	*bord·*na *kar·*ta	**boarding pass**
паспорт m	pas·*port*	**passport**
прекачване n	pre-*kach·*va·ne	**transfer**
транзит m	tran-*zeet*	**transit**

bus & coach

автобусите

Is this a bus stop?
Това ли е автобусната
спирка?
to-*va* lee e av-to-*boos·*na·ta
*speer·*ka

How often do buses come?
Колко често минават
автобусите?
*kol·*ko *ches·*to mee-*na·*vat
av-to-*boo·*see·te

Does it stop at (Plovdiv)?
Спира ли в (Пловдив)?
*spee·*ra lee v (*plov·*deev)

What's the next stop?
Коя е следващата спирка?
ko-*ya* e *sled·*vash·ta·ta *speer·*ka

I'd like to get off at (Koprivshtitsa).
Искам да сляза в
(Копривщица).
*ees·*kam da *slya·*zuh v
(ko-*preev·*shtee·tsa)

bus terminal	депо n	de·*po*
(central) bus station	(централната) автогара f	(tsen-*tral·*na·ta) av-to-*ga·*ra
city bus	градски автобус	*grad·*skee av-to-*boos*
departure bay	платформа f	plat-*for·*ma
intercity bus	междуградски автобус	mezh-doo-*grad·*skee av-to-*boos*
minibus	маршрутка f	marsh-*root·*ka
timetable	разписание n	raz-pee-*sa·*nee·e
trolleybus	тролейбус m	tro-*ley·*boos

For bus numbers, see **numbers & amounts**, page 37.

bus & train station signs		
Забранено за кучета	za·bra·*ne*·no za koo·che·ta	**Dogs Not Allowed**
Заминаващи	za·mee·*na*·vash·tee	**Departures**
Коловоз	ko·lo·*voz*	**Track**
Перон	pe·*ron*	**Platform**
Пристигащи	pree·*stee*·gash·tee	**Arrivals**
Пушенето забранено	poo·she·ne·to za·bra·*ne*·no	**No Smoking**
Разрешено за кучета	raz·re·*she*·no za koo·che·ta	**Dogs Allowed**

train

влакът

What's the next station?
Коя е следващата спирка? ko·*ya* e *sled*·vash·ta·ta *speer*·ka

Does it stop at (Plovdiv)?
Спира ли в (Пловдив)? *spee*·ra lee v (*plov*·deev)

Do I need to change?
Трябва ли да се прехвърля на друг влак? *tryab*·va lee da se pre·*hvuhr*·lyuh na droog vlak

Which carriage is for dining?
Кой е вагон-ресторант? koy e va·gon·res·to·*rant*

Is it ...?	... ли е?	... lee e
direct	Директен	dee·*rek*·ten
express	Експрес	eks·*pres*
fast	Бърз	buhrz
a passenger (slow) train	Пътнически	puht·*nee*·ches·kee

Which carriage is (for) ...?	Кой вагон е ...?	koy va·*gon* e ...
1st class	от първа класа	ot *puhr*·va *kla*·sa
2nd class	от втора класа	ot *vto*·ra *kla*·sa
Sofia	за София	za *so*·fee·ya

transport

train timetable abbreviations

б.в. (бърз влак)	buhrz vlak	**fast train**
Б.Д.Ж. (Български държавни железници)	buhl·gar·skee duhr·zhav·nee zhe·lez·nee·tsee	**Bulgarian State Railways**
екс.в. (експрес влак)	eks·pres vlak	**express train**
ж.п. гара (железопътна гара)	zhe·le·zo·puht·na ga·ra	**train station**
п.в. (пътнически влак)	puht·nee·ches·kee vlak	**passenger (slow) train**
р.с.в. (ресторант-спален вагон)	res·to·rant-spa·len va·gon	**restaurant-sleeper car**

boat

корaб

On the Black Sea, a small boat called *гемия* ge·*mee*·ya can be hired for short distances, while longer distances are covered by the *кометa* ko·*me*·ta (hydrofoil).

What's the river/sea like today?
Как е реката/морето днес?   kak e re·*ka*·ta/mo·*re*·to dnes

Are there life jackets?
Има ли спасителни   *ee*·ma lee spa·*see*·tel·nee
жилетки?   zhee·*let*·kee

Which island/beach is this?
Кой е този остров/плаж?   koy e *to*·zee *os*·trov/plazh

I feel seasick.
Хваща ме морска болест.   *hvash*·ta me *mor*·ska *bo*·lest

boat	корaб m	*ko*·rab
cabin	кабина f	ka·*bee*·na
captain	капитан m	kap·ee·*tan*
(car) deck	палуба (за колите) f	pa·*loo*·ba (za ko·*lee*·te)
ferry	ферибот m	*fe*·ree·bot
lifeboat	спасителна лодка f	spa·*see*·tel·na *lod*·ka
life jacket	спасителна жилетка f	spa·*see*·tel·na zhee·*let*·ka

taxi

I'd like a taxi … Искам да   *ees*·kam da
          поръчам такси …   po·*ruh*·cham tak·*see* …
  at (9am) в (девет часа)   v (*de*·vet cha·*suh*
          сутринта)   soo·treen·*ta*)
  now за сега   za se·*ga*
  tomorrow за утре   za *oot*·re

Where's the taxi rank?
  Къде е таксиметровата   kuh·*de* e tak·see·*met*·ro·va·ta
  стоянка?   sto·*yan*·ka

Is this taxi available?
  Такси́то свободно ли е?   tak·*see*·to svo·*bod*·no lee e

Please take me to (this address).
  Моля да ме закарате   *mol*·yuh da me za·*ka*·ra·te
  до (този адрес).   do (*to*·zee ad·*res*)

Please put the meter on.
  Моля да включите   *mol*·yuh da *vklyoo*·chee·te
  таксиметъра.   tak·see·*me*·tuh·ra

I don't want to pay a flat fare.
  Не искам да платя   ne *ees*·kam da plat·*yuh*
  фиксирана сума.   feek·*see*·ra·na *soo*·ma

How much is the flag fall/hiring charge?
  Колко е първоначалната   *kol*·ko e puhr·vo·na·*chal*·na·ta
  такса?   *tak*·sa

How much is the call-out fee?
  Колко струва   *kol*·ko *stroo*·va
  за повикването?   za po·*veek*·va·ne·to

How much is it to (the airport)?
  Колко струва   *kol*·ko *stroo*·va
  до (летището)?   do (le·*teesh*·te·to)

Please … Моля …   *mol*·yuh …
  come back върнете се   vuhr·*ne*·te se
  at (10 o'clock) в (десет часа)   v (*de*·set cha·*suh*)
  slow down намалете   na·ma·*le*·te
  stop here спрете тук   *spre*·te took
  wait here чакайте тук   *cha*·kai·te took

Благоевград	bla·*go*·ev·grad	**Blagoevgrad**
Бургас	boor·*gas*	**Burgas**
Варна	*var*·na	**Varna**
Велико Търново	ve·*lee*·ko *tuhr*·no·vo	**Veliko Târnovo**
Пловдив	*plov*·deev	**Plovdiv**
Русе	*roo*·se	**Ruse/Rousse**
Сливен	*slee*·ven	**Sliven**
София	so·*fee*·ya	**Sofia**
Стара Загора	*sta*·ra za·*go*·ra	**Stara Zagora**
Шумен	*shoo*·men	**Shumen**

car & motorbike

колите и мотопедите

car & motorbike hire

I'd like to hire a/an …	Искам да взема под наем …	*ees*·kam da *vze*·muh pod *na*·em …
4WD	кола с предаване четири по четири	ko·*la* s pre·*da*·va·ne *che*·tee·ree po *che*·tee·ree
automatic	кола автоматик	ko·*la* av·to·ma·*teek*
car	кола	ko·*la*
manual	кола с ръчни скорости	ko·*la* s *ruhch*·nee *sko*·ros·tee
motorbike	мотопед	mo·to·*ped*
with …	с …	s …
air conditioning	климатик	klee·ma·*teek*
a driver	шофьор	sho·*fyor*
How much for … hire?	Колко струва …?	*kol*·ko *stroo*·va …
daily	на ден	na den
weekly	на седмица	na *sed*·mee·tsa

Does that include insurance?

Включена ли е
застраховката?

*vklyoo·che·na lee e
za·stra·hov·ka·ta*

Does that include mileage?

Включен ли е
километражът?

*vklyoo·chen lee e
kee·lo·me·tra·zhuht*

Do you have a guide to the road rules (in English)?

Имате ли правилник
за движението
по пътищата
(на английски)?

*ee·ma·te lee pra·veel·neek
za dvee·zhe·nee·e·to
po puh·teesh·ta·ta
(na an·gleey·skee)*

Do you have a road map?

Имате ли пътна карта?

ee·ma·te lee puht·na kar·ta

on the road

There are no parking meters in Bulgaria. Instead, you buy a
талон ta·lon (coupon with a certain amount of time on it)
from a ticket machine and display it on the dashboard.

What's the speed limit?

Каква е позволената
скорост?

*kak·va e poz·vo·le·na·ta
sko·rost*

Is this the road to (Blagoevgrad)?

Това ли е пътят за
(Благоевград)?

*to·va lee e puht·yuht za
(bla·go·ev·grad)*

Where's a petrol/gas station?

Къде има
бензиностанция?

*kuh·de ee·ma
ben·zee·no·stan·tsee·ya*

Please fill it up.

Моля напълнете
го до края.

*mol·yuh na·puhl·ne·te
go do kra·yuh*

I'd like (25) litres.

Искам (двайсет и пет)
литра.

*ees·kam (dvai·set ee pet)
leet·ra*

transport

59

безплатно	bez·*plat*·no	**free**
винетка f	vee·*net*·ka	**motorway pass**
регистрационни	re·gee·stra·tsee·o·nee	**registration**
документи m pl	do·koo·*men*·tee	**papers**
шофьорска	sho·*fyor*·ska	**drivers licence**
книжка f	*kneezh*·ka	

diesel	дизел m	*dee*·zel
leaded	оловен бензин m	o·*lo*·ven ben·*zeen*
LPG	газ m	gaz
regular	обикновен	o·beek·no·*ven*
	бензин m	ben·*zeen*
unleaded	безоловен	bez·o·*lo*·ven
super 95/98	супер бензин	*soo*·per ben·*zeen*
	деветдесет и	de·vet·de·*set* ee
	пет/деветдесет	pet/de·vet·de·*set*
	и осем m	ee *o*·sem

Can you check the ...?	Моля да проверите ...	*mol*·yuh da pro·ve·*ree*·te ...
oil	маслото	*mas*·lo·to
tyre pressure	налягането	na·*lya*·ga·ne·to
	на гумите	na *goo*·mee·te
water	водата	vo·*da*·ta

Can I park here?
Мога ли да паркирам тук?   *mo*·guh lee da par·*kee*·ram took

How long can I park here?
Колко време мога   *kol*·ko *vre*·me *mo*·guh
да паркирам тук?   da par·*kee*·ram took

Do I have to pay?
Плаща ли се?   *plash*·ta lee se

problems

I need a mechanic.
Трябва ми монтьор.   *tryab*·va mee mon·*tyor*

I've had an accident.
Имах злополука.   *ee*·mah zlo·po·*loo*·ka

The car/motorbike has broken down (at Knyazhevo).
Колата/Мотопедът   ko·*la*·ta/mo·to·*ped*·uht
претърпя авария   pre·tuhr·*pya* a·va·ree·ya
(в Княжево).   (v *knya*·zhe·vo)

The car/motorbike won't start.
Колата/Мотопедът   ko·*la*·ta/mo·to·*pe*·duht
не запалва.   ne za·*pal*·va

I've run out of petrol.
Нямам бензин.   *nya*·mam ben·*zeen*

I have a flat tyre.
Пукна ми се гумата.   *pook*·na mee se *goo*·ma·ta

I've lost my car keys.
Изгубих си   eez·*goo*·beeh see
ключовете на колата.   *klyoo*·cho·ve·te na ko·*la*·ta

I've locked the keys inside.
Заключих си   za·*klyoo*·cheeh see
ключовете в колата.   *klyoo*·cho·ve·te v ko·*la*·ta

petrol/gas
бензин m
ben·*zeen*

windscreen
предно стъкло n
pred·no stuhk·lo

battery
акумулатор m
a·koo·moo·*la*·tor

engine
мотор m
mo·*tor*

tyre
гума f
goo·ma

headlight
фар m
far

Please call roadside assistance.

Моля да позвънете
на пътна помощ.

mol·yuh da poz·*vuh*·ne·te
na *puht*·na po·mosht

Can you fix it (today)?

Ще можете ли да го
поправите (днес)?

shte *mo*·zhe·te lee da go
po·*pra*·vee·te (dnes)

How long will it take?

Колко ще трае поправката?   *kol*·ko shte *tra*·ye po·*prav*·ka·ta

bicycle

колело

I'd like …	Искам да …	*ees*·kam da …
my bicycle	ми поправят	mee po·*prav*·yuht
repaired	колелото	ko·le·*lo*·to
to buy a bicycle	си купя	see *koop*·yuh
	колело	ko·le·*lo*
to hire a bicycle	взема под	*vze*·muh pod
	наем едно	*na*·em ed·*no*
	колело	ko·le·*lo*

I'd like a … bike.	Искам един	*ees*·kam e·*deen*
	… велосипед.	… ve·lo·see·*ped*
mountain	планински	pla·*neen*·skee
racing	състезателен	suhs·te·*za*·te·len
secondhand	използван	eez·*polz*·van

How much is it per day/hour?

Колко струва на ден/час?   *kol*·ko *stroo*·va na den/chas

Do I need a helmet?

Трябва ли да нося каска?   *tryab*·va lee da *nos*·yuh *kas*·ka

Are there bicycle paths?

Има ли алеи за
велосипедисти?

ee·ma lee a·*le*·ee za
ve·lo·see·pe·*dees*·tee

Is there a bicycle-path map?

Има ли карта с алеи
за велосипедисти?

ee·ma lee *kar*·ta s a·*le*·ee
za ve·lo·see·pe·*dees*·tee

I have a puncture.

Пукнала ми се е гумата.   *pook*·na·la mee se e *goo*·ma·ta

border crossing

граничен пункт

I'm here in transit.

Аз съм транзитен пътник.   az suhm tran·*zee*·ten *puht*·neek

I'm here ...	Тука съм ...	*too*·ka suhm ...
on business	по работа	po *ra*·bo·ta
on holiday	във	vuhv
	ваканция	va·*kan*·tsee·ya

I'm here for ...	Тука съм за ...	*too*·ka suhm za ...
(10) days	(десет) дена	(*de*·set) *de*·na
(three) weeks	(три) седмици	(tree) *sed*·mee·tsee
(two) months	(два) месеца	(dva) *me*·se·tsa

I'm going to (Shumen).

Отивам в (Шумен).   o·*tee*·vam v (*shoo*·men)

I'm staying at the (Sheraton).

Отседнал/Отседнала съм   ot·*sed*·nal/ot·*sed*·na·la suhm
в (Шератон). **m/f**   v (she·ra·*ton*)

The children are on this passport.

Децата са записани   de·*tsa*·ta sa za·*pee*·sa·nee
в този паспорт.   v *to*·zee pas·*port*

---

listen for ...

виза **f**	*vee*·za	**visa**
група **f**	*groo*·pa	**group**
паспорт **m**	pas·*port*	**passport**
печат **m**	pe·*chat*	**stamp**
сам/сама **m/f**	sam/sa·*ma*	**alone**
семейство **n**	se·*meys*·tvo	**family**

at customs

I have nothing to declare.
Нямам нищо за
декларане.
nya·mam *neesh*·to za
dek·la·*ree*·ra·ne

I have something to declare.
Имам какво да
декларирам
ee·mam kak·*vo* da
dek·la·*ree*·ram

Do I have to declare this?
Трябва ли да
декларирам това?
tryab·va lee da
dek·la·*ree*·ram to·*va*

I didn't know I had to declare it.
Не знаех, че трябва
да се декларира.
ne *zna*·yeh che *tryab*·va
da se dek·la·*ree*·ra

That's (not) mine.
Това (не) е мое.
to·*va* (ne) e *mo*·ye

Do you have this form in (English)?
Имате ли този формуляр
на (английски)?
ee·ma·te lee *to*·zee for·moo·*lyar*
na (an·*gleey*·skee)

Could I please have an (English) interpreter?
Може ли да извикате
преводач (който
говори английски)?
mo·zhe lee da eez·*vee*·ka·te
pre·vo·*dach* (*koy*·to
go·*vo*·ree an·*gleey*·skee)

For phrases on payments and receipts, see **money**, page 47, and the box **paperwork**, page 68.

signs		
Безмитен магазин	bez·*mee*·ten ma·ga·*zeen*	Duty-Free Shop
Карантина	ka·ran·*tee*·na	Quarantine
Митница	*meet*·nee·tsa	Customs
Паспортен контрол	pas·*por*·ten kon·*trol*	Passport Control

Where's a/the ...?	Къде има ...?	kuh·*de ee*·ma ...
bank	банка	*ban*·ka
market	пазар	pa·*zar*
tourist	бюро за	byoo·ro za
information	туристическа	too·rees·*tee*·ches·ka
centre	информация	een·for·*ma*·tsee·ya

What's the address?
Какъв е адресът? ka·*kuhv* e a·*dre*·suht

How do I get there?
Как да стигна дотам? kak da *steeg*·nuh do·*tam*

How far is it?
На какво разстояние е? na kak·*vo* ras·to·*ya*·nee·e e

Can you show me (on the map)?
Можете ли да ми *mo*·zhe·te lee da mee
покажете (на картата)? pol po·*ka*·zhe·te (na *kar*·ta·ta)
Можеш ли да ми *mo*·zhesh lee da mee
покажеш (на картата)? inf po·*ka*·zhesh (na *kar*·ta·ta)

listen for ...

In Bulgarian, distance isn't normally measured in terms of time (eg 'an hour's walk from here'), although sometimes the phrase *на пет минути оттука* na pet mee·*noo*·tee ot·*too*·ka (five minutes away) is used with the meaning 'very close'.

Note that the following nouns are given in the counting form (the one that comes after numbers), so you can just slot in the appropriate number.

... километра	... kee·lo·*me*·tra	**... kilometres**
... метра	... *me*·tra	**... metres**
... преки	... *pre*·kee	**... blocks**

For detached houses, the street name comes first followed by the house number – eg *Оборище 16* o·bo·reesh·te shest·nai·set. In the newer parts of larger cities, most people live in big apartment buildings called *блокове* blo·ko·ve (blocks), which are organised into larger complexes. Each such *жилищен комплекс* zhee·leesh·ten kom·pleks (living complex) – abbreviated to *ЖК* zhe·ka – bears a name, such as *Младост* mla·dost (Youth). Although there are streets among the buildings in a complex, addresses don't refer to the streets, but to the building numbers (which can be in the hundreds). Each building has several entrances, labelled in alphabetical order (*А, Б, В, Г* ...). A typical address would look like this:

ЖК Младост	zhe·ka mla·dost	living complex 'Youth'
блок 109	blok sto de·vet	block 109
вх. Б	vhod be	entrance B
5-ти етаж	pe·tee e·tazh	5th floor
ап. 25	a·par·ta·ment dvai·set ee pet	apartment 25

It's ...	... е.	... e
behind ...	Зад ...	zad ...
close	Близо	blee·zo
far away	Далече	da·le·che
here	Тука	too·ka
in front of ...	Пред ...	pred ...
near ...	Близо до ...	blee·zo do ...
next to ...	До ...	do ...
on the corner	На ъгъла	na uh·guh·luh
opposite ...	Срещу ...	sresh·too ...
straight ahead	Направо	na·pra·vo
there	Там	tam
by bus	с автобус	s av·to·boos
by taxi	с такси	s tak·see
by train	с влак	s vlak
on foot	пеша	pe·sha

Turn ...	Завийте ... pol	za·*veey*·te ...
	Завий ... inf	za·*veey* ...
at the corner	на ъгъла	na *uh*·guh·luh
at the traffic lights	при светофара	pree sve·to·*fa*·ruh
left	наляво	na·*lya*·vo
right	надясно	na·*dyas*·no

north	север m	*se*·ver
south	юг m	yoog
east	изток m	*eez*·tok
west	запад m	za·pad

What ... is this?	Как се казва ...?	kak se *kaz*·va ...
square	този площад	*to*·zee plosh·*tad*
street	тази улица	*ta*·zee oo·lee·tsa
town	този град	*to*·zee grad
village	това село	to·*va* se·lo

traffic lights
светофар m
sve·to·*far*

shop
магазин m
ma·ga·*zeen*

pedestrian crossing
пешеходна пътека f
pe·she·*hod*·na puh·*te*·ka

bus
автобус m
av·to·*boos*

intersection
пресечка f
pre·*sech*·ka

corner
ъгъл m
uh·guhl

taxi
такси n
tak·*see*

directions

67

name/surname	име/презиме n	ee·me/pre·zee·me
address	адрес m	ad·res
date of birth	дата на раждане f	da·ta na razh·da·ne
place of birth	място на раждане n	myas·to na razh·da·ne
age	възраст m	vuhz·rast
sex	пол m	pol
nationality	националност f	na·tsee·o·nal·nost
occupation	професия f	pro·fe·see·ya
marital status	семейно положение n	se·mey·no po·lo·zhe·nee·e
single	неженен m	ne·zhe·nen
	неомъжена f	ne·o·muh·zhe·na
married	женен m	zhe·nen
	омъжена f	o·muh·zhe·na
point of departure/ destination	начална/крайна точка на пътуването f	na·chal·na/krai·na toch·ka na puh·too·va·ne·to
entry/exit date	дата на влизането/ излизането f	da·ta na vlee·za·ne·to/ eez·lee·za·ne·to
purpose of visit	цел на пътуването f	tsel na puh·too·va·ne·to
holiday	ваканция f	va·kan·tsee·ya
business	работа f	ra·bo·ta
identification	документ за самоличност m	do·koo·ment za sa·mo·leech·nost
drivers licence	шофьорска книжка f	sho·fyor·ska kneezh·ka
passport number	номер на паспорта m	no·mer na pas·por·tuh
work/study permit	разрешително за работа/ обучение n	raz·re·shee·tel·no za ra·bo·ta/ o·boo·che·nee·e

accommodation
настаняване

finding accommodation

Where's a …?	Къде има …?	kuh·de ee·ma …
camping ground	къмпинг	kuhm·peeng
guesthouse	пансион	pan·see·on
hotel	хотел	ho·tel
motel	мотел	mo·tel
private room	частна квартира	chast·na kvar·tee·ra
subsidised vacation place	почивна станция	po·cheev·na stan·tsee·ya
youth hostel	хостел	hos·tel
Can you recommend somewhere …?	Можете ли да препоръчате нещо …? pol	mo·zhe·te lee da pre·po·ruh·cha·te nesh·to …
	Можеш ли да препоръчаш нещо …? inf	mo·zhesh lee da pre·po·ruh·chash nesh·to …
cheap	евтино	ev·tee·no
good	хубаво	hoo·ba·vo
luxurious	разкошно	raz·kosh·no
nearby	наблизо	na·blee·zo
romantic	романтично	ro·man·teech·no

I'd like something near the ...	Искам нещо близо до ...	ees·kam nesh·to blee·zo do ...
beach	плажа	pla·zhuh
city centre	центъра	tsen·tuh·ruh
lake	езерото	e·ze·ro·to
mountains	планината	pla·nee·na·ta
shops	магазините	ma·ga·zee·nee·te
train station	гарата	ga·ra·ta

Are there any ecolodges here?

Има ли тука екохотели?   ee·ma lee too·ka e·ko·ho·te·lee

I'd like to stay at a locally run hotel.

Искам да отседна в   ees·kam da ot·sed·nuh v
малък частен хотел.   ma·luhk chas·ten ho·tel

What's the address?

Какъв е адресът?   ka·kuhv e a·dre·suht

For responses, see **directions**, page 65.

booking ahead & checking in

I'd like to book a room, please.

Искам да взема   ees·kam da vze·muh
една стая, моля.   ed·na sta·ya mol·yuh

I have a reservation.

Имам резервация.   ee·mam re·zer·va·tsee·ya

listen for ...

За колко нощи?	za kol·ko nosh·tee	How many nights?
баня на етажа f	ban·ya na e·ta·zhuh	shared bathroom
ключ m	klyooch	key
пълен	puh·len	full
рецепция f	re·tsep·tsee·ya	reception
самостоятелна баня f	sa·mo·sto·ya·tel·na ban·ya	ensuite bathroom

My name is …
   Казвам се …   *kaz*·vam se …

For (three) nights/weeks.
   За (три) нощи/седмици.   za (tree) *nosh*·tee/*sed*·mee·tsee

From (2 July) to (6 July).
   От (втори юли) до   ot (*vto*·ree *yoo*·lee) do
   (шести юли).   (*shes*·tee *yoo*·lee)

Do I need to pay upfront?
   Трябва ли да платя   *tryab*·va lee da plat·*yuh*
   предварително?   pred·va·*ree*·tel·no

Can I see it?
   Мога ли да я видя?   *mo*·guh lee da ya *veed*·yuh

I'll take it.
   Ще я взема.   shte ya *vze*·muh

air conditioner
климатик m
klee·ma·*teek*

fan
вентилатор m
ven·*tee*·la·tor

toilet
тоалетна f
to·a·*let*·na

key
ключ m
klyooch

bed
легло n
leg·*lo*

bath
баня f
ban·ya

TV
телевизор m
te·le·*vee*·zor

accommodation

71

Баня	*ban*·ya	**Bathroom**
Има стаи	*ee*·ma *sta*·ee	**Rooms Available**
Квартирно бюро	kvar·*teer*·no *byoo*·ro	**Accommodation Bureau**
Няма стаи	*nya*·ma *sta*·ee	**No Vacancy**
Пералня	pe·*ral*·nya	**Laundry**
Планинска хижа	pla·*neen*·ska *hee*·zha	**Mountain Hut**
Ресторант	res·to·*rant*	**Restaurant**
Свободни стаи	svo·*bod*·nee *sta*·ee	**Vacancy**
Туристическа спалня	too·rees·*tee*·ches·ka *spal*·nya	**Tourist Bedroom**
Туристически дом	too·rees·*tee*·ches·kee dom	**Tourist Home**

How much is it per ...?	Колко е на ...?	*kol*·ko e na ...
night	вечер	*ve*·cher
person	човек	cho·*vek*
week	седмица	*sed*·mee·tsa
Can I pay by ...?	Мога ли да платя с ...?	*mo*·guh lee da plat·*yuh* s ...
credit card	кредитна карта	*kre*·deet·na *kar*·ta
travellers cheque	пътнически чек	puht·*nee*·ches·kee chek
Do you have a ... room?	Има ли стая ...?	*ee*·ma lee *sta*·ya ...
single	с едно единично легло	s ed·*no* e·dee·*neech*·no leg·*lo*
double	с едно двойно легло	s ed·*no* dvoy·no leg·*lo*
twin	с две легла	s dve leg·*la*

For other methods of payment, see **money**, page 47, and **banking**, page 95.

requests & queries

Is breakfast included?
Включена ли е закуската? *vklyoo*·che·na lee e za·*koos*·ka·ta

When/Where is breakfast served?
Кога/Къде сервират ko·*ga*/kuh·*de* ser·*vee*·rat
закуската? za·*koos*·ka·ta

Is there hot water all day?
Има ли топла вода *ee*·ma lee *top*·la vo·*da*
през целия ден? prez *tse*·lee·yuh den

Please wake me at (seven).
Моля, събудете *mol*·yuh suh·boo·*de*·te
ме в (седем). me v (se·dem)

Can I use the …?	Мога ли да използвам …?	*mo*·guh lee da eez·*polz*·vam …
internet	Интернета	*een*·ter·ne·tuh
kitchen	кухнята	*kooh*·nya·ta
laundry	пералнята	pe·*ral*·nya·ta
telephone	телефона	te·le·*fo*·nuh
Do you have a/an …?	Има ли …?	*ee*·ma lee …
elevator/lift	асансьор	a·san·*syor*
laundry service	пералня	pe·*ral*·nya
message board	табло за съобщения	*tab*·lo za suh·ob·*shte*·nee·ya
safe	сейф	seyf
swimming pool	плувен басейн	*ploo*·ven ba·*seyn*
Do you … here?	Има ли при вас …?	*ee*·ma lee pree vas …
arrange tours	организирани екскурзии	or·ga·nee·*zee*·ra·nee eks·*koor*·zee·ee
change money	обмяна на валута	ob·*mya*·na na va·*loo*·ta
offer long-stay discounts	намаление за по-дълъг престой	na·ma·*le*·nee·e za *po*·duh·luhg pre·*stoy*

73

Could I have ..., please?	Дайте ми ..., моля.	*dai*·te mee ... *mol*·yuh
my key	ключа	*klyoo*·chuh
a receipt	квитанция	kvee·*tan*·tsee·ya

Is there a message for me?

| Има ли съобщение за мене? | *ee*·ma lee suh·ob·*shte*·nee·e za *me*·ne |

I'm locked out of my room.

| Забравил/Забравила съм си ключа в стаята. m/f | za·*bra*·veel/za·*bra*·vee·la suhm see *klyoo*·chuh v *sta*·ya·ta |

complaints

It's too ...	Много е ... в стаята.	*mno*·go e ... v *sta*·ya·ta
cold	студено	stoo·*de*·no
dark	тъмно	*tuhm*·no
noisy	шумно	*shoom*·no

It's too ...	... ми е.	... mee e
small	Малко	*mal*·ko
expensive	Скъпо	*skuh*·po

The ... doesn't work.	... не работи.	... ne ra·*bo*·tee
air conditioner	Климатикът	klee·ma·*tee*·kuht
fan	Вентилаторът	ven·tee·*la*·to·ruht
toilet	Тоалетната	to·a·*let*·na·ta

Can I get another ...?	Дайте ми моля още ...	*dai*·te mee *mol*·yuh *osh*·te ...
blanket	едно одеяло	ed·*no* o·de·*ya*·lo
sheet	един чаршаф	e·*deen* char·*shaf*

This ... isn't clean.	Тази ... не е чиста.	*ta*·zee ... ne e *chees*·ta
pillow	възглавница	vuhz·*glav*·nee·tsa
towel	кърпа	*kuhr*·pa

There's no hot water.
    Няма топла вода.   *nya*·ma *top*·la vo·*da*

a knock at the door ...		
Who is it?	Кой е?	koy e
Just a moment.	Един момент.	e·*deen* mo·*ment*
Come in.	Влезте.	*vlez*·te
Come back later, please.	Елате по-късно, моля.	e·*la*·te *po*·kuhs·no *mol*·yuh

checking out

напускане на хотела

What time is checkout?
    Кога трябва да   ko·*ga tryab*·va da
    освободя стаята?   os·vo·bo·*dyuh sta*·ya·ta

Can I have a late checkout?
    Мога ли да остана   *mo*·guh lee da o·*sta*·nuh
    до по-късно?   do *po*·kuhs·no

Can you call a taxi for me (for 11 o'clock)?
    Ще ми поръчате ли   shte mee po·*ruh*·cha·te lee
    едно такси   ed·*no* tak·*see*
    (за единайсет часа)?   (za e·dee·*nai*·set cha·*suh*)

I'm leaving now.
    Тръгвам сега.   *truhg*·vam se·*ga*

There's a mistake in the bill.
    Има грешка в сметката.   *ee*·ma *gresh*·ka v *smet*·ka·ta

Can I leave my bags here?
    Мога ли да оставя   *mo*·guh lee da os·*tav*·yuh
    багажа си тук?   ba·*ga*·zhuh see took

Could I have my ..., please?	Дайте ми ..., моля.	*dai*·te mee ... *mol*·yuh
deposit	моя депозит	*mo*·yuh de·po·*zeet*
passport	моя паспорт	*mo*·yuh pas·*port*
valuables	моите ценности	*mo*·yee·te *tsen*·nos·tee

accommodation

75

I'll be back …
    in (three) days
    on (Thursday)

Ще се върна …
    след (три) дена
    в (четвъртък)

shte se *vurh*·nuh …
    sled (tree) *de*·na
    v (chet·*vurh*·tuhk)

I had a great stay, thanks.
Беше много
приятно, благодаря.

be·she *mno*·go
pree·*yat*·no bla·go·dar·*yuh*

camping

Who do I ask to stay here?
Кого да попитам
за да остана тука?

ko·*go* da po·*pee*·tam
za da o·*sta*·nuh *too*·ka

Can I …?
    camp here
    park next to
    my tent

Мога ли да …?
    лагерувам тук
    паркирам
    колата си до
    палатката

mo·guh lee da …
    la·ge·*roo*·vam took
    par·*kee*·ram
    ko·*la*·ta see do
    pa·*lat*·ka·ta

Do you have …?
    bungalows
    electricity
    a laundry
    a tent site

Имате ли …?
    бунгала
    електричество
    пералня
    свободно
    място за
    палатката

ee·ma·te lee …
    boon·ga·*la*
    e·lek·*tree*·chest·vo
    pe·*ral*·nya
    svo·*bod*·no
    myas·to za
    pa·*lat*·ka·ta

    shower facilities
    tents for hire

    душове
    палатки
    под наем

    doo·sho·ve
    pa·*lat*·kee
    pod *na*·em

Is it coin-operated?
Работи ли с монети?

ra·*bo*·tee lee s mo·*ne*·tee

Is the water drinkable?
Водата може ли
да се пие?

vo·*da*·ta *mo*·zhe lee
da se *pee*·e

Could I borrow …?
Мога ли да взема
под наем …?

mo·guh lee da *vze*·muh
pod *na*·em …

How much is it per ...?	Колко струва на ...?	kol·ko stroo·va na ...
caravan	каравана	ka·ra·va·na
person	човек	cho·vek
tent	палатка	pa·lat·ka
vehicle	кола	ko·la

renting

наемане

I'm here about the ... for rent.	Дойдох да попитам за ... под наем.	doy·doh da po·pee·tam za ... pod na·em.
apartment	апартамента	a·par·ta·men·tuh
cabin	бунгалото	boon·ga·lo·to
house	къщата	kuhsh·ta·ta
(private) room	стая (в частно жилище)	sta·ya (v chast·no zhee·leesh·te)

Do you have a/an ... for rent?	Давате ли ... под наем?	da·va·te lee ... pod na·em
apartment	апартамент	a·par·ta·ment
cabin	бунгало	boon·ga·lo
house	къща	kuhsh·ta
room	стая	sta·ya

furnished	мебелиран	me·be·lee·ran
partly furnished	отчасти мебелиран	ot·chas·tee me·be·lee·ran
unfurnished	без мебели	bez me·be·lee

Is a deposit required?
Необходим ли е депозит?   ne·ob·ho·deem lee e de·po·zeet

Are bills extra?
Режийните включени ли са в цената?   re·zheey·nee·te vklyoo·che·nee lee suh v tse·na·ta

staying with locals

Bulgarians sincerely love entertaining guests and are always delighted when they arrive. Allow your hosts to indicate where you should sit. It's also best to let them direct the topics of conversation. The usual gifts are flowers (just make sure it's an uneven number of stems, as even numbers are for funerals), a bottle of alcohol and sweets (eg chocolates) for the children.

Can I stay at your place?

Може ли да остана	*mo*·zhe lee da o·*sta*·nuh
да спя у вас?	da spyuh oo vas

Is there anything I can do to help?

Да ви помогна с нещо?	da vee po·*mog*·nuh s *nesh*·to

Can I bring anything for dinner/lunch?

Какво да донеса за	*kak*·vo da do·ne·*suh* za
вечеря/обяд?	ve·*che*·rya/o·*byad*

I have my own …	Нося своя …	*nos*·yuh *svo*·yuh …
mattress	дюшек	dyoo·*shek*
sleeping bag	спален чувал	*spa*·len choo·*val*

Can I …?	Може ли да …?	*mo*·zhe lee da …
do the dishes	измия	eez·*mee*·yuh
	съдовете	*suh*·do·ve·te
set/clear the	сложа/	*slo*·zhuh/
table	прибера	pree·be·*ruh*
	масата	*ma*·sa·ta
take out the	изхвърля	eez·*hvuhr*·lyuh
rubbish	боклука	bok·*loo*·kuh

Thanks for your hospitality.

Благодаря ви за	bla·go·dar·*yuh* vee za
гостоприемството.	gos·to·pree·*ems*·tvo·to

To compliment your hosts' cooking, see **eating out**, page 168.

looking for ...

търсене на ...

Are shops open on (24 May)?

Магазините отворени
ли са на (двайсет и
четвърти май)?

ma·ga·*zee*·nee·te ot·*vo*·re·nee
lee suh na (*dvai*·set ee
chet·*vuhr*·tee mai)

What hours are shops open?

Какво е работното
време на магазините?

kak·*vo* e ra·*bot*·no·to
vre·me na ma·ga·*zee*·nee·te

Where can I buy (a padlock)?

Къде мога да си
купя (катинар)?

kuh·*de* mo·guh da see
koop·yuh (ka·tee·*nar*)

Where can I buy locally produced goods?

Къде мога да си купя
нещо направено тук?

kuh·*de* mo·guh da see *koop*·yuh
nesh·to na·*pra*·ve·no took

Where can I buy locally produced souvenirs?

Къде мога да си купя
сувенири направени
тук?

kuh·*de* mo·guh da see *koop*·yuh
soo·ve·*nee*·ree na·*pra*·ve·nee
took

Where's a ...?	**Къде има ...?**	kuh·*de* ee·ma ...
department store	универсален магазин	oo·nee·ver·*sa*·len ma·ga·*zeen*
market	пазар	pa·*zar*
supermarket	супермаркет	soo·per·mar·ket

For more items and shopping locations, see the **dictionary**.

making a purchase

I'm just looking.
Само разглеждам.   sa·mo raz·*gle*·dam

I'd like to buy (an adaptor plug).
Искам да си купя   ees·kam da see *koop*·yuh
(адаптор).   (a·*dap*·tor)

How much is it?
Колко струва?   *kol*·ko *stroo*·va

Can you write down the price?
Моля, напишете цената.   *mol*·yuh na·pee·*she*·te tse·*na*·ta

Do you have any others?
Имате ли други от   *ee*·ma·te lee *droo*·gee ot
този вид?   *to*·zee veed

Can I look at it?
Мога ли да го видя?   *mo*·guh lee da go *veed*·yuh

Is this (220) volts?
Това на (двеста двайсет)   to·*va* na (*dve*·sta *dvai*·set)
волта ли е?   *vol*·ta lee e

street-side shopping

In Bulgaria, many things (both new and secondhand) are sold by street vendors. They display their wares in various ways, ranging from a simple *маса ma*·sa (table) to a *сергия* ser·*gee*·ya (more extended display area), to a *пазар* pa·*zar* (an established set of tables) or a *будка* *bood*·ka (an enclosed kiosk). The latter can be small, selling newspapers, magazines etc, or large, effectively functioning as a one-room store. These displays can be set up on the pavement, set back from the street in what used to be a garage, or in *подлези* pod·le·zee (underground walkways helping pedestrians cross major intersections).

healthy purchases

The acquisition of new possessions is often accompanied by the following good wishes:

Със здраве да го носите/носиш! pol/inf
suhs *zdra*·ve da go
no·see·te/*no*·seesh

May you wear it in good health!
(for clothing)

Със здраве да го използвате/използваш! pol/inf
suhs *zdra*·ve da go
eez·*polz*·va·te/
eez·*polz*·vash

May you use it in good health!
(for appliances, cars, utensils etc)

Do you accept …?	Приемате ли …?	pree·e·ma·te lee …
credit cards	кредитни карти	kre·*deet*·nee *kar*·tee
debit cards	дебитни карти	de·*beet*·nee *kar*·tee
travellers	пътнически	*puht*·nee·ches·kee
cheques	чекове	*che*·ko·ve
Could I have a …, please?	Дайте ми моля …	*dai*·te mee *mol*·yuh …
bag	плик	pleek
receipt	квитанция	kvee·*tan*·tsee·ya

I don't need a bag, thanks.
Не ми трябва плик,
благодаря.

ne mee *tryab*·va pleek
bla·go·dar·*yuh*

Could I have it wrapped?
Моля да го опаковате.

mol·yuh da go o·pa·*ko*·va·te

Does it have a guarantee?
Има ли гаранция?

ee·ma lee ga·*ran*·tsee·ya

Can I have it sent abroad?
Можете ли да го
изпратите в чужбина?

mo·zhe·te lee da go
eez·*pra*·tee·te v choozh·*bee*·na

Can you order it for me?
Можете ли да го
поръчате за мене?

mo·zhe·te lee da go
po·*ruh*·cha·te za *me*·ne

Can I pick it up later?
Мога ли да го взема
по-късно?

mo·guh lee da go *vze*·muh
po·*kuhs*·no

The quality isn't good.
Качеството не е добро.   *ka*·chest·vo·to ne e do·*bro*

I'd like my change, please.
Дайте ми моля ресто.   *dai*·te mee *mol*·yuh *res*·to

I'd like …, please.	Искам да …	*ees*·kam da …
a refund	ми върнете	mee *vurh*·ne·te
	парите	pa·*ree*·te
to return this	върна това	*vuhr*·nuh to·*va*

bargaining

That's too expensive.
Много е скъпо.   *mno*·go e *skuh*·po

Can you lower the price?
Можете ли да свалите   *mo*·zhe·te lee da sva·*lee*·te
цената?   tse·*na*·ta

Do you have something cheaper?
Имате ли нещо   *ee*·ma·te lee *nesh*·to
по-евтино?   po·ev·tee·no

What's your final price?
Каква е най-ниската   kak·*va* e *nai*·nees·ka·ta
ви цена?   vee tse·*na*

I'll give you (five lev/euros).
Ще ви дам (пет лева/евра).   shte vee dam (pet *le*·va/*ev*·ra)

---

faulty things

Има дефект.	*ee*·ma de·*fekt*	It's faulty.
(lit: there's a defect)		(clothes, shoes)
Не работи.	ne ra·*bo*·tee	It's faulty.
(lit: it doesn't work)		(electrical goods, etc)
Развалено е.	raz·va·*le*·no e	It's faulty.
(lit: it's spoiled)		(general: no good, etc)
Повредено е.	po·*vre*·de·no e	It's faulty.
(lit: it's broken)		(general: no good, etc)

82

bargain	изгодно n	eez·god·no
sale n	разпродажба f	raz·pro·dazh·ba
specials	стоки с	sto·kee s
	намаление f pl	na·ma·le·nee·e
(straight-out)	(пладнешки)	(plad·nesh·kee)
rip-off n	обир m	o·beer

books & reading

книги и четене

Do you have ...?	Имате ли ...?	ee·ma·tee lee ...
a book by	някоя книга	nya·ko·ya knee·ga
(Elin Pelin)	на (Елин Пелин)	na (e·leen pe·leen)
an entertainment	справочник	spra·voch·neek
guide	за културни	za kool·toor·nee
	събития	suh·bee·tee·ya

Is there an	Има ли ...	ee·ma lee ...
English-	с книги на	s knee·gee na
language ...?	английски?	an·gleey·skee
bookshop	книжарница	knee·zhar·nee·tsa
section	отделение	ot·de·le·nee·e

I'd like a ...	Търся ...	tuhr·syuh ...
dictionary	речник	rech·neek
newspaper	вестник	vest·neek
(in English)	(на английски)	(na an·gleey·skee)
notepad	бележник	be·lezh·neek

Can you recommend a book for me?

Можете ли да ми	mo·zhe·te lee da mee
препоръчате някоя	pre·po·ruh·cha·te nya·ko·ya
книга?	knee·ga

Do you have Lonely Planet guidebooks/phrasebooks?

Имате ли пътеводители/	ee·ma·te lee puh·te·vo·dee·te·lee/
разговорници на фирма	raz·go·vor·nee·tsee na feer·ma
'Лонли Планет'?	lon·lee pla·net

shopping

83

clothes

My size is …	Моят номер е …	mo·yuht no·mer e …
(40)	(четирийсет)	(chet·tee·ree·set)
small (S)	малък (S)	ma·luhk (es)
medium (M)	среден (M)	sre·den (em)
large (L)	голям (L)	go·lyam (el)

Can I try it on?
Мога ли да го пробвам? *mo*·guh lee da go *prob*·vam

It doesn't fit.
Не ми става. ne mee *sta*·va

hairdressing

I'd like (a) …	Искам да …	ees·kam da …
colour	ми боядисате косата	mee bo·ya·dee·sa·te ko·sa·ta
foils/streaks	ми направите кичури	mee na·pra·vee·te kee·choo·ree
haircut	ме подстрижете	me pod·stree·zhe·te
my beard trimmed	ми подстрижете брадата	mee pod·stree·zhe·te bra·da·ta
my hair washed/ dried	ми измиете/ изсушите косата	mee eez·mee·e·te/ eez·soo·shee·te ko·sa·ta
shave	ме обрьснете	me o·bruhs·ne·te
trim	ми подстрижете крайчетата на косата	mee pod·stree·zhe·te krai·che·ta·ta na ko·sa·ta

Don't cut it too short.
Да не е много късо. da ne e *mno*·go *kuh*·so

Please use a new blade.
Моля, използвайте ново ножче за брьснене. *mol*·yuh eez·*polz*·vai·te *no*·vo *nozh*·che za *bruhs*·ne·ne

Shave it all off!
Обръснете я цялата!   o·bruhs·*ne*·te ya *tsa*·la·ta

I don't like this!
Не ми харесва!   ne mee ha·*res*·va

I should never have let you near me!
Не трябваше да се   ne *tryab*·va·she da se
оставям в ръцете ви!   os·*tav*·yam v ruh·*tse*·te vee

music & DVD

музика и дивиди

I'd like a ...
Искам ...   *ees*·kam ...
  CD   едно сиди   ed·*no* see·dee
  DVD   едно дивиди   ed·*no* dee·vee·*dee*
  video   едно видео   ed·*no* vee·de·o

I'm looking for something by (Teodosi Spassov).
Търся изпълнение   *turh*·syuh eez·puhl·*ne*·nee·e
на (Теодоси Спасов).   na (te·o·*do*·see *spa*·sov)

What's his best recording?
Кой е най-добрият   koy e *nai*·do·*bree*·yuht
му запис?   moo *za*·pees

Can I listen to this?
Мога ли да чуя това?   *mo*·guh lee da *choo*·yuh to·*va*

Will this work on any DVD player?
Това ще работи ли на   to·*va* shte ra·*bo*·tee lee na
всеки дивиди-плейър?   *vse*·kee dee·vee·*dee* ple·yuhr

Can you …?	Можете ли да …?	*mo·zhe·te lee da …*
develop this film	проявите този филм	*pro·ya·vee·te to·zee feelm*
load my film	ми заредите филма	*mee za·re·dee·te feel·muh*
recharge the battery for my digital camera	презаредите батерията на цифровия ми фотоапарат	*pre·za·re·dee·te ba·te·ree·ya·ta na tsee·fro·vee·yuh mee fo·to·a·pa·rat*
transfer photos from my camera to CD	прехвърлите снимките от фотоапарата ми на едно сиди	*pre·hvuhr·lee·te sneem·kee·te ot fo·to·a·pa·ra·tuh mee na ed·no see·dee*

Do you have (a) … or this camera?	Имате ли … за този фотоапарат?	*ee*·ma·te lee … za *to*·zee fo·to·a·pa·*rat*
batteries	батерии	ba·*te*·ree·ee
flash (bulb)	(крушка за) светкавица	(*kroosh*·ka za) svet·*ka*·vee·tsa
(zoom) lens	(варио-) обектив	(*va*·ree·o·) o·bek·*teev*
light meter	светломер	svet·lo·*mer*
memory cards	памет	*pa*·met
Can I connect my … to this computer?	Мога ли да свържа моя … към този компютър?	*mo*·guh lee da *svuhr*·zhuh *mo*·yuh … kuhm *to*·zee kom·*pyoo*·tuhr
camera	фотоапарат	fo·to·a·pa·*rat*
media player	плейър	*ple*·yuhr
portable hard drive	портативен харддиск	por·ta·*tee*·ven *hard*·deesk
USB flash drive	USB флаш памет	yoo·es·*bee* flash *pa*·met
I need a/an … film for this camera.	Трябва ми … филм за този фотоапарат.	*tryab*·va mee … feelm za *to*·zee fo·to·a·pa·*rat*
APS	APS	a·pe·*es*
B&W	черно-бял	cher·no·*byal*
colour	цветен	*tsve*·ten
slide	диапози- тивен	dee·a·po·zee·*tee*·ven

I need a (200)-speed film for this camera.

| Трябва ми филм от скорост (двеста) за този фотоапарат. | *tryab*·va mee feelm ot *sko*·rost (*dve*·sta) za *to*·zee fo·to·a·pa·*rat* |

I need a cable to recharge this battery.

| Трябва ми кабел да презаредя тази батерия. | *tryab*·va mee *ka*·bel da pre·za·red·*yuh* ta·zee ba·*te*·ree·ya |

I need a passport photo taken.

Трябва ми снимка
за паспорт.

tryab·va mee *sneem*·ka
za pas·*port*

I'm not happy with these photos.

Не ми харесват тези
снимки.

ne mee ha·*res*·vat te·zee
sneem·kee

I don't want to pay the full price.

Не искам да платя
цялата цена.

ne *ees*·kam da plat·*yuh*
tsya·la·ta tse·*na*

repairs

Can I have my ... repaired here?

Можете ли да
поправите ... тук?

mo·zhe·te lee da
po·*pra*·vee·te ... took

When will my ...	Кога ще бъде	*ko*·ga shte *buh*·de
be ready?	готов моята ...?	*go*·tov mo·*ya*·ta ...
backpack/ rucksack	раница	*ra*·nee·tsa
bag	чанта	*chan*·ta
camera	фотоапарат	fo·to·a·pa·*rat*

souvenirs

бродерия f	bro·*de*·ree·ya	embroidery
губери m pl	*goo*·be·ree	tufted rugs
дърворезба f	duhr·vo·rez·*ba*	woodcarving
икони f pl	ee·*ko*·nee	icons
килими m pl	kee·*lee*·mee	carpets
китеници f pl	*kee*·te·nee·tsee	fleecy rugs
розово масло n	*ro*·zo·vo *mas*·lo	rose products (eg oil and perfume)
торби f pl	tor·*bee*	bags
Троянска	tro·*yan*·ska	Troyan pottery
керамика f	ke·*ra*·mee·ka	
черги f pl	*cher*·gee	rugs

the internet

интернет

Where's the local internet café?

Къде се намира
най-близкото
Интернет-кафе?

kuh·*de* se na·*mee*·ra
nai·bleez·ko·to
een·ter·net·ka·*fe*

Do you have English-language keyboards?

Имате ли английска
клавиатура?

ee·ma·te lee ang·*lees*·ka
kla·vee·a·*too*·ra

Please change it to the English-language setting.

Моля да смените
настройката на
английски език.

mol·yuh da sme·*nee*·te
na·*stroy*·ka·ta na
an·*gleey*·skee e·*zeek*

I'd like to …	**Искам да …**	*ees*·kam da …
check my email	проверя своя е-мейл	pro·ver·*yuh* svo·yuh *ee*·meyl
download my photos	сваля снимките си	sval·*yuh* *sneem*·kee·te see
get internet access	вляза в Интернета	*vlya*·zuh v *een*·ter·ne·tuh
use a printer/scanner	използвам принтер/скенер	eez·*polz*·vam *preen*·ter/*ske*·ner

Do you have …?	**Имате ли …?**	*ee*·ma·te lee …
Macs	мак	mak
PCs	писи	pee·*see*
a Zip drive	зип драйв	zeep draiv

Can I connect my ... to this computer?	Мога ли да свържа своя ... към този компютър?	mo·guh lee da svuhr·zhuh svo·yuh ... kuhm to·zee kom·pyoo·tuhr
camera	фотоапарат	fo·to·a·pa·rat
iPod	iPod	ai·pod
media player (MP3)	плейър (ем-пи-три)	ple·yuhr (em·pee·tree)
portable hard drive	портативен харддиск	por·ta·tee·ven hard·deesk
USB flash drive (memory stick)	USB флаш драйв (памет)	yoo·es·bee flash draiv (pa·met)

How much per ...?	Колко струва ...?	kol·ko stroo·va ...
hour	на час	na chas
(five) minutes	за (пет) минути	za (pet) mee·noo·tee
page	на страница	na stra·nee·tsa

How do I log on?	Как да вляза?	kak da vlya·zuh
It's crashed.	Счупи се.	s·choo·pee se
I've finished.	Свърших.	svuhr·sheeh

mobile/cell phone

GSM

I'd like a ...	Искам ...	ees·kam ...
charger for my phone	зарядно устройство за моя GSM	zar·yad·no oo·stroys·tvo za mo·yuh dzhee·es·em
mobile/cell phone for hire	да взема под наем GSM	da vze·muh pod na·em dzhee·es·em
prepaid mobile/cell phone	GSM с предплатена карта	dzhee·es·em s pred·pla·te·na kar·ta
SIM card for your network	сим-карта за вашата мрежа	seem kar·ta za va·sha·ta mre·zha

What are the call rates?
Какви са тарифите?   kak·*vee* sa ta·*ree*·fee·te

(40 stotinki) per minute.
(Четирийсет стотинки)   (che·*tee*·ree·set sto·*teen*·kee)
на минута.   na mee·*noo*·ta

(20 cents) per minute.
(Двадесет цента)   (*dva*·de·set *tsen*·ta)
на минута.   na mee·*noo*·ta

phone

телефон

What's your phone number?
Какъв е вашият   ka·*kuhv* e *va*·shee·yuht
телефонен номер?   te·le·*fo*·nen *no*·mer

Where's the nearest telephone centre?
Къде се намира   kuh·*de* se na·*mee*·ra
най-близката телефонна   *nai*·bleez·ka·ta te·le·*fon*·na
централа?   tsen·*tra*·la

Where's the nearest public phone?
Къде се намира   kuh·*de* se na·*mee*·ra
най-близкият   *nai*·bleez·kee·yuht
телефонен автомат?   te·le·*fo*·nen av·to·*mat*

Can I look at a phone book?
Мога ли да погледна   *mo*·guh lee da po·*gled*·nuh
телефонния указател?   te·le·*fon*·nee·yuh oo·ka·*za*·tel

Can I have some coins, please?
Дайте ми моля монети.   *dai*·te mee *mol*·yuh mo·*ne*·tee

How much does … cost?	Колко струва …?	*kol*·ko *stroo*·va …
a (three)-minute call	разговор от (три) минути	*raz*·go·vor ot (tree) mee·*noo*·tee
each extra minute	всяка допълнителна минута	*vsya*·ka do·puhl·*nee*·tel·na mee·*noo*·ta

communications

I want to …	Искам да …	*ees*·kam da …
buy a phonecard	си купя една фонокарта	see *koop*·yuh ed·na fo·no·*kar*·ta
call (Singapore)	се обадя в (Сингапур)	se o·*bad*·yuh v (seen·ga·*poor*)
make a call	се обадя по телефона	se o·*bad*·yuh po te·le·*fo*·na
make a local call	се обадя в града	se o·*bad*·yuh v gra·*duh*
reverse the charges	се обадя за тяхна сметка	se o·*bad*·yuh za *tyah*·na *smet*·ka
speak for (three) minutes	говоря (три) минути	go·*vor*·yuh (tree) mee·*noo*·tee

The number is …
Номерът е …   *no*·me·ruht e …

What's the code for (New Zealand)?
Какъв е кодът за (Нова Зеландия)?   ka·*kuhv* e *ko*·duht za (*no*·va ze·*lan*·dee·ya)

It's engaged.
Дава заето.   *da*·va za·*e*·to

I've been cut off.
Прекъснаха ни.   pre·*kuhs*·na·ha nee

The connection's bad.
Връзката е лоша.   *vruhz*·ka·ta e *lo*·sha

---

dial me up

In Bulgarian, phone numbers with an even number of digits are pronounced in pairs – eg 42 56 21 is che·*tee*·ree·set ee dve pet·de·*set* ee shest *dvai*·set ee ed·*no* (forty-two, fifty-six, twenty-one). If there's an uneven number of digits, either the first number is pronounced separately or the first three digits are rolled into one number, and the other numbers are pronounced in pairs – eg 3 57 21 34 is tree pet·de·*set* ee se·dem *dvai*·set ee ed·*no* tree·set ee che·tee·ree (three, fifty-seven, twenty-one, thirty-four) or tree sto pet·de·*set* ee se·dem *dvai*·set ee ed·*no* tree·set ee che·tee·ree (three hundred and fifty-seven, twenty-one, thirty-four).

Имате грешка.	ee·ma·te gresh·ka	**Wrong number.**
Кой е на телефона?	koy e na te·le·fo·na	**Who's calling?**
Кого търсите?	ko·go tuhr·see·te	**Who do you want to speak to?**
Един момент, моля.	e·deen mo·ment mol·yuh	**One moment, please.**
Няма го/я.	nya·ma go/ya	**He/She isn't here.**

Hello.
Ало.   al·lo

Can I speak to ...?
Може ли да говоря с ...?   mo·zhe lee da go·vor·yuh s ...

It's ...
На телефона е ...   na te·le·fo·na e ...

Can I leave a message?
Мога ли да оставя бележка?   mo·guh lee da o·stav·yuh be·lezh·ka

My number is ...
Моят телефонен номер е ...   mo·yuht te·le·fo·nen no·mer e ...

I don't have a contact number.
Нямам връзка с телефон.   nya·mam vruhz·ka s te·le·fon

I'll call back later.
Ще се обадя по-късно.   shte se o·ba·dyuh po·kuhs·no

What time should I call?
В колко часа да се обадя?   v kol·ko cha·suh da se o·bad·yuh

Please tell (him/her) I called.
Моля, кажете (му/й), че съм се обаждал/обаждала. **m/f**   mol·yuh ka·zhe·te (mu/ee) che suhm se o·bazh·dal/o·bazh·da·la

For telephone numbers, see **numbers & amounts**, page 37.

communications

post office

I want to send a ...	Искам да изпратя ...	*ees*·kam da eez·*prat*·yuh ...
fax	един факс	e·*deen* faks
letter	едно писмо	ed·*no* pees·*mo*
parcel	един колет	e·*deen* ko·*let*
I want to buy a/an ...	Искам да си купя ...	*ees*·kam da see *koop*·yuh ...
envelope	един плик	e·*deen* pleek
stamp	една марка	ed·*na* mar·ka
customs declaration	митническа декларация f	meet·*nee*·ches·ka de·kla·*ra*·tsee·ya
domestic mail	вътрешна поща f	*vuh*·tresh·na *posh*·ta
fragile	чуплив	choop·*leev*
international mail	международна поща f	mezh·doo·na·*rod*·na *posh*·ta
PO box	П.К. f	puh·*kuh*
postcode	пощенски код m	*posh*·ten·skee kod

Please send it by airmail/surface mail to (Australia).
Моля да го изпратите с въздушна/обикновена поща в (Австралия). — *mol*·yuh da go eez·*pra*·tee·te s vuhz·*doosh*·na/o·beek·no·*ve*·na *posh*·ta v (av·*stra*·lee·ya)

It contains (souvenirs).
Съдържа (сувенири). — suh·*duhr*·zha (soo·ve·*nee*·ree)

Is there any mail for me?
Има ли поща за мене? — *ee*·ma lee *posh*·ta za *me*·ne

snail mail

by ...	с ... поща	s ... *posh*·ta
airmail	въздушна	vuhz·*doosh*·na
express mail	бърза	*buhr*·za
sea/surface mail	обикновена	o·beek·no·*ve*·na
by registered mail	препоръчано	pre·po·*ruh*·cha·no

What times is the bank open?

Какво е работното време на банката? · kak·vo e ra·bot·no·to vre·me na ban·ka·ta

What days is the bank open?

В кои дни работи банката? · v ko·yee dnee ra·bo·tee ban·ka·ta

I'd like to …	Искам да …	ees·kam da …
Where can I …?	Къде мога да …?	kuh·de mo·guh da …
cash a cheque	осребря чек	o·sreb·ruh chek
change a travellers cheque	осребря пътнически чек	o·sreb·ruh puht·nee·ches·kee chek
change money	обменя пари	ob·men·yuh pa·ree
get a cash advance	изтегля пари от кредитната си карта	eez·teg·lyuh pa·ree ot kre·deet·na·ta see kar·ta
get change for this note	разваля тази банкнота	raz·va·lyuh ta·zee bank·no·ta
withdraw money	изтегля пари	eez·teg·lyuh pa·ree

What's the …?	Какъв/Каква е …? m/f	ka·kuhv/kak·va e …
charge for that	таксата f	tak·sa·ta
exchange rate	обменният курс на валутата m	ob·men·nee·yuht koors na va·loo·ta·ta

Where's a/an…?	Къде има …?	kuh·de ee·ma …
ATM	банкомат	ban·ko·mat
bank	банка	ban·ka
foreign exchange office	пункт за обмяна на валута	poonkt za ob·mya·na na va·loo·ta

The ATM took my card.
Банкоматът ми взе
картата.

ban·ko·*ma*·tuht mee vze
kar·ta·ta

I've forgotten my PIN.
Забравих си пин-кода.

za·*bra*·veeh see *peen*·ko·da

Can I use my credit card to withdraw money?
Мога ли да изтегля
пари от кредитната си
карта?

mo·guh lee da eez·*teg*·lyuh
pa·*ree* ot kre·*deet*·na·ta see
kar·ta

Has my money arrived yet?
Моите пари
пристигнаха ли вече?

mo·yee·tee pa·*ree*
pree·*steeg*·na·ha lee *ve*·che

How long will it take to arrive?
След колко време ще
пристигнат?

sled *kol*·ko *vre*·me shte
pree·*steeg*·nuht

For other useful phrases, see **money**, page 47.

For other useful phrases, see **money**, page 47.

---

listen for ...

документ за	do·koo·*ment* za	**identification**
самоличност m	sa·mo·*leech*·nost	
паспорт m	pas·*port*	**passport**
твърда валута f	*tvuhr*·da va·*loo*·ta	**hard currency**

Има проблем.
ee·ma prob·*lem*   **There's a problem.**

На вашата сметка няма пари.
na *va*·sha·ta *smet*·ka   **You have no funds left.**
nya·ma pa·*ree*

Не можем да направим това.
ne *mo*·zhem da   **We can't do that.**
na·*pra*·veem to·*va*

Подпишете тука.
pod·pee·*she*·te *too*·ka   **Sign here.**

sightseeing

разглеждане на забележителности

I'd like a/an …	Искам …	*ees*·kam …
audio set	аудио-гид	*a*·oo·dee·o·geed
catalogue	каталог	ka·ta·*log*
guide	пътеводител	puh·te·vo·*dee*·tel
(in English)	(на английски)	(na an·*gleey*·skee)
(local) map	карта	*kar*·ta
	(на района)	(na ra·*yo*·nuh)

Do you have information on … sights?	Имате ли информация за … забележителности?	ee·ma·te lee een·for·*ma*·tsee·ya za … za·be·le·*zhee*·tel·nos·tee
cultural	културните	kool·*toor*·nee·te
historical	историческите	ees·to·*ree*·ches·kee·te
natural	природните	pree·*rod*·nee·te
religious	религиозните	re·lee·gee·*oz*·nee·te

I'd like to go somewhere off the beaten track.

Искам да отида някъде, където ходят малко хора.	*ees*·kam da o·*tee*·duh *nya*·kuh·de kuh·*de*·to *ho*·dyuht *mal*·ko *ho*·ra

I'd like to see …

Искам да видя …	*ees*·kam da *vee*·dyuh …

What's that?

Какво е това?	kak·*vo* e to·*va*

Who built/made it?

Кой го е построил/ направил?	koy go e po·stro·*yeel*/ na·*pra*·veel

How old is it?

Колко е старо?	*kol*·ko e *sta*·ro

Could you take a photo (of me/us)?
Можете ли да (ме/ни)   *mo*·zhe·te lee da (me/nee)
снимате? pol   *snee*·ma·te

Could you take a photo (of me/us)?
Можеш ли да (ми/ни)   *mo*·zhesh lee da (mee/nee)
снимаш? inf   *snee*·mash

Can I take a photo (of you)?
Може ли да (ви/те)   *mo*·zhe lee da (vee/te)
снимам? pol/inf   *snee*·mam

I'll send you the photo.
Ще ви/ти изпратя   shte vee/tee eez·*pra*·tyuh
снимката. pol/inf   *sneem*·ka·ta

getting in

What time does it open/close?
В колко часа отварят/   v *kol*·ko cha·*suh* ot·*var*·yuht/
затварят?   zat·*var*·yuht

What's the admission charge?
Каква е входната такса?   kak·*va* e *vhod*·na·ta *tak*·sa

Is there a discount for ...?	Има ли намаление за ...?	*ee*·ma lee na·ma·*le*·nee·e za ...
children	деца	de·*tsa*
families	семейства	se·*meys*·tva
groups	групи	*groo*·pee
military personnel	войници	voy·*nee*·tsee
older people	възрастни хора	*vuhz*·rast·nee *ho*·ra
pensioners	пенсионери	pen·see·o·*ne*·ree
pupils	ученици	oo·che·*nee*·tsee
students	студенти	stoo·*den*·tee

tours

Can you recommend a …?	Можете ли да ми препоръчате …?	*mo*·zhe·te lee da mee pre·po·*ruh*·cha·te …
When's the next …?	Кога е следващата …?	ko·*ga* e *sled*·vash·ta·ta …
boat trip	лодка	*lod*·ka
day trip	екскурзия	eks·*koor*·zee·ya
(sightseeing) tour	с гид обиколка (на забележителностите)	s geed o·bee·*kol*·ka (na za·be·le·*zhee*·tel·nos·tee·te)
Is … included?	Включен/ Включена ли е …? m/f	*vklyoo*·chen/ *vklyoo*·che·na lee e …
accommodation	нощувката f	nosh·*toov*·ka·ta
food	храната f	hra·*na*·ta
transport	транспортът m	trans·*por*·tuht
Are there any … tours?	Организирате ли …?	or·ga·nee·*zee*·ra·te lee …
cultural	културен туризъм	kool·*too*·ren too·*ree*·zuhm
ecotourism	екотуризъм	e·ko·too·*ree*·zuhm

Do you employ local guides?

Местни екскурзоводи ли използвате? *mest*·nee eks·koor·zo·*vo*·dee lee eez·*polz*·va·te

I'd like to hire a local guide.

Искам да наемам местен екскурзовод. *ees*·kam da na·e·mam *mes*·ten eks·koor·zo·*vod*

Does the guide speak the local dialect?

Екскурзоводът разбира ли местния диалект? eks·koor·zo·*vo*·duht raz·*bee*·ra lee *mest*·nee·yuh dee·a·*lekt*

The guide will pay.

Екскурзоводът ще плати. eks·koor·zo·*vo*·duht shte pla·*tee*

How long is the tour?

Колко трае екскурзията?　*kol*·ko *tra*·ye eks·*koor*·zee·ya·ta

What time should we be back?

В колко часа ще се　　　　v *kol*·ko cha·*suh* shte se
върнем?　　　　　　　　　*vuhr*·nem

I'm with them.

Аз съм с тях.　　　　　　az suhm s tyah

I've lost my group.

Загубих си групата.　　　za·*goo*·beeh see *groo*·pa·ta

signs

Аварvиен изход	a·va·*ree*·en *eez*·hod	**Emergency Exit**
Вход	vhod	**Entrance**
Вход безплатен	vhod bez·*pla*·ten	**Free Admission**
Жени	zhe·*nee*	**Women**
Забранено	za·bra·*ne*·no	**Prohibited**
Запазено	za·*pa*·ze·no	**Reserved**
Затворено	zat·*vo*·re·no	**Closed**
Изход	*eez*·hod	**Exit**
Информация	een·for·*ma*·tsee·ya	**Information**
Мъже	muh·*zhe*	**Men**
Отворено	ot·*vo*·re·no	**Open**
Пушенето	*poo*·she·ne·to	**No Smoking**
забранено	za·bra·*ne*·no	
Студено	stoo·*de*·no	**Cold**
Телефон	te·le·*fon*	**Telephone**
Тоалетни	to·a·*let*·nee	**Toilets**
Топло	*top*·lo	**Hot**
Фотографирането	fo·to·gra·*fee*·ra·ne·to	**No Photography**
забранено	za·bra·*ne*·no	

doing business

търговия

I'm attending a …	На … съм.	na … suhm
business meeting	деловата среща	de·lo·va·ta sresh·ta
conference	конференция	kon·fe·ren·tsee·ya
course	курс	koors
trade fair	търговски панаир	tuhr·gov·skee pa·na·eer

I'm with …	Тука съм с …	too·ka suhm s …
the EU	Европейския съюз	ev·ro·pey·skee·yuh suh·yooz
my colleague/ colleagues	колегата/ колегите си	ko·le·ga·ta/ ko·le·gee·te see
some others	другите	droo·gee·te
(two) others	още (двама) души	osh·te (dva·ma) doo·shee

I'm alone.
Сам/Сама съм. m/f   sam/sa·ma suhm

I have an appointment with …
Имам среща с …   ee·mam sresh·ta s …

I'm staying at the (Ganesh), room (205).
Отседнал/Отседнала   ot·sed·nal/ot·sed·na·la
съм в (Ганеш),   suhm v (ga·nesh)
стая (двеста и пет). m/f   sta·ya (dve·sta ee pet)

I'm here for (two) days.
Тука съм за (два) дена.   too·ka suhm za (dva) de·na

I'm here for (two) weeks.
Тука съм за (две)   too·ka suhm za (dve)
седмици.   sed·mee·tsee

Can I please have your business card?

Дайте ми моля вашата
визитна картичка.

dai·te mee *mol*·yuh va·*sha*·ta
vee·*zeet*·na *kar*·teech·ka

Here's my business card.

Заповядайте моята
визитна картичка.

za·po·*vya*·dai·te *mo*·ya·ta
vee·*zeet*·na *kar*·teech·ka

Here's my ...	Заповядайте моя ...	za·po·*vya*·dai·te *mo*·yuh ...
What's your ...?	Какъв е вашият ...?	ka·*kuhv* e va·shee·yuht ...
(email) address	(и·мейл) адрес	(*ee*·meyl) ad·*res*
fax number	номер на факса	*no*·mer na *fak*·suh
mobile/cell phone number	номер на GSM-а	*no*·mer na dzhee·es·*em*·uh
pager number	номер на пейджъра	*no*·mer na *pey*·dzhuh·ruh
work number	служебен телефон	sloo·*zhe*·ben te·le·*fon*
Where's the ...?	Къде е ...?	kuh·*de* e ...
business centre	бизнес центърът	*beez*·nes *tsen*·tuh·ruht
conference	конференцията	kon·fe·*ren*·tsee·a·ta
meeting	срещата	*sresh*·ta·ta
I need (a/an) ...	Трябва ми ...	*tryab*·va mee ...
computer	компютър	kom·*pyoo*·tuhr
internet connection	Интернет връзка	*een*·ter·net *vruhz*·ka
interpreter who speaks (English)	преводач говорещ (английски)	pre·vo·*dach* go·vo·resht (an·*gleey*·skee)
space to set up my presentation	място да подредя презентацията си	*myas*·to da pod·re·*dyuh* pre·zen·*ta*·tsee·ya·ta see

I need more business cards.
Трябват ми още
визитни картички.

tryab·vat mee *osh*·te
vee·*zeet*·nee *kar*·teech·kee

I need to send a fax.
Трябва да изпратя факс.

tryab·va da eez·*prat*·yuh faks

That went very well.
Това мина много добре.

to·*va* mee·na *mno*·go do·*bre*

Thank you for your time.
Благодаря за вашето
време.

bla·go·da·*ryuh* za va·she·to
vre·me

Shall we go for a drink/meal?
Хайде да пийнем/хапнем
нещо.

hai·de da *peey*·nem/*hap*·nem
nesh·to

It's on me.
Аз черпя.

az *cher*·pyuh

looking for a job

Where are jobs advertised?
Къде се обявяват
работните места?

kuh·*de* se ob·ya·*vya*·vat
ra·*bot*·nee·te mes·*ta*

I'm enquiring about the position advertised.
Интересува ме
обявеното място.

een·te·re·*soo*·va me
ob·*ya*·ve·no·to *myas*·to

What's the wage?
Каква е надницата?

kak·*va* e *nad*·nee·tsa·ta

I'm looking for … work.	Търся работа като …	*tuhr*·syuh *ra*·bo·ta *ka*·to …
bar	барман	bar·*man*
English-teaching	преподавател по английски	pre·po·da·*va*·tel po an·*gleey*·skee
fruit-picking	берач на плодове	be·*rach* na plo·do·*ve*
labouring	работник	ra·*bot*·neek
waitering	сервитьор	ser·vee·*tyor*

Do I need to ...?	Трябва ли да ...?	tryab·va lee da ...
complete	попълня	po·puhl·nyuh
paperwork	документи	do·koo·men·tee
have insurance	имам	ee·mam
	застраховка	za·stra·hov·ka
provide my	имам собствен	ee·mam sobs·tven
own transport	транспорт	trans·port
sign a contract	подпиша	pod·pee·shuh
	трудов договор	troo·dov do·go·vor

Here is/are my ...	Заповядайте ...	za·po·vya·dai·te ...
bank account	информаци-	een·for·ma·tsee·
details	ята за моята	ya·ta za mo·ya·ta
	банкова сметка	ban·ko·va smet·ka
CV	моята авто-	mo·ya·ta av·to·
	биография	bee·o·gra·fee·ya
visa	моята виза	mo·ya·ta vee·za

I can start ...	Мога да	mo·guh da
	започна ...	za·poch·nuh ...
at (eight) o'clock	в (осем) часа	v (o·sem) cha·suh
today	днес	dnes
tomorrow	утре	oo·tre
next week	следващата	sled·vash·ta·ta
	седмица	sed·meet·tsa

What time do I ...?	В колко часа ...?	v kol·ko cha·suh ...
start	започвам	za·poch·vam
	работа	ra·bo·ta
have a break	имам	ee·mam
	почивка	po·cheev·ka
finish	свършвам	svuhr·shvam
	работния ден	ra·bot·nee·ya den

advertisement	обява f	ob·ya·va
contract n	трудов договор m	troo·dov do·go·vor
employee	служител m	sloo·zhee·tel
	служителка f	sloo·zhee·tel·ka
employer	работодател m	ra·bo·to·da·tel
job	работа f	ra·bo·ta
work experience	професионален	pro·fe·see·o·na·len
	опит m	o·peet

senior & disabled travellers

I have a disability.
Аз съм инвалид. — *az suhm een·va·leed*

I need assistance.
Трябва ми помощ. — *tryab·va mee po·mosht*

I'm deaf.
Глух/Глуха съм. m/f — *glooh/gloo·ha suhm*

I have a hearing aid.
Имам слухов апарат. — *ee·mam sloo·hov a·pa·rat*

My travelling companion's blind.
Моят съпътник е сляп. m — *mo·yuht suh·puht·neek e slyap*
Моята съпътница
е сляпа. f — *mo·ya·ta suh·puht·nee·tsa e slya·pa*

What services do you have for people with a disability?
Какви услуги — *kak·vee oo·sloo·gee*
предлагате за инвалиди? — *pred·la·ga·te za een·va·lee·dee*

Are guide dogs permitted?
Разрешени ли са — *raz·re·she·nee lee sa*
кучетата водачи? — *koo·che·ta·ta vo·da·chee*

Are there disabled parking spaces?
Има ли места за — *ee·ma lee mes·ta za*
паркиране за инвалиди? — *par·kee·ra·ne za een·va·lee·dee*

Is there wheelchair access?
Има ли достъп за — *ee·ma lee do·stuhp za*
инвалидни колички? — *een·va·leed·nee ko·leech·kee*

How wide is the entrance?
Каква е ширината — *kak·va e shee·ree·na·ta*
на входа? — *na vho·duh*

How many steps are there?
Колко стъпала има? — *kol·ko stuh·pa·la ee·ma*

Is there an elevator/lift?
Има ли асансьор? — *ee·ma lee a·san·syor*

Are there disabled toilets?

Има ли тоалетни
за инвалиди?

*ee·*ma lee to·a·*let·*nee
za een·va·*lee·*dee

Are there rails in the bathroom?

Има ли парапети
в банята?

*ee·*ma lee pa·ra·*pe·*tee
v *ban·*ya·ta

Could you call me a disabled taxi?

Можете ли да ми
поръчате такси за
инвалида?

*mo·*zhe·te lee da mee
po·*ruh·*cha·te tak·*see* za
een·va·*lee·*duh

Could you help me cross the street safely?

Можете ли да ми
помогнете да
пресека улицата?

*mo·*zhe·te lee da mee
po·*mog·*ne·te da
pre·se·*kuh* oo·lee·tsa·ta

Is there somewhere I can sit down?

Има ли място където
мога да седна?

*ee·*ma lee *myas·*to kuh·*de·*to
*mo·*guh da *sed·*nuh

guide dog	куче водач m	*koo·*che vo·*dach*
older man	възрастен човек m	*vuhz·*ras·ten cho·*vek*
older woman	възрастна жена f	*vuhz·*rast·na zhe·*na*
person with a disability	инвалид m	een·va·*leed*
ramp	склон m	sklon
walking frame	помощна рамка за ходене f	po·*mosht·*na *ram·*ka za *ho·*de·ne
walking stick	бастун m	bas·*toon*
wheelchair	инвалидна количка f	een·va·*leed·*na ko·*leech·*ka

---

animal talk

бау-бау	*ba·*oo·*ba·*oo	(dog)
бе-е	be·*e*	(sheep)
грох-грох	*groh·*groh	(pig)
кукуригу	koo·koo·ree·*goo*	(rooster)
ме-е	me·*e*	(goat)
му-у	moo·*oo*	(cow)
мяу	*mya·*oo	(cat)
па-па-па	*pa·*pa·pa	(duck)

travelling with children

пътуване с деца

Is there a ...?	Има ли ...?	ee·ma lee ...
baby change room	стая за преобличане на бебета	sta·ya za pre·o·blee·cha·ne na be·be·ta
child-minding service	служба осигуряваща услуги на бавачки	sloozh·ba o·see·goor·ya·vash·ta oo·sloo·gee na ba·vach·kee
child's portion	детска порция	det·ska por·tsee·ya
children's menu	детско меню	det·sko men·yoo
crèche	детски ясли	det·skee yas·lee
discount for children	намаление за децата	na·ma·le·nee·e za de·tsa·ta
family ticket	семеен билет	se·me·en bee·let

Do you sell ...?	Продавате ли ...?	pro·da·va·te lee ...
baby wipes	мокри кърпички за бебета	mo·kree kuhr·peech·kee za be·be·ta
disposable nappies	пелени за еднократка употреба	pe·le·nee za ed·no·krat·ka oo·po·tre·ba
painkillers for babies	болкоуспо- коутелни лекарства за бебета	bol·ko·oos·po· ko·ee·tel·nee le·kars·tva za be·be·ta
tissues	хартиени кърпички	har·tee·e·nee kuhr·peech·kee

I need a/an ...	Трябва ми ...	*tryab*·va mee ...
baby seat	детска седалка	*det*·ska se·*dal*·ka
(for the car)	(за кола)	(za ko·*la*)
(English-speaking) babysitter	бавачка (говореща английски)	ba·*vach*·ka (go·*vo*·resh·ta an·*gleey*·skee)
booster seat	детска седалка	*det*·ska se·*dal*·ka
cot	детско легло	*det*·sko leg·*lo*
highchair	високо детско столче за хранене	vee·*so*·ko *det*·sko *stol*·che za *hra*·ne·ne
plastic bag	найлонова торбичка	nai·*lo*·no·va tor·*beech*·ka
plastic sheet	найлонов чаршаф	nai·*lo*·nov char·*shaf*
potty	гърне	guhr·*ne*
pram	бебешка количка	*be*·besh·ka ko·*leech*·ka
pushchair/ stroller	детска количка	*det*·ska ko·*leech*·ka
sick bag	торбичка за повръщане	tor·*beech*·ka za po·*vruh*·shta·ne

Where's the nearest ...?	Къде е най-близкият/ най-близката ...? m/f	kuh·*de* e *nai*·bleez·kee·yuht/ *nai*·bleez·ka·ta ...
drinking fountain	чешма f	chesh·*ma*
playground	детска площадка f	*det*·ska plosh·*tad*·ka
puppet theatre	куклен театър m	*kook*·len te·*a*·tuhr
swimming pool	плувен басейн m	*ploo*·ven ba·*seyn*
tap	чешма f	chesh·*ma*
theme park	детски универсален парк m	*det*·skee oo·nee·ver·*sa*·len park
toyshop	магазин за детски играчки m	ma·ga·*zeen* za *det*·skee ee·*grach*·kee

Are there any good places to take children around here?

Има ли в района добри	*ee*·ma lee v ra·*yo*·nuh do·*bree*
места за разходка с деца?	mes·*ta* za raz·*hod*·ka s de·*tsa*

Are children allowed?

Разрешено ли е за деца?	raz·re·*she*·no lee e za de·*tsa*

Is there space for a pram?

Има ли място за	*ee*·ma lee *myas*·to za
бебешка количка?	be·besh·ka ko·*leech*·ka

Where can I change a nappy?

Къде мога да сменя	kuh·*de mo*·guh da smen·*yuh*
бебешките пелени?	be·besh·kee·te pe·le·*nee*

Could I have some paper and pencils, please?

Ще ми дадете/дадеш ли	shte mee da·*de*·te/da·*desh* lee
моля хартия и	*mol*·yuh har·*tee*·ya ee
моливи? pol/inf	*mo*·lee·vee

Is this suitable for (six)-year-old children?

Това подходящо ли е	to·*va* pod·hod·*yash*·to lee e
за (шест)годишни деца?	za (shest·)go·*deesh*·nee de·*tsa*

Do you know a dentist/doctor who is good with children?

Можете ли да	*mo*·zhe·te lee da
препоръчате детски	pre·po·*ruh*·cha·te *det*·skee
зъболекар/лекар?	zuh·bo·*le*·kar/*le*·kar

If your child is sick, see **health**, page 193.

talking with children

разговор с деца

In this section, phrases are in the informal 'you' form only. For more information, see the box **all about you**, page 138.

What's your name?

Как се казваш?	kak se *kaz*·vash

How old are you?

На колко си години?	na *kol*·ko see go·*dee*·nee

Do you go to school?

Ходиш ли на училище?	*ho*·deesh lee na oo·*chee*·leesh·te

What grade are you in?
В кой клас си?   v koy klas see

Do you learn (English)?
Учиш ли (английски)?   *oo*·cheesh lee (an·*gleey*·skee)

What do you do after school?
Какво правиш след   kak·*vo pra*·veesh sled
училище?   oo·*chee*·leesh·te

talking about children

Avoid complimenting children, as it's believed to bring bad luck. For the same reason, Bulgarians don't bring gifts for unborn children.

When's the baby due?
Кога очаквате/   ko·*ga* o·*chak*·va·te/
очакваш да се роди   o·*chak*·vash da se ro·*dee*
бебето? **pol/inf**   be·be·to

What are you going to call the baby?
Как ще кръстите/   kak shte *kruh*·stee·te/
кръстиш бебето? **pol/inf**   *kruh*·steesh be·be·to

Is this your first child?
Това вашето/твоето   to·*va va*·she·to/*tvo*·ye·to
първо дете ли е? **pol/inf**   *puhr*·vo de·*te* lee e

How many children do you have?
Колко деца имате/   *kol*·ko de·*tsa* ee·ma·te/
имаш? **pol/inf**   ee·mash

What's his/her name?
Как се казва?   kak se *kaz*·va

How old is he/she?
На колко години е?   na *kol*·ko go·*dee*·nee e

Does he/she go to school?
Ходи ли на училище?   *ho*·dee lee na oo·*chee*·leesh·te

He/She looks like you.
Прилича на вас. **pol**   pree·*lee*·cha na vas
Прилича на тебе. **inf**   pree·*lee*·cha na *te*·be

basics

основни неща

Yes.	Да.	da
No.	Не.	ne
Please.	Моля.	*mol*·yuh
Thank you (very much).	(Много) Благодаря.	(*mno*·go) bla·go·dar·*yuh*
You're welcome.	Няма защо.	*nya*·ma zash·*to*
Excuse me. (to get attention)	Моля.	*mol*·ya
Excuse me. (to get past)	Извинете.	eez·vee·*ne*·te
Sorry.	Съжалявам.	suh·zhal·*ya*·vam

hello goodbye

The greeting extended to a new arrival is *Добре дошли!* *do*·bre dosh·*lee* (welcome) to a group or in the polite form, and *Добре дошъл!* *do*·bre do·*shuhl* (to a man) or *Добре дошла!* *do*·bre dosh·*la* (to a woman) in the informal form. The response, less commonly used, is *Добре заварили!* *do*·bre za·*va*·ree·lee (lit: well met), spoken in the polite form or on behalf of a group. In the informal form, the equivalent is *Добре заварила!* *do*·bre za·*va*·ree·la (said by a woman) or *Добре заварил!* *do*·bre za·*va*·reel (said by a man). When someone departs on a long trip it's traditional to throw water in front of them and say *Да ви/ти върви по вода!* pol/inf da vee/tee vuhr·*vee* po vo·*da* (May all go smoothly for you!).

It's customary to shake hands when introduced. Old friends hug each other and kiss on both cheeks.

Hello.	Здравейте. pol	zdra·*vey*·te
Hi.	Здравей. inf	zdra·*vey*
Good morning.	Добро утро.	dob·*ro* oot·ro
Good day.	Добър ден.	do·buhr den
Good afternoon.	Добър ден.	do·buhr den
Good evening.	Добър вечер.	do·buhr *ve*·cher

How are you?
Как сте/си? pol/inf — kak ste/see

Fine, thanks. And you?
Добре, благодаря. — dob·*re* bla·go·dar·*yuh*
А вие/ти? pol/inf — a *vee*·e/tee

What's your name?
Как се казвате/казваш? pol/inf — kak se *kaz*·va·te/*kaz*·vash

My name is …
Казвам се … — *kaz*·vam se …

I'd like to introduce you to (Petar Petrov).
Искам да ви/ти — *ees*·kam da vee/tee
представя (Петър — pred·*stav*·yuh (*pe*·tuhr
Петров). pol/inf — pet·*rov*)

I'm pleased to meet you.
Приятно ми е да се — pree·*yat*·no mee e da se
запозная с вас/тебе. pol/inf — za·poz·*na*·yuh s vas/*te*·be

This is my …	Това е … ми.	to·*va* e … mee
child	детето	de·*te*·to
colleague	колегата	ko·*le*·ga·ta
friend	приятелят m	pree·*ya*·tel·yuht
	приятелката f	pree·*ya*·tel·ka·ta
husband	мъжът	muh·*zhuht*
partner	приятелят m	pree·*ya*·tel·yuht
(romantic)	приятелката f	pree·*ya*·tel·ka·ta
wife	жена	zhe·*na*

See you later.	До скоро виждане.	do *sko*·ro *veezh*·da·ne
Bye.	Чао.	*cha*·o
Goodbye.	Довиждане.	do·*veezh*·da·ne
Good night.	Лека нощ.	*le*·ka nosht
Bon voyage!	Приятно пътуване!	pree·*yat*·no puh·*too*·va·ne

addressing people

The words for 'Sir/Madam' are given below in the vocative form, which is the form used when addressing someone. The other words are given in the neutral form, used when talking about a person. The term *госпожице* gos·po·*zhee*·tse ('Miss' in the vocative form) should be avoided if the female in question looks over 20 or so, as it implies you think that the woman isn't married, which is considered impolite. The phrase *Дами и господа* da·mee ee gos·po·da (Ladies and gentlemen) is also used as a form of address, just like in English.

Sir	Господине	gos·po·*dee*·ne
Madam	Господжо	gos·*po*·zho
Mr	Господин	gos·po·*deen*
Mrs/Ms	Господжа	gos·po·*zha*
Ms/Miss	Господжица	gos·po·zhee·tsa

hey there!

The words *колега* ko·*le*·ga (colleague), *приятел* pree·*ya*·tel (friend) and *мой човек* moy cho·*vek* (my man) are often used as neutral forms of address (without implying that the person is a colleague or a friend). The latter two are only for men, whereas the first one can be used for both men and women. The colloquial term *бе* be (buddy, mate) is often used in expressions such as *Хайде бе!* hai·de be (Come on, pal!) or *Стига бе!* stee·ga be (That's enough, mate!). It refers to both men and women. The phrase *моето момиче* mo·e·to mo·*mee*·che (my girl) can be used for addressing women, but only if you know them relatively well.

making conversation

What's new?
Какво ново? — kak·vo no·vo

What's up?
Какво правиш? — kak·vo pra·veesh

What a beautiful day!
Какъв прекрасен ден! — ka·kuhv pre·kra·sen den

Nice/Awful weather, isn't it?
Хубаво/Ужасно време, нали? — hoo·ba·vo/oo·zhas·no vre·me na·lee

Do you live here?
Вие тука ли живеете? pol — vee·e too·ka lee zhee·ve·e·te
Ти тука ли живееш? inf — tee too·ka lee zhee·ve·esh

Where are you going?
Къде отивате/отиваш? pol/inf — kuh·de o·tee·va·te/o·tee·vash

What are you doing?
Какво правите/правиш? pol/inf — kak·vo pra·vee·te/pra·veesh

Do you like it here?
Харесва ли ви/ти тука? pol/inf — ha·res·va lee vee/tee too·ka

I love it here.
Много ми хареса тука. — mno·go mee ha·res·va too·ka

etiquette tips

- Wait to be invited before sitting down, taking food or drinking (even when it's clearly meant for consumption).
- Maintain eye contact during conversation. Keep your hands in view, especially when in small towns.
- Lively facial expressions and frequent touching on the shoulder are a normal part of conversation.
- Avoid asking personal questions about religion, finances or family. It's also impolite to ask a woman's age.

SOCIAL

114

Hey!	Хей!	hey
Great!	Супер!	soo·per
Sure.	Естествено.	es·test·ve·no
Maybe.	Може би.	mo·zhe bee
No way!	Няма начин!	nya·ma na·cheen
Just a minute.	Един момент.	e·deen mo·ment
Just joking.	Шегувам се.	she·goo·vam se
It's OK.	Добре.	do·bre
No problem.	Няма проблем.	nya·ma prob·lem

What's this called?
Това как се казва? — to·va kak se kaz·va

That's (beautiful), isn't it?
Това е (хубаво), нали? — to·va e (hoo·ba·vo) na·lee

Can I take a photo (of you)?
Мога ли да (ви/те) снимам? pol/inf — mo·guh lee da (vee/te) snee·mam

I'll send you the photo.
Ще ви/ти изпратя снимката. pol/inf — shte vee/tee eez·prat·yuh sneem·ka·ta

How long are you here for?
Колко ще останете/останеш тук? pol/inf — kol·ko shte o·sta·ne·te/o·sta·nesh took

I'm here for (four) weeks/days.
Тука съм (четири) седмици/дена. — too·ka suhm (che·tee·ree) sed·mee·tsee/de·na

Are you here on holiday?
Вие във ваканция ли сте тука? pol — vee·e vuhv va·kan·tsee·ya lee ste too·ka
Ти във ваканция ли си тука? inf — tee vuhv va·kan·tsee·ya lee see too·ka

I'm here … — Тука съм … — too·ka suhm …
for a holiday	във ваканция	vuhv va·kan·tsee·ya
on business	по работа	po ra·bo·ta
to study	за да уча	za da oo·chuh

meeting people

115

nationalities

Where are you from?
Откъде сте/си? pol/inf · ot·kuh·*de* ste/see

I'm from …	Аз съм от …	az suhm ot …
Australia	Австралия	av·*stra*·lee·ya
Canada	Канада	ka·*na*·da
Ireland	Ирландия	eer·*lan*·dee·ya
New Zealand	Нова	*no*·va
	Зеландия	ze·*lan*·dee·ya
the UK	Велико-	ve·lee·ko·
	британия	bree·*ta*·nee·ya
the USA	САЩ	sasht

age

възраст

How old …?	На колко	na *kol*·ko
	години …?	go·*dee*·nee …
are you	сте/си pol/inf	ste/see
is your	е дъщеря	e duhsh·ter·*ya*
daughter	ви/ти pol/inf	vee·tee
is your son	е синът	e see·*nuht*
	ви/ти pol/inf	vee·tee

I'm … years old.
Аз съм на … години. · az suhm na … go·*dee*·nee

He/She is … years old.
Той/Тя е на … години. · toy/tya e na … go·*dee*·nee

Too old!
Прекалено стар/стара! m/f · pre·ka·*le*·no star/*sta*·ra

I'm younger than I look.
По-млад/По-млада съм · *po*·mlad/*po*·mla·da suhm
отколкото изглеждам. m/f · ot·*kol*·ko·to eez·*glezh*·dam

For your age, see **numbers & amounts**, page 37.

SOCIAL

116

occupations & studies

What's your occupation?

| Какво работите/ | kak·vo ra·bo·tee·te/ |
| работиш? pol/inf | ra·bo·teesh |

I'm a ...   Аз съм ...   az suhm ...

chef	готвач	got·vach
journalist	журналист m	zhoor·na·leest
	журналистка f	zhoor·na·leest·ka
teacher	учител m	oo·chee·tel
	учителка f	oo·chee·tel·ka

I work in ...   Работя в ...   ra·bo·tyuh v ...

banking	банка	ban·ka
education	учебно	oo·cheb·no
	заведение	za·ve·de·nee·e
sales & marketing	търговията	tuhr·go·vee·ya·ta
transport	транспорта	trans·por·tuh

I'm ...   Аз съм ...   az suhm ...

retired	пенсионер m	pen·see·o·ner
	пенсионерка f	pen·see·o·ner·ka
unemployed	без работа	bez ra·bo·ta

I'm self-employed.

| Имам частен бизнис. | ee·mam chas·ten beez·nees |

What are you studying?

| Какво следвате/ | kak·vo sled·va·te/ |
| следваш? pol/inf | sled·vash |

I'm studying ...   Следвам ...   sled·vam ...

Bulgarian	български	buhl·gar·skee
	език	e·zeek
chemistry	химия	hee·mee·ya
history	история	ees·to·ree·ya
philology	филология	fee·lo·lo·gee·ya
physics	физика	fee·zee·ka

family

Do you have a ...?	Имате/Имаш ли ...? pol/inf	ee·ma·te/ee·mash lee ...
I have a ...	Имам ...	ee·mam ...
I don't have a ...	Нямам ...	nya·mam ...
brother	брат	brat
daughter	дъщеря	duhsh·te·rya
granddaughter	внучка	vnooch·ka
grandson	внук	vnook
husband	мъж	muhzh
partner (romantic)	приятел m	pree·ya·tel
	приятелка f	pree·ya·tel·ka
sister	сестра	ses·tra
son	син	seen
wife	жена	zhe·na

Are you married?

| | Женен ли сте/си? m pol/inf | zhe·nen lee ste/see |
| | Омъжена ли сте/си? f pol/inf | o·muh·zhe·na lee ste/see |

I live with someone.

| | Живея с някого. | zhee·ve·ya s nya·ko·go |

I'm ...	Аз съм ...	az suhm ...
divorced	разведен m	raz·ve·den
	разведена f	raz·ve·de·na
married	женен m	zhe·nen
	омъжена f	o·muh·zhe·na
single	неженен m	ne·zhe·nen
	неомъжена f	ne·o·muh·zhe·na

The system of names for family members in Bulgarian is very complex, reflecting the norm, in the past, of large extended families. There are a number of different terms for both 'aunt' and 'uncle', depending on whether it's the father's or the mother's sibling, and on whether the relationship is by blood or by marriage. As family units become increasingly nuclear, the system of names is becoming simpler. Everyone distinguishes the names for mother-in-law and father-in-law – although both bride and groom are expected to call their mother-in-law simply *майка* mai·ka (mother).

father-in-law and mother-in-law:

свекър	*sve*·kuhr	husband's father
свекърва	sve·*kuhr*·va	husband's mother
тъст	tuhst	wife's father
тъща	*tuhsh*·ta	wife's mother

brother-in-law:

баджанак	bad·zha·*nak*	wife's sister's husband
девер	*de*·ver	husband's brother
зет	zet	sister's husband
шурей	*shoo*·rey	wife's brother

sister-in-law:

балдъза	bal·*duh*·za	wife's sister
етърва	e·*tuhr*·va	husband's brother's wife
зълва	*zuhl*·va	husband's sister
снаха	sna·*ha*	brother's wife
шуренайка	shoo·re·*nai*·ka	wife's brother's wife

uncle:

вуйчо	*vooy*·cho	mother's brother
свако	*sva*·ko	mother's or father's sister's husband
чичо	*chee*·cho	father's brother

aunt:

вуйна	*vooy*·na	mother's brother's wife
леля	*lel*·ya	father's or mother's sister
стринка	*streen*·ka	father's brother's wife

farewells

Tomorrow is my last day here.

Утре ми е последният
ден тука.

oo·tre mee e po·*sled*·nee·yuht
den *too*·ka

If you come to (Scotland), you can stay with me.

Ако дойдете в
(Шотландия), ще можете
да отседнете при мен. pol

a·ko *doy*·de·te v
(shot·*lan*·dee·ya) shte *mo*·zhe·te
da ot·*sed*·ne·te pree men

Ако дойдеш в
(Шотландия), ще можеш
да отседнеш при мен. inf

a·ko *doy*·desh v
(shot·*lan*·dee·ya) shte *mo*·zhesh
da ot·*sed*·nesh pree men

Keep in touch!

Да поддържаме връзка!

da pod·*durh*·zha·me *vruhz*·ka

It's been great meeting you.

Много ми беше приятно
да се запознаем.

mno·go mee *be*·she pree·*yat*·no
da se za·po·*zna*·yem

Here's my …	Заповядайте/	za·po·*vya*·dai·te/
	Заповядай	za·po·*vya*·dai
	моя … pol/inf	*mo*·yuh …
What's your …?	Какъв е вашият/	ka·*kuhv* e va·shee·yuht/
	твоят …? pol/inf	*tvo*·yuht …
(email) address	(и-мейл) адрес	(*ee*·meyl) ad·*res*
phone number	телефонен	te·le·*fo*·nen
	номер	*no*·mer

well-wishing

Bless you!	Наздраве!	na·*zdra*·ve
Congratulations!	Честито!	ches·*tee*·to
Good luck!	Успех!	oo·*speh*
Happy birthday!	Честит рожден	ches·*teet* rozh·*den*
	ден!	den
Happy holiday!	Честит празник!	ches·*teet* *praz*·neek
Happy name day!	Честит имен ден!	ches·*teet* *ee*·men den

n this chapter, phrases are in the informal *mu* tee (you) form
nly. For more information, see the box **all about you**, page 138.

common interests

общи интереси

What do you do in your spare time?

Какво правиш в свободното си време?	kak·*vo* pra·veesh v svo·*bod*·no·to see *vre*·me

Do you like ...?	Обичаш ли ...?	o·*bee*·chash lee ...
(don't) like ...	(Не) Обичам ...	(ne) o·*bee*·cham ...
computer games	компютър-ните игри	kom·*pyoo*·tuhr-nee·te ee·*gree*
cooking	готвенето	*got*·ve·ne·to
gardening	градинарството	gra·dee·*narst*·vo·to
music	музиката	*moo*·zee·ka·ta
photography	фотографията	fo·to·*gra*·fee·ya·ta
sport	спорта	*spor*·tuh

Do you like ...?	Обичаш ли да ...?	o·*bee*·chash lee da ...
dancing	танцуваш	tan·*tsoo*·vash
drawing	рисуваш	ree·*soo*·vash
films	гледаш филми	*gle*·dash *feel*·mee
painting	рисуваш	ree·*soo*·vash
reading	четеш	che·*tesh*
shopping	пазаруваш	pa·za·*roo*·vash
socialising	си сред хората	see sred *ho*·ra·ta
surfing the internet	сърфираш Интернета	suhr·*fee*·rash *een*·ter·ne·tuh
travelling	пътуваш	puh·*too*·vash
watching TV	гледаш телевизия	*gle*·dash te·le·*vee*·zee·ya

I (don't) like …	(He) Обичам да …	(ne) o·bee·cham da …
dancing	танцувам	tan·tsoo·vam
drawing	рисувам	ree·soo·vam
films	гледам филми	gle·dam feel·mee
painting	рисувам	ree·soo·vam
reading	чета	che·tuh
shopping	пазарувам	pa·za·roo·vam
socialising	съм сред хората	suhm sred ho·ra·ta
surfing the internet	сърфирам интернета	suhr·fee·ram een·ter·ne·tuh
travelling	пътувам	puh·too·vam
watching TV	гледам телевизия	gle·dam te·le·vee·zee·ya

For types of sport, see **sport**, page 149, and the **dictionary**.

traditional pastimes

Older men in Bulgaria frequently play games such as *табла tab·la* (backgammon) and *карти kar·tee* (cards), while older women often entertain themselves by doing *ръкоделие ruh·ko·de·lee·e* (needlework).

music

музика

Do you …?		
dance	Танцуваш ли?	tan·tsoo·vash lee
go to concerts	Ходиш ли на концерти?	ho·deesh lee na kon·tser·tee
listen to music	Слушаш ли музика?	sloo·shash lee moo·zee·ka
play an instrument	Свириш ли някакъв инструмент?	svee·reesh lee nya·ka·kuhv een·stroo·ment
sing	Пееш ли?	pe·esh lee

in the folk groove

Bulgarian traditional music presents a contrast between the Byzantine elements found in Orthodox church music and the Turkish influence evident in the folk songs and dances of the villages. Here are some traditional folk instruments:

гъдулка f	guh·*dool*·ka	small pear-shaped fiddle, also known as *ребек* m *re*·bek
гайда f	*gai*·da	goatskin bagpipe
даире n	dai·*re*	similar to a tambourine
кавал m	ka·*val*	long, open flute, held diagonally when played
тамбура f	tam·boo·*ra*	four-stringed, long-necked lute, also called *дрънка* f *druhn*·ka
тъпан m	*tuh*·pan	large, cylindrical, double-headed drum

Which ... do you like?	Какви ... харесваш?	kak·*vee* ... ha·*res*·vash
bands	оркестри	or·*kes*·tree
performers	изпълнители	eez·puhl·*nee*·te·lee
singers	певци	pev·*tsee*
choral music	хорова музика f	*ho*·ro·va moo·zee·ka
classical music	класическа музика f	kla·*see*·ches·ka moo·zee·ka
contemporary music	съвременна музика f	suh·*vre*·men·na moo·zee·ka
electronic music	електронна музика f	e·lek·*tron*·na moo·zee·ka
folk music	народна музика f	na·*rod*·na moo·zee·ka
pop	естрадна музика f	es·*trad*·na moo·zee·ka
world music	музика на други народи f	moo·zee·ka na *droo*·gee na·*ro*·dee

Planning to go to a concert? See **tickets**, page 51, and **going out**, page 133.

interests

123

cinema & theatre

I feel like going to a/an …	Ходи ми се на …	*ho*·dee mee se na …
ballet	балет	ba·*let*
film	кино	*kee*·no
opera	опера	*o*·pe·ra
performance	представление	pred·stav·*le*·nee·e
play	театър	te·*a*·tuhr

Did you like the …?	Хареса ли ти …?	ha·*re*·sa lee tee …
ballet	балетът	ba·*le*·tuht
film	филмът	*feel*·muht
opera	операта	*o*·pe·ra·ta
performance	представле-ниeто	pred·stav·*le*·nee·e·to
play	пиесата	pee·*e*·sa·ta

What's showing at the cinema/theatre tonight?
Какво дават в киното/ театъра довечера? kak·*vo da*·vat v *kee*·no·to/ te·*a*·tuh·ruh do·*ve*·che·ra

Is it in (English)?
На (английски) ли е? na (an·*glee*·skee) lee e

Does it have (English) subtitles?
Има ли субтитри (на английски)? *ee*·ma lee *soob*·tee·tree (na an·*glee*·skee)

Is it dubbed?
Дублиран ли е? doob·*lee*·ran lee e

Is this seat taken?
Това място заето ли е? to·*va myas*·to za·*e*·to lee e

Do you have tickets for …?
Имате ли билети за …? *ee*·ma·te lee bee·*le*·tee za …

Are there any extra tickets?
Има ли още билети? *ee*·ma lee *osh*·te bee·*le*·tee

I'd like cheap/the best tickets.
Искам евтини/ най-хубавите билети. *ees*·kam *ev*·tee·nee/ nai·hoo·ba·vee·te bee·*le*·tee

s there a matinée show?

Има ли дневно представление?		ee·ma lee dnev·no pred·stav·le·nee·e

Have you seen (The Peach Thief)?

Гледал/Гледала ли си (Крадецът на праскови)? m/f		gle·dal/gle·da·la lee see (kra·de·tsuht na pras·ko·vee)

Who's in it?

Кой играе в него?	koy ee·gra·ye v ne·go

stars (Hristo Shopov).

В главната роля е (Христо Шопов).	v glav·na·ta rol·ya e (hrees·to sho·pov)

thought it	Мисля, че	mees·lya che
was …	беше …	be·she …
excellent	страхотно	stra·hot·no
long	много дълго	mno·go duhl·go
OK	добре	do·bre

(don't) like …	(Не) Харесвам …	(ne) ha·res·vam …
action movies	приключенски филми	pree·klyoo·chen·skee feel·mee
animated films	анимационни филми	a·nee·ma·tsee·on·nee feel·mee
(Bulgarian) cinema	(българското) кино	(buhl·gar·sko·to) kee·no
comedies	комедии	ko·me·dee·ee
documentaries	документални филми	do·koo·men·tal·nee feel·mee
drama	драма	dra·ma
horror movies	филми на ужасите	feel·mee na oo·zha·see·te
sci-fi	фантастични филми	fan·tas·teech·nee feel·mee
short films	кратко-метражни филми	krat·ko·me·trazh·nee feel·mee
thrillers	криминални филми	kree·mee·nal·nee feel·mee
war movies	военни филми	vo·yen·nee feel·mee

Like father, like son.
> Крушата не пада   *kroo*·sha·ta ne *pa*·da
> по-далеч от дървото.   *po*·da·lech ot duhr·*vo*·to
> (lit: The pear doesn't fall any further than the tree.)

Talk is cheap.
> Дума дупка не прави.   *doo*·ma *doop*·ka ne *pra*·vee
> (lit: A word doesn't make a hole.)

Best to keep your head down.
> Преклонена глава   prek·lo·*ne*·na gla·*va*
> сабя не я сече.   sab·*ya* ne ya se·*che*
> (lit: Swords don't cut off the bowed head.)

Mind your own business.
> Всяка жаба да си   *vsya*·ka *zha*·ba da see
> знае гьола.   *zna*·e *gyo*·la
> (lit: Each frog needs to know its own pond.)

There's strength in numbers.
> Сговорна дружина   sgo·*vor*·na droo·*zhee*·na
> планина повдига.   pla·nee·*na* pov·*dee*·ga
> (lit: A harmonious group can raise a mountain.)

A bad penny always turns up.
> Черен гологан   *che*·ren go·lo·*gan*
> не се губи.   ne se *goo*·bee
> (lit: A black coin doesn't get lost.)

Every dog has its day.
> Всяко чудо за три дена.   *vsya*·ko *choo*·do za tree *de*·na
> (lit: Each miracle lasts three days.)

eelings

чувства

n this section, phrases are in the informal *mu* tee (you) form
nly. For more information, see the box **all about you**, page 138.

re you …?	… ли си?	… lee see
m (not) …	Аз (не) съм …	az (ne) suhm …
annoyed	раздразнен m	raz-*draz*-nen
	раздразнена f	raz-*draz*-ne-na
disappointed	разочарован m	ra-zo-cha-*ro*-van
	разочарована f	ra-zo-cha-*ro*-va-na
embarrassed	притеснен m	pree-tes-*nen*
	притеснена f	pree-tes-*ne*-na
happy	щастлив m	shtast-*leev*
	щастлива f	shtast-*lee*-va
homesick	обзет/обзета от	ob-*zet*/ob-*ze*-ta ot
	носталгия m/f	nos-*tal*-gee-ya
hungry	гладен m	*gla*-den
	гладна f	*glad*-na
surprised	изненадан m	eez-ne-*na*-dan
	изненадана f	eez-ne-*na*-da-na
sad	тъжен m	*tuh*-zhen
	тъжна f	*tuhzh*-na
thirsty	жаден m	*zha*-den
	жадна f	*zhad*-na
tired	уморен m	oo-mo-*ren*
	уморена f	oo-mo-*re*-na
re you worried?	Притесняваш ли се?	pree-tes-*nya*-vash lee se
m worried.	Притеснявам се.	pree-tes-*nya*-vam se
'm not worried.	Не се притеснявам.	ne se pree-tes-*nya*-vam

Are you ...?	... ли ти е?	... lee tee e
I'm ...	... ми е.	... mee e
cold	Студено	stoo·*de*·no
hot	Горещо	go·*resh*·to
I'm not ...	Не ми е ...	ne mee e ...
cold	студено	stoo·*de*·no
hot	горещо	go·*resh*·to

If you're not feeling well, see **health**, page 193.

mixed emotions

not at all	никак	*nee*·kak

I don't care at all.
Никак не ме вълнува.   *nee*·kak ne me vuhl·*noo*·va

a little	малко	*mal*·ko

I'm a little sad.
Малко съм тъжен/   *mal*·ko suhm *tuh*·zhen/
тъжна. m/f   *tuhzh*·na

very	много	*mno*·go

I feel very happy.
Чувствам се много   *chuvs*·tvam se *mno*·go
щастлив/щастлива. m/f   shtast·*leev*/shtast·*lee*·va

extremely	страшно	*strash*·no

I'm extremely sorry.
Страшно съжалявам.   *strash*·no suh·zhal·*ya*·vam

opinions

Did you like it?
Това хареса ли ви/ти? pol/inf   to·*va* ha·*re*·sa lee vee/tee

What do you think of it?
Какво мислите/мислиш   kak·*vo* mees·lee·te/mees·lees·
за това? pol/inf   za to·*va*

I thought it was ...	Мисля, че беше ...	mees·lyuh che be·she ...
It's ...	Това е ...	to·va e ...
awful	ужасно	oo·zhas·no
beautiful	много хубаво	mno·go hoo·ba·vo
boring	досадно	do·sad·no
(too) expensive	(много) скъпо	(mno·go) skuh·po
great	чудесно	choo·des·no
interesting	интересно	een·te·res·no
OK	добре	do·bre
strange	странно	stran·no

politics & social issues

политика и обществени проблеми

Tread carefully when discussing politics in Bulgaria – it's best not to ask which political party someone belongs to or how they vote. The issue of ethnic minorities, especially *Рома ro·*ma (the Roma people) but also *Помаци* po·*ma·*tsee (Bulgarian Muslims, or Pomaks), is a sensitive one.

I support the ... party.	Подкрепям ... партия.	pod·*krep*·yam ... *par*·tee·ya
I'm a member of the ... party.	Член съм на ... партия.	chlen suhm na ... *par*·tee·ya
communist	комунисти-ческата	ko·moo·nees·*tee·*ches·ka·ta
conservative	консерватив-ната	kon·ser·va·*teev·*na·ta
democratic	демократи-ческата	de·mo·kra·*tee·*ches·ka·ta
green	зелената	ze·*le·*na·ta
liberal	либералната	lee·be·*ral·*na·ta
social democratic	социал-демо-кратическата	so·tsee·yal·de·mo·kra·*tee·*ches·ka·ta
socialist	социалисти-ческата	so·tsee·a·lees·*tee·*ches·ka·ta

I'm (Australian), but I didn't vote for …

Аз съм (австралиец/
австралийка), но не
гласувах за … **m/f**

az suhm (av·stra·*lee*·ets/
av·stra·*leey*·ka) no ne
gla·*soo*·vah za …

Did you hear about …?

Чухте/Чу ли за …? **pol/inf**

chooh·te/choo lee za …

Do you agree with …?

Съгласни ли сте с …? **pol**
Съгласен/Съгласна
ли си с …? **inf m/f**

suh·*glas*·nee lee ste s …
suh·*gla*·sen/suh·*glas*·na
lee see s …

I (don't) agree with …

Аз (не) съм съгласен/
съгласна с … **m/f**

az (ne) suhm suh·*gla*·sen/
suh·*glas*·na s …

How do people feel about …?

Какво мислят хората
за …?

kak·*vo* *mees*·lyuht *ho*·ra·ta
za …

How can we protest against …?

Как можем да
протестираме против …?

kak *mo*·zhem da
pro·tes·*tee*·ra·me pro·*teev* …

How can we support …?

Как можем да
подкрепим …?

kak *mo*·zhem da
pod·*kre*·peem …

abortion	абортите **m pl**	a·*bor*·tee·te
animal rights	закрилата на	za·*kree*·la·ta na
	животните **f pl**	zhee·*vot*·nee·te
civil liberties	гражданските	grazh·*dan*·skee·te
	права **n pl**	pra·*va*
corruption	корупцията **f**	ko·*roop*·tsee·ya·ta
crime	престъпността **f**	pre·stuhp·nost·*ta*
drugs	наркотиците **m pl**	nar·ko·*tee*·tsee·te
the economy	икономиката **f**	ee·ko·*no*·mee·ka·ta
education	образованието **n**	o·bra·zo·*va*·nee·e·to
the EU	Европейският	ev·ro·*pey*·skee·yuht
	съюз **m**	suh·*yooz*

euthanasia	евтаназията f	ev·ta·*na*·zee·ya·ta
freedom of the press	свободата на печата f	svo·bo·*da*·ta na pe·*cha*·tuh
globalisation	глобализацията f	glo·ba·lee·*za*·tsee·ya·ta
human rights	човешките права n pl	cho·*vesh*·kee·te pra·*va*
immigration	имиграцията f	ee·mee·*gra*·tsee·ya·ta
party politics	партийната политика f	par·*teey*·na·ta po·*lee*·tee·ka
poverty	бедността f	bed·nost·*ta*
privatisation	приватизацията f	pree·va·te·za·tsee·ya·ta
racism	расизмът m	ra·*seez*·muht
sexism	сексизмът m	sek·*seez*·muht
social welfare	социалното обезпечаване n	so·tsee·*yal*·no·to o·bez·pe·*cha*·va·ne
terrorism	тероризмът m	te·ro·*reez*·muht
tourism	туризмът m	too·*reez*·muht
unemployment	безработицата f	bez·ra·*bo*·tee·tsa·ta
the war (in ...)	войната (в ...) f	voy·*na*·ta (v ...)

Is there help for (the) ...?	Отпускат ли се помощи за ...?	ot·*poos*·kat lee se po·mosh·tee za ...
aged	възрастните	*vuhz*·rast·nee·te
beggars	просяците	*pros*·ya·tsee·te
disabled	инвалидите	een·va·*lee*·dee·te
homeless	бездомните	bez·*dom*·nee·te
street kids	безпризорните деца	bez·pree·*zor*·nee·te de·*tsa*
unemployed	безработните	bez·ra·*bot*·nee·te

the environment

Is there a ... problem here?

| Има ли тук проблеми с ...? | ee·ma lee took pro·*ble*·mee s ... |

What should be done about ...?

| Какво трябва да се направи за ...? | kak·*vo tryab*·va da se na·*pra*·vee za ... |

alternative energy sources	алтернативните източници на енергия m pl	al·ter·na·teev·nee·te eez·toch·nee·tsee na e·ner·gee·ya
climate change	промяната на климата f	pro·mya·na·ta na klee·ma·ta
conservation	опазването на околната среда n	o·paz·va·ne·to na o·kol·na·ta sre·da
deforestation	изсичането на горите n	eez·see·cha·ne·to na go·ree·te
drought	сушата f	soo·sha·ta
ecosystem	екосистемата f	e·ko·sees·te·ma·ta
endangered species	застрашените видове m pl	za·stra·she·nee·te vee·do·ve
genetically modified food	генетически модифицираните храни f pl	ge·ne·tee·ches·kee mo·dee·fee·tsee·ra·nee·te hra·nee
global warming	глобалното затопляне n	glo·bal·no·to za·top·le·nee·e
hunting	ловът m	lo·vuht
hydroelectricity	токът от водно-електрическите централи m	to·kuht ot vod·no·e·lek·tree·ches·kee·te tsen·tra·lee
irrigation	напояването n	na·po·ya·va·ne·to
nuclear energy	атомната енергия f	a·tom·na·ta e·ner·gee·ya
nuclear testing	ядрените опити m pl	ya·dre·nee·te o·pee·tee
ozone layer	озоновият слой m	o·zo·no·vee·yuht sloy
pesticides	пестицидите m pl	pes·tee·tsee·dee·te
pollution	замърсяването n	za·muhr·sya·va·ne·to
recycling programme	програмата за преработване на отпадъците f	pro·gra·ma·ta za pre·ra·bot·va·ne na ot·pa·duh·tsee·te
toxic waste	токсичните отпадъци m pl	tok·seech·nee·te ot·pa·duh·tsee
water supply	водоизточ-ниците m pl	vo·do·eez·toch·nee·tsee·te

n this chapter, phrases are in the informal *mu* tee (you) form
only. For more information, see the box **all about you**, page 138.

where to go

къде да отидем

What's there to do in the evenings?

Какво се прави тука вечер?		kak·vo se pra·vee too·ka ve·cher

What's on …?

	Какво се предлага …?	kak·vo se pred·la·ga …
locally	наоколо	na·o·ko·lo
today	днес	dnes
tonight	довечера	do·ve·che·ra
this weekend	този уикенд	to·zee oo·ee·kend

Where can I find …?

	Къде има …?	kuh·de ee·ma …
clubs	клубове	*kloo*·bo·ve
gay/lesbian venues	гей клубове	gey *kloo*·bo·ve
music venues	музикални клубове	moo·zee·*kal*·nee *kloo*·bo·ve
places to eat	места за хапване	mes·*ta* za *hap*·va·ne
pubs	кръчми	kruhch·*mee*

Is there a local … guide?

	Има ли програма на …?	ee·ma lee pro·*gra*·ma na …
entertainment	развлеченията	raz·vle·che·nee·ya·ta
film	филмите	*feel*·mee·te
gay/lesbian	гей клубовете	gey *kloo*·bo·ve·te
music	концертите	kon·*tser*·tee·te

133

I feel like going to a/an ...	Ходи ми се на ...	*ho*·dee mee se na ...
ballet	балет	ba·*let*
bar	бар	bar
café	кафене	ka·fe·*ne*
concert	концерт	kon·*tsert*
film	кино	*kee*·no
karaoke bar	кариоки	ka·ree·*o*·kee
nightclub	нощен клуб	*nosh*·ten kloob
opera	опера	*o*·pe·ra
party	купон	koo·*pon*
(folk) performance	концерт (на народна музика)	kon·*tsert* (na na·*rod*·na *moo*·zee·ka)
play	театър	te·*a*·tuhr
pub	кръчма	kruhch·*ma*
restaurant	ресторант	res·to·*rant*

For more on bars, drinks and partying, see **romance**, page 139, and **eating out**, page 163.

invitations

What are you doing now?
Какво правиш сега? kak·*vo pra*·veesh se·*ga*

What are you doing ...?	Какво ще правиш ...?	kak·*vo* shte *pra*·veesh ...
tonight	довечера	do·*ve*·che·ra
this weekend	този уикенд	*to*·zee oo·*ee*·kend

Would you like to go (for a) ...?	Искаш ли да излезем ...?	*ees*·kash lee da eez·*le*·zem ...
I feel like going (for a) ...	Иска ми се да изляза ...	*ees*·ka mee se da eez·*lya*·zuh ...
dancing	на танци	na *tan*·tsee
out somewhere	някъде	*nya*·kuh·de
walk	на разходка	na raz·*hod*·ka

Would you like	Искаш ли да	*ees*·kash lee da
to go for a …?	излезем …?	eez·*le*·zem …
coffee	за по едно	za po ed·*no*
	кафе	ka·*fe*
drink	да пийнем	da *peey*·nem
	по нещо	po *nesh*·to
meal	да хапнем	da *hap*·nem
	по нещо	po *nesh*·to

I feel like going	Иска ми се	*ees*·ka mee se
for a …	да изляза …	da eez·*lya*·zuh …
coffee	за едно кафе	za ed·*no* ka·*fe*
drink	да пийна нещо	da *peey*·nuh *nesh*·to
meal	да хапна нещо	da *hap*·nuh *nesh*·to

Do you know a good restaurant?
Знаеш ли някой *zna*·yesh lee *nya*·koy
добър ресторант? do·*buhr* res·to·*rant*

Do you want to come to the concert with me?
Искаш ли да дойдеш *ees*·kash lee da *doy*·desh
с мен на концерт? s men na kon·*tsert*

We're having a party.
Ще правим купон. shte *pra*·veem koo·*pon*

You should come.
Ела непременно. e·*la* ne·pre·*men*·no

what's in a name?

Luckily for modern-day travellers, Bulgarian nouns have lost nearly all elements of the case system (ie endings on nouns which indicate their role in a sentence). The only exception is the vocative – the noun form used for addressing people. It still remains in men's names, which change form when used to address a person. As for women's names, using them in the vocative form is avoided as it's considered archaic and even rude. Here are some common men's names, in the subject form followed by the vocative:

Петър	*pe*·tuhr	Петре	*pe*·tre
Димитър	dee·*mee*·tuhr	Димитре	dee·*mee*·tre
Иван	ee·*van*	Иване	ee·*va*·ne

going out

135

responding to invitations

Sure!
Разбира се!   raz·*bee*·ra se

Yes, I'd love to.
Да, с удоволствие.   da s oo·do·*vols*·tvee·e

That's very kind of you.
Това е много мило   to·*va* e *mno*·go *mee*·lo
от твоя страна.   ot *tvo*·ya stra·*na*

Where shall we go?
Къде ще отидем?   kuh·*de* shte o·*tee*·dem

No, I'm afraid I can't.
Съжалявам, не мога.   suh·zhal·*ya*·vam ne *mo*·guh

Sorry, I can't sing/dance.
Съжалявам, не мога   suh·zhal·*ya*·vam ne *mo*·guh
да пея/танцувам.   da *pe*·yuh/tan·*tsoo*·vam

What about tomorrow?
А утре?   a *oo*·tre

I'm looking forward to it.
Радвам се.   *rad*·vam se

---

colourful bulgarian

Nonsense!
Вятър и мъгла!   *vya*·tuhr ee muh·*gla*
(lit: wind and fog)

on occasion
от дъжд на вятър   ot duhzhd na *vya*·tuhr
(lit: from rain to wind)

completely
от глава до пети   ot gla·*va* do pe·*tee*
(lit: from head to heels)

from the frying pan into the fire
от трън та на глог   ot truhn ta na glog
(lit: from the thorn
into the bush)

arranging to meet

What time will we meet?
По кое време ще се срещнем?
po ko·*ye* vre·me shte se *sresht*·nem

Where will we meet?
Къде ще се срещнем?
kuh·*de* shte se *sresht*·nem

Let's meet at … Нека да се *ne*·ka da se
срещнем … *sresht*·nem …
(eight) o'clock в (осем) часа v (*o*·sem) cha·*suh*
the entrance при входа pree *vho*·da

I'll pick you up.
Ще те взема.
shte te *vze*·muh

Are you ready?
Готов/Готова ли си? m/f
go·*tov*/go·*to*·va lee see

I'm ready.
Готов/Готова съм. m/f
go·*tov*/go·*to*·va suhm

I'll be coming later.
Ще дойда по-късно.
shte *doy*·duh po·kuhs·no

Where will you be?
Къде ще бъдеш?
kuh·*de* shte *buh*·desh

OK!
Добре!
do·*bre*

I'll see you then.
Ще те видя тогава.
shte te *vee*·dyuh to·*ga*·va

See you later/tomorrow.
Ще се видим
по-късно/утре.
shte se *vee*·deem
po·kuhs·no/*oo*·tre

Sorry I'm late.
Съжалявам, че
закъснях.
suh·zhal·*ya*·vam che
za·kuhs·*nyah*

Never mind.
Няма защо.
nya·ma zash·*to*

drugs

I don't take drugs.
Аз не взимам наркотици.   az ne *vzee*·mam nar·*ko*·tee·tsee

I take … occasionally.
Използвам … понякога.   eez·*polz*·vam … po·*nya*·ko·ga

Do you want to have a smoke?
Искаш ли да ходим   *ees*·kash lee da *ho*·deem
да пушим?   da *poo*·sheem

Do you have a light?
Имаш ли огънче?   *ee*·mash lee o·*guhn*·che

If the police are talking to you about drugs, see **police**, page 190, for useful phrases.

all about you

In Bulgarian, the informal form of address is used when speaking to children, animals, God, among students and with those you know well. It's appropriate to use the polite form with people older than you, and with those you don't know well. However, the informal mode of address is becoming more common. It's always been the norm in rural settings, where the polite form is rarely used.

The two forms are reflected in the use of the pronoun 'you' – *mu* tee inf or *вие* vee·e pol – and the verb endings accompanying them. For more information on pronouns and verbs, see the **phrasebuilder**.

In this book we've given the appropriate form for the situation that the phrase is used in – this is normally the polite form, unless marked otherwise. For phrases where either form might be suitable, we've given both.

romance
любов

In this chapter, phrases are in the informal *mu* tee (you) form only. For more information, see the box **all about you**, page 138.

asking someone out

да поканиш някого

Where would you like to go (tonight)?

Къде искаш да отидем
(довечера)?

kuh·*de* ees·kash da o·*tee*·dem
(do·*ve*·che·ra)

Would you like to do something (tomorrow)?

Искаш ли (утре) да
отидем някъде заедно?

ees·kash lee (*oo*·tre) da
o·*tee*·dem *nya*·kuh·de za·*ed*·no

Yes, I'd love to.

Да, с удоволствие.

da s oo·do·*vols*·tvee·e

Sorry, I can't.

Съжалявам, не мога.

suh·zhal·*ya*·vam ne *mo*·guh

pick-up lines

запознаване

Would you like a drink?

Да ти почерпя едно
питие?

da tee po·*cher*·pyuh ed·*no*
pee·tee·*e*

Don't I know you from somewhere?

Не се ли познаваме
от някъде?

ne se lee poz·*na*·va·me
ot *nya*·kuh·de

You're a fantastic dancer.

Страхотно танцуваш.

stra·*hot*·no tan·*tsoo*·vash

romance

139

Can I …?	Може ли да …?	*mo·zhe lee da …*
dance with you	танцувам с теб	*tant·soo·vam s teb*
sit here	седна тука	*sed·nuh too·ka*
take you home	те изпратя	*te eez·prat·yuh*

rejections

I'm here with my girlfriend/boyfriend.

Тука съм с приятелката/
приятеля си.

*too·ka suhm s pree·ya·tel·ka·ta
pree·ya·tel·ya see*

I'd rather not.

Не трябва.

ne tryab·va

No, thank you.

Не, благодаря.

ne bla·go·da·ryuh

Excuse me, I have to go now.

Извинявай, трябва
да си тръгвам.

*eez·vee·nya·vai tryab·va
da see truhg·vam*

---

hard talk

Here are some phrases that might come in handy if you're
being hassled.

Leave me alone, please.

Ако обичаш, остави
ме на мира.

*a·ko o·bee·chash o·sta·vee
me na mee·ra*

Leave me alone!

Остави ме на мира!

o·sta·vee me na mee·ra

Go away!	Разкарай се!	*raz·ka·rai se*
Get lost!	Махай се!	*ma·hai se*
Piss off!	Чупката!	*choop·ka·ta*

getting closer

I really like you.
Много те харесвам.   *mno*·go te ha·*res*·vam

You're great.
Чудесен/Чудесна си. **m/f**   choo·*de*·sen/choo·*des*·na see

Can I kiss you?
Може ли да те целуна?   *mo*·zhe lee da te tse·*loo*·nuh

Do you want to come inside for a while?
Искаш ли да влезеш   *ees*·kash lee da *vle*·zesh
за малко?   za *mal*·ko

Do you want a massage?
Искаш ли да ти   *ees*·kash lee da tee
направя масаж?   na·*prav*·yuh ma·*sazh*

Would you like to stay over?
Искаш ли да останеш   *ees*·kash lee da o·*sta*·nesh
да спиш тука?   da speesh *too*·ka

Can I stay over?
Може ли да остана   *mo*·zhe lee da o·*sta*·nuh
да спа тука?   da spuh *too*·ka

romance

Kiss me.	Целуни ме.	tse·loo·*nee* me
I want you.	Желая те.	zhe·*la*·yuh te
Let's go to bed.	Да си лягаме.	da see *lya*·ga·me
Touch me here.	Докосни ме тук.	do·kos·*nee* me took
Do you like this?	Харесва ли ти това?	ha·*res*·va lee tee to·*va*
I like that.	Харесва ми.	ha·*res*·va mee
I don't like that.	Не ми хареса.	ne mee ha·*res*·va
I think we should stop now.	Стига толкова.	*stee*·ga tol·ko·va

Do you have a (condom)?

Имаш ли (презерватив)?   ee·mash lee (pre·zer·va·*teev*)

Let's use a (condom).

Нека да използваме (презерватив).   *ne*·ka da eez·*polz*·va·me (pre·zer·va·*teev*)

I won't do it without protection.

Не искам да го правим без предпазни мерки.   ne *ees*·kam da go *pra*·veem bez pred·*paz*·nee *mer*·kee

It's my first time.

Това ми е за първи път.   to·*va* mee e za *puhr*·vee puht

It helps to have a sense of humour.

Хубаво е, човек да има чувство за хумор.   *hoo*·ba·vo e cho·*vek* da ee·ma *choovs*·tvo za *hoo*·mor

Oh my god!	О боже!	o *bo*·zhe
That's great.	Това е върха.	to·*va* e vuhr·*huh*
Easy tiger!	Полека!	po·*le*·ka

That was …	Това беше …	to·*va* be·she …
amazing	страхотно	stra·*hot*·no
romantic	романтично	ro·man·*teech*·no
wild	диво	*dee*·vo

love

любов

I think we're good together.
Мисля, че се разбираме
добре.
mees·lyuh che se raz·*bee*·ra·me
do·*bre*

I love you.
Обичам те.
o·*bee*·cham te

Will you go out with me?
Ще излезеш ли с мен?
shte eez·*le*·zesh lee s men

Will you marry me? (to a man)
Ще се ожениш ли за мен?
shte se o·*zhe*·neesh lee za men

Will you marry me? (to a woman)
Ще се омъжеш ли за мен?
shte se o·*muh*·zhesh lee za men

Will you meet my parents?
Съгласен/Съгласна ли
си да те представя
на родителите си? m/f
suh·*gla*·sen/suh·*glas*·na lee
see da te pred·*stav*·yuh
na ro·*dee*·te·lee·te see

sweet talk		
бубенце n	*boo*·ben·tse	little bug
котенце n	*ko*·ten·tse	kitten
маце n	*ma*·tse	dear cat
миличко n	*mee*·leech·ko	dear little one
пиленце n	*pee*·len·tse	little chick
слънчице n	*sluhn*·chee·tse	little sun

romance

143

problems

I don't think it's working out.
Нещо не върви
между нас.

nesh·to ne vuhr·*vee*
mezh·*doo* nas

Are you seeing another man/woman?
С друг/друга ли
излизаш? m/f

s droog/droo·*ga* lee
eez·*lee*·zash

He's just a friend.
Той е само добър познат.

toy e *sa*·mo do·*buhr* poz·*nat*

She's just a friend.
Тя е само добра позната.

tya e *sa*·mo dob·*ra* poz·*na*·ta

You're just using me for sex.
Използваш ме само
за секс.

eez·*polz*·vash me *sa*·mo
za seks

I never want to see you again.
Не искам да те видя
повече.

ne *ees*·kam da te *vee*·dyuh
po·ve·che

We'll work it out.
Ще намерим решение.

shte na·*me*·reem re·*she*·nee·e

leaving

I have to leave (tomorrow).
(Утре) Трябва да тръгвам.

(*oo*·tre) *tryab*·va da *truhg*·vam

I'll …	Ще …	shte …
keep in touch	поддържам връзка с теб	pod·*duhr*·zham *vruhz*·ka s teb
miss you	ми липсваш	mee *leeps*·vash
visit you	ти дойда на гости	tee *doy*·duh na *gos*·tee

eligion

What's your religion?
Каква вяра изповядвате/ kak·*va vya*·ra ees·pov·*yad*·va·te/
изповядваш? pol/inf ees·pov·*yad*·vash

I'm not religious.
Не съм религиозен/ ne suhm re·lee·gee·*o*·zen/
религиозна. m/f re·lee·gee·*oz*·na

I'm (a/an) …	Аз съм …	az suhm …
agnostic	агностик m	ag·nos·*teek*
	агностичка f	ag·nos·*teech*·ka
atheist	атеист m	a·te·*eest*
	атеистка f	a·te·*eest*·ka
Catholic	католик m	ka·to·*leek*
	католичка f	ka·to·*leech*·ka
Christian	християнин m	hrees·tee·*ya*·neen
	християнка f	hrees·tee·*yan*·ka
Dunovist	дъновист m	duh·no·*veest*
	дъновистка f	duh·no·*veest*·ka
Jewish	евреин m	ev·*re*·yeen
	еврейка f	ev·*rey*·ka
Muslim	мохамеданин m	mo·ha·me·*da*·neen
	мохамеданка f	mo·ha·me·*dan*·ka
Orthodox	православен m	pra·vo·*sla*·ven
	православна f	pra·vo·*slav*·na
Protestant	протестант m	pro·tes·*tant*
	протестантка f	pro·tes·*tant*·ka

I (don't) believe in …	(Не) Вярвам в …	(ne) *vyar*·vam v …
astrology	астрологията	as·tro·*lo*·gee·ya·ta
fate	съдбата	suhd·*ba*·ta
God	Бога	*bo*·ga

Where can I …?	Къде мога да …?	kuh·de mo·guh da …
attend a service	посетя църковна служба	po·set·yuh tsuhr·kov·na sloozh·ba
pray	се помоля	se po·mol·yuh

cultural differences

културни различия

I didn't mean to do/say anything wrong.
Аз нямах предвид да направя/кажа нищо нередно.
az nya·mah pred·veed da na·prav·yuh/ka·zhuh neesh·to ne·red·no

I don't want to offend you.
Не искам да ви/те обидя. pol/inf
ne ees·kam da vee/te o·bee·dyuh

I respect your beliefs.
Уважавам вашата/ твоята вяра. pol/inf
oo·va·zha·vam va·sha·ta/ tvo·ya·ta vya·ra

I'm not used to this.
Не съм свикнал/ свикнала с това. m/f
ne suhm sveek·nal/ sveek·na·la s to·va

I'd rather not join in.
Предпочитам да не участвам.
pred·po·chee·tam da ne oo·chast·vam

I'm sorry, it's against my …	Съжалявам, но това е против …	suh·zhal·ya·vam no to·va e pro·teev…
beliefs	моите вярвания	mo·yee·te vyar·va·nee·ya
religion	моята религия	mo·ya·ta re·lee·gee·ya

This is …	Това е …	to·va e …
different	различно	raz·leech·no
fun	забавно	za·bav·no
interesting	интересно	een·te·res·no

When's the gallery/museum open?

Какво е работното време
на галерията/музея?
kak·*vo* e ra·*bot*·no·to *vre*·me
na ga·*le*·ree·ya·ta/moo·*ze*·yuh

What kind of art are you interested in?

От какво изкуство се
интересувате/
интересуваш? **pol/inf**
ot kak·*vo* eez·*koost*·vo se
een·te·re·*soo*·va·te/
een·te·re·*soo*·vash

What's in the collection?

Какво има в колекцията?
kak·*vo* ee·ma v ko·*lek*·tsee·ya·ta

What do you think of …?

Какво мислите/
мислиш за …? **pol/inf**
kak·*vo* *mees*·lee·te/
mees·leesh za …

It's an exhibition of …

Това е изложба на …
to·*va* e eez·*lozh*·ba na …

I'm interested in …

Интересувам се от …
een·te·re·*soo*·vam se ot …

I like the works of …

Харесвам работите на …
ha·*res*·vam *ra*·bo·tee·te na …

It reminds me of …

Това ми напомня за …
to·*va* mee na·*pom*·nya za …

… art	… изкуство	… eez·*koost*·vo
abstract	абстрактното	ab·*strakt*·no·to
contemporary	съвременното	suh·*vre*·men·no·to
modern	модерното	mo·*der*·no·to
performance	изпълнител-	eez·puhl·*nee*·tel·
	ното	no·to
religious	религиозното	re·lee·gee·*oz*·no·to

... art		
graphic	графиката f	*gra*·fee·ka·ta
icon painting	иконописът m	ee·ko·no·*pee*·suht
impressionist	импресио-н/измът m	eem·pre·see·o·*neez*·muht
inlaid	инкрус-тацията f	een·kroos·*ta*·tsee·ya·ta
Renaissance	ренесансът m	re·ne·*san*·suht
textiles	текстилът m	teks·*tee*·luht
architecture	архитектура f	ar·hee·tek·*too*·ra
artwork	произведение на изкуството n	pro·eez·ve·*de*·nee·e na eez·*koost*·vo·to
curator	куратор m	koo·*ra*·tor
design n	дизайн m	dee·*zain*
embroidery	бродерия f	bro·*de*·ree·ya
etching	гравюра f	grav·*yoo*·ra
exhibit n	изложба f	eez·*lozh*·ba
exhibition hall	изложбена галерия f	eez·*lozh*·be·na ga·*le*·ree·ya
installation	инсталация f	een·sta·*la*·tsee·ya
opening	откриване n	ot·*kree*·va·ne
painter	художник m	hoo·*dozh*·neek
	художничка f	hoo·*dozh*·neech·ka
painting (artwork)	картина f	kar·*tee*·na
painting (technique)	живопис n	zhee·vo·*pees*
period	период m	pe·ree·*od*
permanent collection	постоянна експозиция f	po·sto·*yan*·na eks·po·*zee*·tsee·ya
pottery	керамика f	ke·*ra*·mee·ka
print n	копие n	*ko*·pee·e
sculptor	скулптор m	*skoolp*·tor
	скулпторка f	*skoolp*·tor·ka
sculpture	скулптура f	skoolp·*too*·ra
statue	статуя f	*sta*·too·a
studio	ателие n	a·te·lee·*e*
style n	стил m	steel
technique	техника f	*teh*·nee·ka
weaving	тъкан m	tuh·*kan*
woodcarving n	дърворезба f	duhr·vo·rez·*ba*

Sporting interests

спортни интереси

Popular sports in Bulgaria, in addition to those given in the list below, are *художествена гимнастика* hoo·do·zhest·ve·na jeem·*nas*·tee·ka (rhythmic gymnastics), *фигурно пързаляне* fee·goor·no puhr·*za*·lya·ne (figure skating), as well as *борба* bor·ba (wrestling) and *вдигане на тежести* vdee·ga·ne na te·zhes·tee (weightlifting). For more sports, see the **dictionary**.

What sport do you follow?

От какъв спорт се интересувате/интересуваш? pol/inf	ot ka·*kuhv* sport se een·te·re·*soo*·va·te/een·te·re·*soo*·vash

What sport do you play?

С какъв спорт се занимавате/занимаваш? pol/inf	s ka·*kuhv* sport se za·nee·*ma*·va·te/za·nee·*ma*·vash

I follow athletics.

Интересувам се от лека атлетика.	een·te·re·*soo*·vam se ot *le*·ka at·*le*·tee·ka

I do athletics.

Занимавам се с лека атлетика.	za·nee·*ma*·vam se s *le*·ka at·*le*·tee·ka

I follow …	Интересувам се от …	een·te·re·*soo*·vam se ot …
I play/do …	Играя …	ee·*gra*·yuh …
basketball	баскетбол	*bas*·ket·bol
boxing	бокс	boks
football (soccer)	футбол	*foot*·bol
karate	карате	ka·*ra*·te
tennis	тенис	*te*·nees
volleyball	волейбол	*vo*·ley·bol

I ...	Аз ...	az ...
cycle	карам колело	*ka*·ram ko·le·*lo*
run	бягам	*bya*·gam
Who's your favourite ...?	Кой е любимия ви/ти ...? pol/inf	koy e lyoo·*bee*·mee·yu vee/tee ...
sportsperson	спортист m	spor·*teest*
	спортистка f	spor·*teest*·ka
team	отбор	ot·*bor*

Do you like (basketball)?
Обичате/Обичаш ли (баскетбол)? pol/inf
o·*bee*·cha·te/o·*bee*·chash lee (*bas*·ket·bol)

Yes, very much.
Да, много.
da *mno*·go

Not really.
Не особено.
ne o·*so*·be·no

going to a game

ходене на ма◆

Would you like to go to a game?
Искате/Искаш ли да отидем на мач? pol/inf
ees·ka·te/*ees*·kash lee da o·*tee*·dem na mach

Who are you supporting?
Кого подкрепяте/ подкрепяш? pol/inf
ko·*go* pod·*kre*·pya·te/ pod·*kre*·pyash

Who's playing/winning?
Кой играе/печели?
koy ee·*gra*·ye/pe·*che*·lee

What's the score?
Какъв е резултатът?
ka·*kuhv* e re·zool·*ta*·tuht

scoring		
draw/even	равен резултат	*ra*·ven re·zool·*tat*
love (zero)	нула на нула	*noo*·la na *noo*·la
match-point	мач-пойнт	*mach*·poynt
nil (zero)	нулев резултат	*noo*·lev re·zool·*tat*

sports talk

What a …!	Какъв …!	ka·*kuhv* …
goal	гол	gol
hit	удар	*oo*·dar
kick	шут	shoot
pass	пас	pas

That was a … game!	Това беше … мач!	to·*va be*·she … mach
bad	лош	losh
great	страхотен	stra·*ho*·ten

playing sport

Do you want to play?
Искате ли да играете? inf
ees·ka·te lee da ee·*gra*·ye·te

Искаш ли да играеш? inf
ees·kash lee da ee·*gra*·yesh

Can I join in?
Може ли да участвам?
mo·zhe lee da oo·*chast*·vam

That would be great.
Това би било чудесно.
to·*va* bee bee·*lo* choo·*des*·no

I can't.
Не мога.
ne *mo*·guh

I have an injury.
Имам контузия.
ee·mam kon·*too*·zee·ya

Kick/Pass it to me!
Подай ми го! inf
po·*dai* mee go

Your/My point.
Точка за теб/мен. inf
toch·ka za teb/men

You're a good player.
Вие сте добър играч. pol
vee·e ste do·*buhr* ee·*grach*

Ти си добър играч. inf
tee see do·*buhr* ee·*grach*

Thanks for the game.
Благодаря за играта.
bla·go·dar·*yuh* za ee·*gra*·ta

Where's a good place to …?	Къде има хубаво място за …?	kuh·de ee·ma hoo·ba·vo myas·to za …
fish	риболов	ree·bo·lov
go hiking	туризъм	too·ree·zuhm
go horse riding	конна езда	kon·na ez·da
paraglide	летене с делтапланер	le·te·ne s del·ta·pla·ner
run	бягане	bya·ga·ne
scuba dive	гмуркане	gmoor·ka·ne
ski	каране на ски	ka·ra·ne na skee
windsurf	уинд-сърфинг	oo·eend·suhr·feeng
Where's the nearest …?	Къде е най-близкият/най-близкото …? m/n	kuh·de e nai·bleez·kee·yuht/nai·bleez·ko·to …
gym	фитнес център m	feet·nes tsen·tuhr
swimming pool	плувен басейн m	ploo·ven ba·seyn
tennis court	тенискорт m	te·nees·kort

Do I have to be a member to attend?

Трябва ли да съм член за да мога да участвам?	tryab·va lee da suhm chlen za da mo·guh da oo·chast·vam

Is there a women-only session?

Има ли женска секция?	ee·ma lee zhen·ska sek·tsee·ya

Where are the changing rooms?

Къде са съблекалните?	kuh·de suh suh·ble·kal·nee·te

Can I hire a court?

Мога ли да си запазя час за корта?	mo·guh lee da see za·paz·yuh chas za kor·tuh

Can I hire a …?	Мога ли да взема под наем …?	mo·guh lee da vze·muh pod na·em …
ball	една топка	ed·na top·ka
bicycle	едно колело	ed·no ko·le·lo
racquet	една ракета	ed·na ra·ke·ta

What's the charge per ...?	Колко струва ...?	kol·ko stroo·va ...
day	на ден	na den
game	за една игра	za ed·na ee·gra
hour	на час	na chas

cheering on

Go ...!	Давай ...!	da·vai ...
Down with ...!	Долу ...!	do·loo ...
A goal for ...!	Гол за ...!	gol za ...

fishing

риболов

Where are the good spots?
Рибата къде кълве? — ree·ba·ta kuh·de kuhl·ve

Do I need a fishing permit?
Нужен ли е риболовен билет? — noo·zhen lee e ree·bo·lo·ven bee·let

Do you do fishing tours?
Правите ли риболовни излети? — pra·vee·te lee ree·bo·lov·nee eez·le·tee

What's the best bait?
Коя е най-добрата стръв? — ko·ya e nai·do·bra·ta struhv

What kind of fish are you landing?
Какво ловите/ловиш? pol/inf — kak·vo lo·vee·te/lo·veesh

How much does it weigh?
Колко тежи? — kol·ko te·zhee

bait	стръв f	struhv
fishing line	корда f	kor·da
float n	плувка f	ploov·ka
hooks	въдици f pl	vuh·dee·tsee
lures	мамки f pl	mam·kee
rod	прът m	pruht
sinkers	оловни тежести f pl	o·lov·nee te·zhes·tee

sport

153

skiing

How much is a pass?
Колко струва един
абонамент?
kol·ko stroo·va e·deen
a·bo·na·ment

Can I take lessons?
Може ли да взимам
уроци?
mo·zhe lee da vzee·mam
oo·ro·tsee

I'd like to hire ...	Искам да взема под наем ...	*ees·kam da vze·muh pod na·em ...*
boots	скиорски обувки	*skee·or·skee o·boov·kee*
goggles	скиорски очила	*skee·or·skee o·chee·la*
poles	щеки	*shte·kee*
a ski suit	скиорски костюм	*skee·or·skee kos·tyoom*

Is it possible to go ...?	Може ли тука да ...?	*mo·zhe lee too·ka da ...*
Alpine skiing	карам ски	*ka·ram skee*
cross-country skiing	се занимавам със ски-бягане	*se za·nee·ma·vam suhs skee·bya·ga·ne*
snowboarding	се пързалям със сноуборд	*se puhr·za·lyam suhs sno·oo·bord*
tobogganing	спускам с тобоган	*spoos·kam s to·bo·gan*

What are the conditions like ...?	Какви са условията ...?	*kak·vee suh oo·slo·vee·ya·ta ...*
higher up	по-нагоре	*po·na·go·re*
on that run	на онази писта	*na o·na·zee pees·ta*

Which are the ... slopes?	Кои са пистите за ...?	*koy·ee suh pees·tee·te za ...*
beginner	начинаещи	*na·chee·na·esh·tee*
intermediate	средно-напреднали	*sred·no·na·pred·na·lee*
advanced	напреднали	*na·pred·na·lee*

able car	кабинков лифт m	ka-*been*-kov leeft
hairlift	седалков лифт m	se-*dal*-kov leeft
nstructor	инструктор m	een-*strook*-tor
esort	курорт m	koo-*rort*
ki lift	лифт m	leeft
led	шейна f	shey-*na*

occer/football

футбол

Vho plays for (Levski)?
Кой играе за (Левски)? koy ee-*gra*-ye za (*lev*-skee)

le's a great (player).
Той е страхотен (играч). toy e stra-*ho*-ten (ee-*grach*)

Vhich team is at the top of the league?
Кой отбор е лидер koy ot-*bor* e *lee*-der
в групата? v *groo*-pa-ta

Vhat a great/terrible team!
Какъв чудесен/ужасен ka-*kuhv* choo-*de*-sen/oo-*zha*-sen
отбор! ot-*bor*

all	топка f	*top*-ka
oach n	треньор m	tre-*nyor*
xpulsion	изгонване n	iz-*gon*-va-ne
an	запалянко m	za-pa-*lyan*-ko
ree kick	свободен удар m	svo-*bo*-den *oo*-dar
oal (structure)	врата f	vra-*ta*
oalkeeper	вратар m	vra-*tar*
ffside	засада f	za-*sa*-da
enalty (kick)	наказателен удар m	na-ka-*za*-te-len *oo*-dar
layer	играч m	ee-*grach*
ed card	червен картон m	cher-*ven* kar-*ton*
eferee	съдия m	suh-dee-*ya*
triker	нападател m	na-pa-*da*-tel
hrow in v	хвърлям тъч	*hvuhr*-lyam tuhch
ellow card	жълт картон m	zhuhlt kar-*ton*

Off to see a match? Check out **going to a game**, page 150.

water sports

Can I book a lesson?
Мога ли да си запиша
време за инструкция?

mo·guh lee da see za·*pee*·shu
vre·me za een·*strook*·tsee·ya

Can I hire (a) …?
Мога ли да
взема под
наем …?

mo·guh lee da
vze·muh pod
na·em …

boat	лодка	*lod*·ka
life jacket	спасителна	spa·*see*·tel·na
	жилетка	zhee·*let*·ka
snorkelling	екипировка	e·kee·pee·*rov*·ka
gear	със шнорхел	suhs *shnor*·hel
water-skis	водни ски	*vod*·nee skee
wetsuit	неопренов	ne·o·*pre*·nov
	костюм	kos·*tyoom*

Are there any …? Има ли …? *ee*·ma lee …
reefs	рифове	*ree*·fo·ve
rips	мъртво	*muhrt*·vo
	вълнение	vuhl·*ne*·nee·e
water hazards	подводни	pod·*vod*·nee
	опасности	o·*pas*·nos·tee

guide n	водач m	vo·*dach*
motorboat	моторница f	mo·*tor*·nee·tsa
oars	гребла n pl	greb·*la*
sailboard	сърф m	suhrf
sailboarding	каране на сърф n	*ka*·ra·ne na suhrf
sailing boat	платноходка f	plat·no·*hod*·ka
surfboard	сърф m	suhrf
surfing	сърфиране n	suhr·*fee*·ra·ne
wave n	вълна f	vuhl·*na*

outdoors
сред природата

iking

туризъм

Where can I ...?	Къде мога да ...?	kuh·de mo·guh da ...
buy supplies	си купя	see koop·yuh
	всичко	vseech·ko
	необходимо	ne·ob·ho·dee·mo
find someone	намеря	na·mer·yuh
who knows	човек, който	cho·vek koy·to
this area	знае околността	zna·e o·kol·nost·ta
get a map	взема карта	vze·muh kar·ta
hire hiking	взема под наем	vze·muh pod na·em
gear	туристическа	too·ree·stee·ches·ka
	екипировка	e·kee·pee·rov·ka

Do we need a guide?
Трябва ли водач?   tryab·va lee vo·dach

Are there guided treks?
Има ли групови   ee·ma lee groo·po·vee
екскурзии?   eks·koor·zee·ee

Is it safe?
Безопасно ли е?   be·zo·pas·no lee e

Is there a hut?
Има ли хижа?   ee·ma lee hee·zha

When does it get dark?
В колко часа се мръква?   v kol·ko cha·suh se mruhk·va

How high is the climb?
Каква височина ще   kak·va vee·so·chee·na shte
вземем?   vze·mem

How long is the trail?
Колко дълга е пътеката?   kol·ko duhl·ga e puh·te·ka·ta

Is the track well marked?
Пътеката добре ли   puh·te·ka·ta do·bre lee
е означена?   e o·zna·che·na

outdoors

157

Is the track ...?	Пътеката ... ли е?	puh·*te*·ka·ta ... lee e
open	открита	ot·*kree*·ta
scenic	с изгледи	s *eez*·gle·dee

Which is the ... route?	Кой е ... път?	koy e ... puht
easiest	най-лекият	*nai*·le·kee·yuht
most interesting	най-интересният	*nai*· een·te·res·nee·yuk
shortest	най-краткият	*nai*·krat·kee·yuht

Do we need to take ...?	Тряба ли да носим ...?	*tryab*·va lee da *no*·seem ...
food	храна	hra·*na*
water	вода	vo·*da*

Where can I find the ...?	Къде се намира ...?	kuh·*de* se na·*mee*·ra ...
camping ground	къмпингът	*kuhm*·peeng·uht
nearest village	най-близкото село	*nai*·bleez·ko·to *se*·lo

Where can I find the ...?	Къде се намират ...?	kuh·*de* se na·*mee*·rat ...
showers	душовете	*doo*·sho·ve·te
toilets	тоалетните	to·a·*let*·nee·te

Where have you come from?
Откъде идвате/идваш? pol/inf   ot·kuh·*de* eed·va·te/*eed*·vas

How long did it take you?
За колко време взехте/взе прехода? pol/inf   za *kol*·ko *vre*·me *vzeh*·te/ vze pre·*ho*·duh

Does this path go to (Knyazhevo)?
Тази пътека води ли до (Княжево)?   ta·zee puh·*te*·ka vo·dee lee do (knya·zhe·vo)

beach & pool signs		
Плуването забранено	*ploo*·va·ne·to za·bra·*ne*·no	**No Swimming**
Скачането забранено	*ska*·cha·ne·to za·bra·*ne*·no	**No Diving**

an I go through here?
Мога ли да мина оттук?   *mo*·guh lee da *mee*·nuh ot·*took*

the water OK to drink?
Тази вода може ли да   *ta*·zee vo·*da mo*·zhe lee da
се пие?   se *pee*·e

each

here's the ...	Къде се намира	kuh·*de* se na·*mee*·ra
each?	... плаж?	... plazh
best	най-хубавият	*nai*·hoo·ba·vee·yuht
nearest	най-близкият	*nai*·bleez·kee·yuht
nudist	нудисткият	noo·*deest*·kee·yuht
public	общественият	ob·*shtest*·ve·nee·yuht

listen for ...

Внимавайте/Внимавай мъртво вълнение! **pol/inf**
vnee·*ma*·vai·te/vnee·*ma*·vai
muhr·tvo vuhl·*ne*·nee·e **Be careful of the undertow!**

Опасно е!
o·*pas*·no e **It's dangerous!**

Is it safe to dive/swim here?
Безопасно ли е
гмуркането/плуването
тук?
be·zo·*pas*·no lee e
gmoor·ka·ne·to/*ploo*·va·ne·to
took

What time is high/low tide?
В колко часа е
приливът/отливът?
v *kol*·ko cha·*suh* e
pree·lee·vuht/*ot*·lee·vuht

Do we have to pay?
Плаща ли се?
plash·ta lee se

How much to rent a/an ...?	Колко струва да се наеме ...?	*kol*·ko *stroo*·va da se na·*e*·me ...
chair	столче	*stol*·che
hut	бунгало	boon·*ga*·lo
umbrella	чадър	cha·*duhr*

weather

времето

What's the weather like?
Какво е времето?
kak·*vo* e *vre*·me·to

What will the weather be like tomorrow?
Какво ще бъде
времето утре?
kak·*vo* shte *buh*·de
vre·me·to *oo*·tre

It's freezing.
Много е студено.
mno·go e stoo·*de*·no

It's raining/snowing.
Вали дъжд/сняг.
va·*lee* duhzhd/snyag

It's …	… е.	… e
cloudy	Облачно	*o*·blach·no
cold	Студено	stoo·*de*·no
fine	Хубаво	*hoo*·ba·vo
hot	Горещо	go·*resh*·to
sunny	Слънчево	*sluhn*·che·vo
warm	Топло	*top*·lo
windy	Ветровито	ve·tro·*vee*·to

Where can I buy a/an …?	Къде мога да си купя …?	kuh·*de* mo·guh da see *koop*·yuh …
rain jacket	дъждобран	duhzh·do·*bran*
umbrella	чадър	cha·*duhr*

flora & fauna

растения и животни

What … is that?	Какво е това …?	kak·*vo* e to·*va* …
animal	животно	zhee·*vot*·no
flower	цвете	*tsve*·te
plant	растение	ras·*te*·nee·e
tree	дърво	duhr·*vo*

local plants & animals

chamomile	лайка f	*lai*·ka
fir	елха f	el·*ha*
(Bulgarian) geranium	здравец m	*zdra*·vets
marigold	невен m	ne·*ven*
rose	роза f	*ro*·za
summer savoury	чубрица f	*choo*·bree·tsa
bear	мечка f	*mech*·ka
eagle	орел m	o·*rel*
ferret	пор m	por
fox	лисица f	lee·*see*·tsa
stork	щъркел m	*shtuhr*·kel
wolf	вълк m	vuhlk

outdoors

Is it ...?	... ли е?	... lee e
common	Разпространено	ras·pros·tra·*ne*·no
dangerous	Опасно	o·*pas*·no
endangered	Застрашено	za·stra·*she*·no
poisonous	Отровно	o·*trov*·no
protected	Защитено	zash·tee·*te*·no

Is this a protected ...?	Това защитен/ защитена ... ли е? m/f	to·*va* zash·tee·*ten*/ zash·tee·*te*·na ... lee e
forest	гора f	go·*ra*
park	парк m	park
species	вид m	veed

What's it used for?

За какво се използва?   za kak·*vo* se eez·*polz*·va

Can you eat the fruit?

Яде ли се плодът му?   ya·*de* lee se plo·*duht* moo

For geographical and agricultural terms and names of animals and plants, see the **dictionary**.

---

names across borders

Many 'international' names are also found in Bulgaria, but the local version has a distinctively Bulgarian flavour (especially considering the written, Cyrillic, form). If you'd like to adopt the Bulgarian version of your name while travelling, here are some equivalents:

Andrew	Андрей	an·*drey*
George	Георги	ge·*or*·gee
John	Иван	ee·*van*
Michael	Михаил	mee·ha·*eel*
Paul	Павел	*pa*·vel
Barbara	Варвара	var·*va*·ra
Elizabeth	Елисавета	e·lee·sa·*ve*·ta
Helen	Елена	e·*le*·na
Irene	Ирина	ee·*ree*·na
Katherine	Екатерина	e·ka·te·*ree*·na

basics

основни неща

breakfast	закуска f	za·*koos*·ka
lunch	обед m	*o*·bed
dinner	вечеря f	ve·*cher*·ya
snack	закуска f	za·*koos*·ka
eat v	ям	yam
drink v	пия	*pee*·yuh
I'd like …	Искам …	*ees*·kam …
Please.	Моля.	*mol*·yuh
Thank you.	Благодаря.	bla·go·dar·*yuh*
I'm starving!	Много съм	*mno*·go suhm
	гладен/гладна. m/f	*gla*·den/*glad*·na

the meal deal

A typical Bulgarian breakfast consists of sweet pastries and/or bread, butter and jam, *сирене* see·re·ne (soft white cheese) or *кашкавал* kash·ka·*val* (hard yellow cheese), sliced ham and coffee or tea.

The main meal can be taken either at lunchtime or at dinnertime. If lunch is the main meal, it begins with salad, often accompanied by *ракия* ra·*kee*·ya (grape brandy), followed by soup, then a cooked main dish usually containing meat and vegetables, and either a sweet or fruit for dessert. If lunch is the lighter meal, it's frequently a sandwich.

If dinner is the main meal, it follows the model above. If it's the lighter meal, it's either cheese, yogurt and bread, *баница* ba·*nee*·tsa (savoury cheese pastry), eggs and tomatoes, a toasted sandwich or something similar. Classic snacks are sandwiches or small savoury pastries.

eating out

163

finding a place to eat

Can you recommend a ...?	Можете ли да препоръчате ...? pol	mo·zhe·te lee da pre·po·ruh·cha·te ...
	Можеш ли да препоръчаш ...? inf	mo·zhesh lee da pre·po·ruh·chash ...
bar	бар	bar
café	кафене	ka·fe·ne
pub	кръчма	kruhch·ma
restaurant	ресторант	res·to·rant
tavern	механа	me·ha·na

Where would you go for ...?	Къде ходите да ...?	kuh·de ho·dee·te da ...
a celebration	опразнувате нещо	o·praz·noo·va·te nesh·to
a cheap meal	хапнете евтино	hap·ne·te ev·tee·no
local specialities	опитате местните специалитети	o·pee·ta·te mest·nee·te spe·tsee·a·lee·te·te

I'd like to reserve a table for ...	Искам да запазя една маса за ...	ees·kam da za·paz·yuh ed·na ma·sa za ...
(two) people	(двама) души	(dva·ma) doo·shee
(eight) o'clock	(осем) часа	(o·sem) cha·suh

Are you still serving food?
Сервирате ли все още? ser·vee·ra·te lee vse osh·te

How long is the wait?
Колко се чака? kol·ko se cha·ka

---

listen for ...

Затворено е.	zat·vo·re·no e	We're closed.
Няма места.	nya·ma mes·ta	We're full.
Един момент.	e·deen mo·ment	One moment.

at the restaurant

Summon the waiter using the phrase *ако обичате* a·ko ·bee·cha·te (lit: if you like). To ask for the bill, say *сметката, моля* smet·ka·ta mol·yuh (lit: the bill, please) – the waiter will not bring the bill until it's specifically requested. Tips are normally minimal. Unless the service has been exceptional, or you wish to make a gesture for some other reason, just round the bill off slightly upwards.

What would you recommend?
Какво ще препоръчате?   kak·vo shte pre·po·*ruh*·cha·te

What's in that dish?
Какво има в това блюдо?   kak·vo ee·ma v to·*va* blyoo·do

What's that called?
Как се казва това?   kak se *kaz*·va to·*va*

I'll have that.
Ще го взема.   shte go *vze*·muh

Does it take long to prepare?
Дълго ли се готви?   *duhl*·go lee se *got*·vee

Is it self-serve?
На самообслужване ли е?   na sa·mo·ob·*sloozh*·va·ne lee e

Is there a cover/service charge?
Плаща ли се кувертът/   *plash*·ta lee se koo·*ver*·tuht/
обслужването?   ob·*sloozh*·va·ne·to

Is service included in the bill?
Обслужването   ob·*sloozh*·va·ne·to
включено ли е в сметката?   vklyoo·che·no lee e v *smet*·ka·ta

Are these complimentary?
Тези безплатни ли са?   te·zee bez·*plat*·nee lee suh

Could I see the wine list, please?
Моля, дайте ми   *mol*·yuh *dai*·te mee
листата с вината.   *lees*·ta·ta s vee·*na*·ta

Can you recommend a good local wine?
Можете ли да ми   *mo*·zhe·te lee da mee
препоръчате някое   pre·po·*ruh*·cha·te *nya*·koy·e
хубаво местно вино?   *hoo*·ba·vo *mest*·no vee·no

I'd like (a/the) …, please.	Дайте ми …, моля.	*dai*·te mee … *mol*·yuh
children's menu	детското меню	*det*·sko·to me·*nyoo*
drink list	листата с напитките	*lees*·ta·ta s na·*peet*·kee·te
half portion	половин порция	po·lo·*veen* *por*·tsee·ya
local speciality	някой местен специалитет	*nya*·koy *mes*·ten spe·tsee·a·lee·*tet*
meal fit for a king	царска трапеза	*tsar*·ska tra·*pe*·za
menu	менюто	me·*nyoo*·to
(in English)	(на английски)	(na an·*glee*·skee)
(non)smoking section	маса за (не)пушачи	*ma*·sa za (ne·)poo·*sha*·chee
table for (five)	маса за (пет) човека	*ma*·sa za (pet) cho·*ve*·ka
that dish	онова блюдо	o·no·*va blyoo*·do

Къде искате да седнете?
kuh·*de* ees·ka·te da sed·ne·te
Where would you like to sit?

Какво ще желаете?
kak·*vo* shte zhe·*la*·ye·te
What can I get for you?

Заповядайте!
za·po·*vya*·dai·te
Here you go!

Добър апетит.
do·*buhr* a·pe·*teet*
Enjoy your meal.

Обичате ли …?
o·*bee*·cha·te lee …
Do you like …?

Препоръчвам …
pre·po·*ruhch*·vam …
I suggest the …

Как искате да го приготвим?
kak ees·*ka*·te da go pree·*got*·veem
How would you like that cooked?

Предястия	pred·*yas*·tee·ya	Appetisers
Ордьоври	or·*dyo*·vree	Entrées
Супи	*soo*·pee	Soups
Салати	sa·*la*·tee	Salads
Основни ястия	os·*nov*·nee *yas*·tee·ya	Main Courses
Аламинути	a·la·mee·*noo*·tee	Prepared to Order
Скара	*ska*·ra	From the Grill
Гарнитури	gar·nee·*too*·ree	Side Dishes
Десерти	de·*ser*·tee	Desserts
Аперитиви	a·pe·ree·*tee*·vee	Apéritifs
Безалкохолни напитки	bez·al·ko·*hol*·nee na·*peet*·kee	Soft Drinks
Алкохолни напитки	al·ko·*hol*·nee na·*peet*·kee	Spirits
Бири	*bee*·ree	Beers
Шумящи вина	shoo·*myash*·tee vee·*na*	Sparkling Wines
Бели вина	*be*·lee vee·*na*	White Wines
Червени вина	cher·*ve*·nee vee·*na*	Red Wines
Десертни вина	de·*sert*·nee vee·*na*	Dessert Wines

For additional items, see the **menu decoder**, page 181.

I'd like it with/ without ...	Моля, дайте ми го с/без ...	*mol*·yuh *dai*·te mee go s/bez ...
cheese	кашкавал	kash·ka·*val*
chilli	люти чушки	*lyoo*·tee *choosh*·kee
chilli sauce	чили сос	*chee*·lee sos
garlic	чесън	*che*·suhn
ketchup	кетчуп	*ket*·choop
nuts	ядки	*yad*·kee
oil	олио	o·*lee*·o
pepper	пипер	pee·*per*
salt	сол	sol
tomato sauce	доматен сос	do·*ma*·ten sos
vinegar	оцет	o·*tset*

For other specific meal requests, see **vegetarian & special meals**, page 179.

at the table

Please bring a/the …	Моля, донесете …	mol·yuh do·ne·se·te …
bill	сметката	smet·ka·ta
cutlery	прибори	pree·bo·ree
(wine)glass	чаша (за вино)	cha·sha (za vee·no)
serviette	салфетка	sal·fet·ka
tablecloth	покривка	po·kreev·ka

I didn't order this.
Аз не съм поръчвал/ поръчвала това. m/f   az ne suhm po·ruhch·val/ po·ruhch·va·la to·va

There's a mistake in the bill.
В сметката има грешка.   v smet·ka·ta ee·ma gresh·ka

street eats

баничках f pl	ba·neech·kee	cheese pastries
гевреци m pl	ge·vre·tsee	large pretzels
дюнер кебаб m	dyoo·ner ke·bab	doner kebab
палачинки f pl	pa·la·cheen·kee	pancakes
сладолед m	sla·do·led	ice cream
слънчогледови семки f pl	sluhn·cho·gle·do·vee sem·kee	sunflower seeds
тиквени семки f pl	teek·ve·nee sem·kee	pumpkin seeds
фъстъци m pl	fuh·stuh·tsee	peanuts
царевица f	tsa·re·vee·tsa	corn on the cob

talking food

That was delicious!
Това беше много вкусно!   to·va be·she mno·go vkoos·no

I'm full.
Преядох.   pre·ya·doh

love this dish.

Много харесвам това ястие. f	mno·go ha·res·vam to·va yas·tee·e

love the local cuisine.

Много харесвам местната кухня.	mno·go ha·res·vam mest·na·ta kooh·nya

My compliments to the chef.

Моите поздравления за готвача.	mo·yee·te poz·drav·le·nee·ya za got·va·chuh

This is stale.

Това не е прясно.	to·va ne e pryas·no

This is …	Това е …	to·va e …
burnt	изгорено	eez·go·re·no
(too) cold	(прекалено) студено	(pre·ka·le·no) stoo·de·no
(too) spicy	(прекалено) люто	(pre·ka·le·no) lyoo·to
superb	отлично	ot·leech·no

poon
лъжица f
uh-zhee·tsa

ork
вилица f
vee·lee·tsa

plate
чиния f
chee·nee·ya

knife
нож m
nozh

wineglass
чаша за вино f
cha·sha za vee·no

glass
чаша f
cha·sha

table
маса f
ma·sa

methods of preparation

I'd like it …	Предпочитам	pred·po·*chee*·tam
	да е …	da e …
I don't want it …	Предпочитам	pred·po·*chee*·tam
	да не е …	da ne e …
boiled	варено	va·*re*·no
broiled	печено	pe·che·no
deep-fried	пържено	*puhr*·zhe·no
fried	пържено	*puhr*·zhe·no
grilled	на скара	na *ska*·ra
mashed	на пюре	na pyoo·*re*
medium	средно	*sred*·no
	изпечено	eez·*pe*·che·no
rare	алангле	a·*lan*·gle
reheated	претоплено	pre·*top*·le·no
steamed	варено на пара	va·*re*·no na *pa*·ra
well-done	добре	do·*bre*
	изпечено	eez·*pe*·che·no
without …	без …	bez …
with the	със соса	suhs *so*·sa
dressing on	отделно	ot·*del*·no
the side		

coffee, anyone?

black coffee	кафе без мляко n	ka·*fe* bez *mlya*·ko
cappuccino	капучино n	ka·poo·*chee*·no
decaffeinated	без кофеин	bez ko·fe·*een*
espresso	еспресо n	es·*pre*·so
iced coffee	айскафе n	*ais*·ka·fe
instant coffee	нескафе n	nes·ka·*fe*
strong coffee	силно кафе n	*seel*·no ka·*fe*
Turkish coffee	турско кафе n	*toor*·sko ka·*fe*
Viennese coffee	виенско кафе n	vee·*en*·sko ka·*fe*
weak coffee	слабо кафе n	*sla*·bo ka·*fe*
white coffee	кафе с мляко n	ka·*fe* s *mlya*·ko

nonalcoholic drinks

(cup of) coffee ...	(чаша) кафе ...	(*cha*·sha) ka·*fe* ...
(cup of) tea ...	(чаша) чай ...	(*cha*·sha) chai ...
with (milk)	с (мляко)	s (*mlya*·ko)
without (sugar)	без (захар)	bez (*za*·har)
... mineral water	... минерална вода	... mee·ne·*ral*·na vo·*da*
sparkling	газирана	ga·*zee*·ra·na
still	негазирана	ne·ga·*zee*·ra·na
(orange) juice	(портокалов) сок m	(por·to·*ka*·lov) sok
soft drink	безалкохолна напитка f	bez·al·ko·*hol*·na na·*peet*·ka
(boiled) water	(преварена) вода f	(pre·va·*re*·na) vo·*da*

alcoholic drinks

beer	бира f	*bee*·ra
(local) brandy	ракия f	ra·*kee*·ya
champagne	шампанско n	sham·*pan*·sko
a shot of whisky	едно малко уиски	ed·*no* mal·ko oo·*ees*·kee
a shot of ...	един малък ...	e·*deen* ma·luhk ...
gin	джин	dzheen
rum	ром	rom
a shot of ...	една малка ...	ed·*na* mal·ka ...
tequila	текила	te·*kee*·la
vodka	водка	*vod*·ka

a bottle/glass	бутилка/чаша	boo·*teel*·ka/*cha*·sha
of ... wine	... вино	... *vee*·no
dessert	десертно	de·*sert*·no
red	червено	cher·*ve*·no
sparkling	шумящо	shoo·*myash*·to
white	бяло	*bya*·lo
a ... of beer	... бира	... *bee*·ra
glass	чаша	*cha*·sha
jug	кана	*ka*·na
large bottle	голяма	go·*lya*·ma
	бутилка	boo·*teel*·ka
small bottle	малка бутилка	*mal*·ka boo·*teel*·ka

For additional items, see the **menu decoder**, page 181, and the dictionary.

---

local drinks

Bulgarians' favourite alcoholic drinks are beer, wine and *ракия* ra·*kee*·ya (brandy usually made from grapes, but sometimes from plums or apricots). Red wines from Melnik and Asenovgrad are made from the *мавруд* mav·*rood* and *гъмза* *guhm*·za grapes, which aren't found anywhere else in the world. Vodka, whisky, gin, *мента* *men*·ta (crème de menthe) and *мастика* mas·*tee*·ka (ouzo) are also popular.

---

in the bar

в бара

Before taking a sip, wait until everyone in the group is served and someone offers a toast, either in spoken form or by means of eye contact and a raised glass. Common toasts are *Да сме живи и здрави!* da sme *zhee*·vee ee *zdra*·vee (May we live in health!) and *За много години!* za *mno*·go go·*dee*·nee (To many years!). 'Topping up' isn't done in Bulgaria: a glass should be drained before it's refilled.

xcuse me!
Моля.
mol·yuh

m next.
Аз съм на ред.
az suhm na red

'll have a brandy.
За мене ракия.
za *me*·ne ra·*kee*·ya

ame again, please.
Същото, моля.
suhsh·to·to *mol*·yuh

lo ice, thanks.
Без лед, моля.
bez led *mol*·yuh

'll buy you a drink.
Аз черпя.
az *cher*·pyuh

Vhat would you like?
Какво ще пиете/пиеш? pol/inf
kak·*vo* shte *pee*·e·te/*pee*·esh

don't drink alcohol.
Не пия алкохол.
ne *pee*·yuh al·ko·*hol*

t's my round.
Сега е моят ред
да почерпя.
se·*ga* e *mo*·yuht red
da po·*cherp*·yuh

low much is that?
Колко струва?
kol·ko *stroo*·va

Do you serve meals here?
Тука сервирате ли храна?
too·ka ser·*vee*·ra·te lee hra·*na*

ready to order?

Beer and wine are ordered either by the glass or by the
bottle. Spirits are ordered according to standard sizes –
50 grams (small), 100 grams (large), 200 grams (double) – eg
една малка/голяма/двойна ракия ed·*na mal*·ka/go·*lya*·ma/
dvoy·na ra·*kee*·ya (a small/large/double brandy) or *един
малък/голям/двоен джин* e·*deen ma*·luhk/go·*lyam/dvo*·yen
dzheen (a small/large/double gin). A minibottle of spirits
(eg as served on a plane) is called a *патронче* pa·*tron*·che.

eating out

173

drinking up

Cheers!
На здраве!   na *zdra*·ve

This is hitting the spot.
Това е върхът.   to·*va* e vuhr·*huht*

I feel fantastic!
Чувствам се страхотно!   *choovs*·tvam se stra·*hot*·no

I think I've had one too many.
Май се понапих.   mai se po·na·*peeh*

I'm feeling drunk.
Пиян/Пияна съм. m/f   pee·*yan*/pee·*ya*·na suhm

I'm pissed.
Аз съм кьоркютук   az suhm kyor·kyoo·*took*
пиян/пияна. m/f   pee·*yan*/pee·*ya*·na

I feel ill.
Не ми е добре.   ne mee e do·*bre*

Where's the toilet?
Къде е тоалетната?   kuh·*de* e to·a·*let*·na·ta

I'm tired, I'd better go home.
Уморен/Уморена съм,   oo·mo·*ren*/oo·mo·*re*·na suhm
по-добре да се   po·do·*bre* da se
прибирам. m/f   pree·*bee*·ram

I don't think you should drive.
Не трябва да карате/   ne *tryab*·va da *ka*·ra·te/
караш кола. pol/inf   *ka*·rash ko·*la*

listen for ...

Какво пиете/пиеш? pol/inf
kak·*vo* pee·e·te/*pee*·esh   **What are you having?**

Стига толкова.
stee·ga *tol*·ko·va   **I think you've had enough.**

Последна поръчка.
po·*sled*·na po·*ruhch*·ka   **Last orders.**

FOOD

самостоятелно пазаруване и готвене

buying food

купуване на храна

What's the local speciality?
Какъв е местният
специалитет?

ka·*kuhv* e *mest*·nee·yuht
spe·tsee·a·lee·*tet*

Is this locally produced?
Това местно
производство ли е?

to·*va mest*·no
pro·eez·*vods*·tvo lee e

What's that?
Какво е това?

kak·*vo* e to·*va*

Can I taste it?
Мога ли да го пробвам?

mo·guh lee da go *prob*·vam

Can I have a bag, please?
Дайте ми един плик, моля.

dai·te mee e·*deen* pleek *mol*·yuh

I don't need a bag, thanks.
Не ми трябва плик,
благодаря.

ne mee *tryab*·va pleek
bla·go·dar·*yuh*

How much is (a kilo of cheese)?
Колко струва (един
килограм кашкавал)?

kol·ko *stroo*·va (e·*deen*
kee·lo·*gram* kash·ka·*val*)

food stuff

cooked	сготвен	*sgot*·ven
cured	пушен	*poo*·shen
dried	сушен	*soo*·shen
fresh	пресен	*pre*·sen
frozen	замразен	za·*mra*·zen
home-made	домашен	do·*ma*·shen
raw	суров	*soo*·rov
smoked	пушен	*poo*·shen
steamed	сварен на пара	sva·*ren* na *pa*·ra

I'd like ...	Дайте ми, моля ...	dai·te mee mol·yuh ...
(200) grams	(двеста) грама	(dve·sta) gra·ma
half a dozen	половин дузина	po·lo·veen doo·zee·na
a dozen	дузина	doo·zee·na
half a kilo	половин кило	po·lo·veen kee·lo
a kilo	едно кило	ed·no kee·lo
(two) kilos	(две) кила	(dve) kee·la
a bottle	една бутилка	ed·na boo·teel·ka
a jar	един буркан	e·deen boor·kan
a packet	една опаковка	ed·na o·pa·kov·ka
a piece	едно парче	ed·no par·che
(three) pieces	(три) парчета	(tree) par·che·ta
a slice	една филия	ed·na fee·lee·ya
(six) slices	(шест) филии	(shest) fee·lee·e
a tin	една кутия	ed·na koo·tee·ya
(just) a little	(само) малко	(sa·mo) mal·ko
more	още	osh·te
some	няколко	nya·kol·ko
that one	онова там	o·no·va tam
this one	това тук	to·va took
Less.	По-малко.	po·mal·ko
Enough.	Достатъчно.	do·sta·tuhch·no
More.	Повече.	po·ve·che

listen for ...

С какво мога да ви помогна?	s kak·vo mo·guh da vee po·mog·nuh	Can I help you?
Какво желаете?	kak·vo zhe·la·ye·te	What would you like?
Още нещо?	osh·te nesh·to	Anything else?
Няма.	nya·ma	There isn't any.

here can I find	Къде се намира	kuh·de se na·mee·ra
...e ... section?	отделът за ...?	ot·de·luht za ...
dairy	млечни	mlech·nee
	продукти	pro·dook·tee
fish	риби	ree·bee
frozen goods	замразени	za·mra·ze·nee
	стоки	sto·kee
fruit and	плодове и	plo·do·ve ee
vegetable	зеленчуци	ze·len·choo·tsee
health-food	здравословни	zdra·vo·slov·nee
	храни	hra·nee
meat	месо	me·so
poultry	домашни	do·mash·nee
	птици	ptee·tsee

or food items, see the **menu decoder**, page 181, and the
ictionary.

Do you have …?	Имате ли …?	*ee*·ma·te lee …
anything	нещо	*nesh*·to
cheaper	по-евтино	*po*·ev·tee·no
other kinds	други видове	*droo*·gee vee·do·v

cooking utensils

кухненски съдове и прибор

I need a …	Трябва ми …	*tryab*·va mee …
Could I please	Моля, мога ли	*mol*·yuh *mo*·guh lee
borrow a …?	да взема	da *vze*·muh
	назаем …?	na·*za*·em …
chopping	дъска за	duhs·*ka* za
board	рязане	*rya*·za·ne
frying pan	тиган	tee·*gan*
knife	нож	nozh
saucepan	тенджера	*tend*·zhe·ra

For more cooking implements, see the **dictionary**.

diminutives

Bulgarian is rich in diminutives – these are words (created by the addition of certain endings) that sometimes express the idea of smallness, but more often they indicate familiarity or affection (like 'doggy' in English) – for example, *пиле* n *pee*·le (chick) becomes *пиленце* n *pee*·len·tse (sweetheart). Personal names, nouns, adjectives and even verbs can all be transformed into diminutives in Bulgarian. Here are some more examples of the base word followed by the diminutive form:

Милена f (name) mee·*le*·na	Миленче n mee·*len*·che
нож m (knife) nozh	ножче n *nozh*·che
ракия f (brandy) ra·*kee*·ya	ракийка f ra·*keey*·ka
салата f (salad) sa·*la*·ta	салатка f sa·*lat*·ka
спя v (sleep) spyuh	спинкам *speen*·kam
хубав a (nice) *hoo*·bav	хубавички *hoo*·ba·veech·kee

ordering food

o you have . food?	Имате ли … храна?	*ee*·ma·te lee … hra·*na*
kosher	кашер	ka·*sher*
vegetarian	вегетарианска	ve·ge·ta·ree·*an*·ska
s it cooked /with …?	С … ли е сготвено?	s … lee e *sgot*·ve·no
butter	краве масло	*kra*·ve *mas*·lo
eggs	яйца	yai·*tsa*
fish	риба	*ree*·ba
fish stock	рибен бульон	*ree*·ben boo·*lyon*
meat	месо	me·*so*
meat stock	месен бульон	*me*·sen boo·*lyon*
oil	олио	o·lee·o
pork	свинско месо	*sveen*·sko me·*so*
poultry	домашни птици	do·*mash*·nee *ptee*·tsee
red meat	червено месо	cher·*ve*·no me·*so*
s this …?	Това … ли е?	to·*va* … lee e
decaffeinated	без кофеин	bez ko·fe·*een*
free of animal produce	без животински продукти	bez zhee·vo·*teen*·skee pro·*dook*·tee
genetically modified	генетически модифи- цирано	ge·ne·*tee*·ches·kee mo·dee·fee· *tsee*·ra·no
gluten-free	без глутен	bez *gloo*·ten
low-fat	ниско на мазнина	*nees*·ko na maz·nee·*na*
low in sugar	с малко захар	s *mal*·ko *za*·har
organic	органично	or·ga·*neech*·no
salt-free	безсолно	bez·*sol*·no

special diets & allergies

I'm on a special diet.
Аз съм на специална
диета.
az suhm na spe·tsee·*al*·na
dee·*e*·ta

I'm a vegan.
Аз съм пълен
вегетарианец. m
az suhm *puh*·len
ve·ge·ta·ree·*a*·nets
Аз съм пълна
вегетарианка. f
az suhm *puhl*·na
ve·ge·ta·ree·*an*·ka

I'm a vegetarian.
Аз съм вегетарианец/
вегетарианка. m/f
az suhm ve·ge·ta·ree·*a*·nets/
ve·ge·ta·ree·*an*·ka

I don't eat …
Аз не ям …
az ne yam …

**I'm allergic
to …**
Аз съм
алергичен/
алергична
към … m/f
az suhm
a·ler·*gee*·chen/
a·ler·*geech*·na
kuhm …

dairy produce	млечни продукти	*mlech*·nee pro·*dook*·tee
eggs	яйца	yai·*tsa*
gelatine	желатин	zhe·la·*teen*
gluten	глутен	*gloo*·ten
honey	мед	med
MSG	MSG	em·es·*dzhee*
nuts	ядки	*yad*·kee
peanuts	фъстъци	fuh·*stuh*·tsee
seafood	морски продукти	*mor*·skee pro·*dook*·tee

To explain your dietary restrictions with reference to religious
beliefs, see **beliefs & cultural differences**, page 145.

menu decoder
готварски речник

is miniguide to Bulgarian cuisine is designed to help you get the most out of your stronomic experience by providing you with food terms that you may see on enus. Nouns have their gender indicated by ⓜ (masculine), ⓕ (feminine) or ⓝ euter). If it's a plural noun, you'll also see pl. Adjectives are given in the masculine rm only. For more information, see the **phrasebuilder**.

This **menu decoder** has been ordered according to the Cyrillic alphabet, shown below in both roman and italic text:

Аа Бб Вв Гг Дд Ее Жж Зз Ии Йй Кк Лл Мм Нн Оо Пп
Аа Бб Вв Гг Дд Ее Жж Зз Ии Йй Кк Лл Мм Нн Оо Пп

Рр Сс Тт Уу Фф Хх Цц Чч Шш Щщ Ъъ ь Юю Яя
Рр Сс Тт Уу Фф Хх Цц Чч Шш Щщ Ъъ ь Юю Яя

А

нешка главичка ⓕ
ag-nesh-ka gla-veech-ka lamb's head

нешка курбан-чорба ⓕ
ag-nesh-ka kur-ban-chor-ba
boiled lamb cut into cubes with chopped onion, paprika, rice, parsley & eggs

нешка яхния ⓕ *ag-nesh-ka yah-nee-ya stewed lamb with onion*

нешко ⓝ *ag-nesh-ko lamb*

нешко филе с горчица ⓝ
ag-nesh-ko fee-le s gor-chee-tsa
lamb fillet with mustard sauce

нешко шкембе-чорба ⓝ
ag-nesh-ko shkem-be-chor-ba
seasoned lamb in milk

нешки кебап ⓜ *ag-nesh-kee ke-bap lamb shish kebab*

йрян ⓜ *ai-ryan liquefied yogurt drink*

йскафе ⓝ *ais-ka-fe iced coffee*

кула ⓕ *a-koo-la shark*

пангле *a-lan-gle rare (of meat)*

пкохолни напитки ⓕ pl
al-ko-hol-nee na-peet-kee alcoholic drinks

нанас ⓜ *a-na-nas pineapple*

перитиви ⓜ pl *a-pe-ree-tee-vee apéritifs*

артишок ⓜ *ar-tee-shok artichoke*

аспержи as-*per-zhee asparagus*

ашуре *a-shoo-re*
milk soup with bulgur (cracked wheat)

Б

бадеми ⓜ pl *ba-de-mee almonds*

баклава ⓕ *bak-la-va*
flaky pastry with walnuts or pistachios & cinnamon, honey or sugar syrup

банан ⓜ *ba-nan banana*

баница ⓕ *ba-nee-tsa*
flaky pastry stuffed with white cheese

банички ⓕ pl *ba-neech-kee cheese pastries*

безалкохолни напитки ⓕ pl
bez-al-ko-hol-nee na-peet-kee
soft drinks

без кофеин *bez ko-fe-een decaffeinated*

бекон ⓜ *be-kon bacon*

биволско мляко ⓝ *bee-vol-sko mlya-ko*
water buffalo milk

билки ⓕ pl *beel-kee herbs*

билков чай ⓜ *beel-kov chai herbal tea*

бира ⓕ *bee-ra beer*

бисквита ⓕ *beesk-vee-ta biscuit*

бисквити с орехи ⓕ pl
beesk-vee-tee s o-re-hee
biscuits made with crushed walnuts

бифтек ⓜ *beef-tek steak*
боб ⓜ *bob seasoned bean soup*
бобово растение ⓝ
  bo-bo-vo ras-te-nee-e legume
боза ⓕ *bo-za*
  millet ale (also made from other grains)
брашно ⓝ *brash-no flour*
бульон ⓜ *boo-lyon consommé • stock*
бъркан *buhr-kan scrambled*
бъркани яйца с печени чушки ⓝ pl
  *buhr-ka-nee yai-tsa s pe-che-nee
  choosh-kee scrambled eggs with diced
  roasted peppers & grated white cheese*
бяло вино ⓝ *bya-lo vee-no white wine*

В

варен *va-ren boiled*
варено жито ⓝ *va-re-no zhee-to
  boiled wheat*
вечеря ⓕ *ve-cher-ya dinner*
виенско кафе ⓝ *vee-en-sko ka-fe
  Viennese coffee*
вино ⓝ *vee-no wine*
вита баница ⓕ *vee-ta ba-nee-tsa
  thin flaky pastry stuffed with white
  cheese, yogurt & eggs*
вишни ⓕ pl *veesh-nee sour cherries*
вода ⓕ *vo-da water*
водка ⓕ *vod-ka vodka*
вретено ⓝ *vre-te-no seasoned pork
  burger filled with melted cheese*

Г

газирана минерална вода ⓕ
  *ga-zee-ra-na mee-ne-ral-na vo-da
  sparkling mineral water*
гарнитура ⓕ *gar-nee-too-ra
  garnish • side dish*
гевреци ⓜ pl *ge-vre-tsee
  large ring-shaped pretzels*
гола праскова ⓕ *go-la pras-ko-va
  nectarine*
горчица ⓕ *gor-chee-tsa mustard*
градинарска чорба ⓕ
  *gra-dee-nar-ska chor-ba
  soup of celery, carrots, parsley, cabbage
  & potatoes, with white cheese & milk*
грах ⓜ *grah peas*

грозде ⓝ *groz-de grapes*
гроздова ракия ⓕ *groz-do-va ra-kee
  brandy made from grapes*
гъби ⓕ pl *guh-bee mushrooms*
гювеч ⓜ *gyoo-vech
  stew – peppers, tomatoes, aubergine
  onions, potatoes, zucchini, carrots &
  sometimes meat, cooked in the oven*
гювеч с овнешко месо ⓜ
  *gyoo-vech s ov-nesh-ko me-so
  mutton & vegetable stew baked in an
  earthenware dish*

Д

десерт ⓜ *de-sert dessert*
десертно вино ⓝ *de-sert-no vee-no
  dessert wine*
джин ⓜ *dzheen gin*
дивеч ⓜ *dee-vech game (meat)*
диня ⓕ *deen-ya watermelon*
добре изпечен *do-bre eez-pe-chen
  well-done (of meat)*
добуш торта ⓕ *do-boosh tor-ta
  layered chocolate cake*
доматен сос ⓜ *do-ma-ten sos
  tomato sauce*
домати pl *do-ma-tee tomatoes*
домашни птици ⓕ pl
  do-mash-nee ptee-tsee poultry
домашно вино ⓝ *do-mash-no vee-no
  home-made wine*
дреболии ⓕ pl *dre-bo-lee-ee giblets*
дроб-сарма ⓕ *drob-sar-ma
  boiled lamb's liver & intestines with
  rice & onions, wrapped in fat & baked
  in the oven*
друсан кебап ⓜ *droo-san ke-bap large
  cubes of meat fried in fat, then boiled,
  with spices, onions & parsley*
дюли ⓕ pl *dyoo-lee quinces*
дюнер кебаб ⓜ *dyoo-ner ke-bab
  doner kebab*

Е

едра скарида ⓕ *ed-ra ska-ree-da prawn*
език ⓜ *e-zeek tongue*
есетра ⓕ *e-se-tra sturgeon*
еспресо ⓝ *es-pre-so espresso coffee*

ушен za·doo·shen *braised · poached*

шко ⓝ za·esh·ko *rabbit*

уска ① za·koos·ka *breakfast · snack*

ар ① za·har *sugar*

е ⓝ ze·le *cabbage*

ена чушка ① ze·le·na choosh·ka
reen pepper

ен лук ⓜ ze·len look *spring onion*

ен фасул ⓜ ze·len fa·sool
reen beans

енчук ⓜ ze·len·chook *vegetable*

тин ⓝ zeh·teen *olive oil*

л фасул ⓜ zryal fa·sool
*oiled kidney beans with onions, carrots,
elery, dried red pepper & mint*

арма ⓝ ka·var·ma
*neat or vegetable stew (usually pork or
hicken), served in an earthenware pot*

аиф ⓜ ka·da·yeef
hredded wheat stuffed with nuts in syrup

има ① kai·ma *mincemeat*

йсиева ракия ① kai·see·e·va ra·kee·ya
randy made from apricots

йсия ① kai·see·ya *apricot*

ао ⓝ ka·ka·o *cocoa*

кан ⓜ kal·kan *turbot (fish)*

мар ⓜ kal·mar *calamari*

пама ① ka·pa·ma *meat, rice &
auerkraut (or other ingredients)
immered & served in a clay pot*

пучино ⓝ ka·poo·chee·no
rappuccino

рантия ① ka·ran·tee·ya *offal*

ртофи ⓜ pl kar·to·fee *potatoes*

ртофи със сирене ⓜ pl
kar·to·fee suhs see·re·ne *fried potatoes
opped with white cheese*

фиол ⓜ kar·fee·ol *cauliflower*

фе ⓝ ka·fe *coffee*

фе без захар ⓝ ka·fe bez za·har
coffee without sugar

фе без кофеин ⓝ ka·fe bez ko·fe·een
decaffeinated coffee

фе без мляко ⓝ ka·fe bez mlya·ko
black coffee

кафе с мляко ⓝ ka·fe s mlya·ko
white coffee

качамак ⓜ ka·cha·mak *polenta*

кашкавал ⓜ kash·ka·val
hard yellow cheese

кашкавал пане ⓝ kash·ka·val pa·ne
fried yellow cheese in batter

кашу ⓝ ka·shoo *cashew*

кебабчета ⓝ pl ke·bap·che·ta
grilled spicy meat sausages

кебап ⓜ ke·bap *kebab*

кебапчета на скара ⓝ pl
ke·bap·che·ta na ska·ra
*grilled, sausage-shaped pork meatballs
mixed with finely chopped onion*

кекс ⓜ keks *loaf cake*

керевиз ⓜ ke·re·veez *celery*

кестени ⓜ pl kes·te·nee *chestnuts*

кисело мляко ⓝ ke·se·lo mlya·ko
yogurt

кифла с мармалад ①
keef·la s mar·ma·lad jam-filled croissant

козе мляко ⓝ ko·ze mlya·ko *goat's milk*

козунак ⓜ ko·zoo·nak
plaited sweet bread

козуначена кифла ①
ko·zoo·na·che·na keef·la
*small bread roll made from slightly
sweetened dough & flavoured with
marmalade*

кокосов орех ⓜ ko·ko·sov o·reh
coconut

коктейл ⓜ kok·teyl *cocktail*

конфитюр ⓜ kon·fee·tyoor *jam*

коняк ⓜ kon·yak *cognac*

костур ⓜ kos·toor *perch*

котлет на скара ⓜ kot·let na ska·ra
grilled cutlet

краве масло ⓝ kra·ve mas·lo *butter*

краве мляко ⓝ kra·ve mlya·ko
cow's milk

краставица ① kras·ta·vee·tsa *cucumber*

крем карамел ⓜ krem ka·ra·mel *custard*

круша ① kroo·sha *pear*

къпана баница ① kuh·pa·na ba·nee·tsa
*'bathed bread' – ceremonial bread that's
wrapped in cheesecloth & placed in a
large pot of tepid water prior to baking*

къпини ① pl kuh·pee·nee *blackberries*

menu decoder

183

кьопоолу ⓜ kyo-po-o-loo
eggplant purée with garlic, salt, vinegar, parsley & slices of tomato
кюфтета ⓒ pl kyoof-te-ta round meatballs similar to **кюфте татарско**
кюфте татарско ⓝ kyoof-te ta-tar-sko
pork burger filled with melted cheese

Л

лайм ⓜ laim lime
лед ⓜ led ice
лефер ⓜ le-fer bluefish
лешници ⓜ pl lesh-nee-tsee hazelnuts
леща ⓒ pl lesh-ta lentils
лимон ⓜ lee-mon lemon
лимонада ⓒ lee-mo-na-da lemonade
локум ⓜ lo-koom Turkish delight
лук ⓜ look onion
луканка ⓒ loo-kan-ka
flat sausage, usually made from dried pork, beef & spices
лют ⓜ lyoot hot (spicy)
лютеница ⓒ lyoo-te-nee-tsa
piquant sauce of red peppers & herbs •
roasted pepper spread
люти чушки ⓒ pl lyoo-tee choosh-kee
chilli • hot peppers

М

магданоз ⓜ mag-da-noz parsley
майонеза ⓒ ma-yo-ne-za mayonnaise
макарони ⓒ ma-ka-ro-nee pasta
малини ⓒ pl ma-lee-nee raspberries
мандарина ⓒ man-da-ree-na mandarine
маргарин ⓜ mar-ga-reen margarine
маруля ⓒ ma-roo-lya lettuce
маслина ⓒ mas-lee-na olive
масло ⓝ mas-lo butter
мастика ⓒ mas-tee-ka ouzo
мед ⓜ med honey
меденка ⓒ me-den-ka
honeyed round loaf
мента ⓜ men-ta crème de menthe • mint
ментов чай ⓜ men-tov chai mint tea
месен бульон ⓜ me-sen boo-lyon
meat stock
месо ⓝ me-so meat
мешана салата ⓒ me-sha-na sa-la-ta
mixed salad

миди ⓒ pl mee-dee mussels
миди цигане ⓒ pl mee-dee tsee-ga-r
mussels sautéed with a spicy cheese mustard sauce
минерална вода ⓒ mee-ne-ral-na vo
mineral water
миш-маш ⓜ meesh-mash
scrambled eggs with peppers, tomate onions & grated white cheese
млечна баница ⓒ mlech-na ba-nee-t
sweet pastry made with milk & eggs
млечни продукти ⓜ pl
mlech-nee pro-dook-tee dairy produc
мляко ⓝ mlya-ko milk
мляко от соя ⓝ mlya-ko ot so-ya
soy milk
мозък ⓜ mo-zuhk brains
морков ⓜ mor-kov carrot
морски кефал ⓜ mor-skee ke-fal
grey mullet
морски костур ⓜ mor-skee kos-toor
sea bass
морски продукти ⓜ pl
mor-skee pro-dook-tee seafood
морски рак ⓜ mor-skee rak crab
мусака ⓒ moo-sa-ka moussaka
мусака от телешко месо ⓒ
moo-sa-ka ot te-lesh-ko me-so
minced veal, sliced eggplant, tomatoes, covered with a white sauce & baked
мюсли ⓒ myoos-lee muesli

Н

… на гюведже … na gyoo-ved-zhe
casserole of …
наденица ⓒ na-de-nee-tsa sausage
наливна бира ⓒ na-leev-na bee-ra
draught beer
напитки ⓒ pl na-peet-kee drinks
на пюре na pyoo-re mashed
на скара na ska-ra grilled
натурален сок ⓜ na-too-ra-len sok
fruit juice not freshly squeezed (unlike **фреш от …**)
негазирана минерална вода ⓒ
ne-ga-zee-ra-na mee-ne-ral-na vo-da
still mineral water
нескафе ⓝ nes-ka-fe instant coffee

ед ⓜ o-bed *lunch*
езмаслено мляко ⓝ
·bez·mas·le·no *mlya·*ko *skim milk*
сени ядки ⓜ pl o·ve·se·nee *yad·kee*
atmeal
ешко ⓝ ov·nesh·ko *mutton*
ешко-пилаф ⓜ ov·nesh·ko·pee·laf
ubed mutton fried with rice, onions,
easonings & tomatoes, then cooked
е мляко ⓝ ov·che *mlya·*ko *ewe's milk*
ло ⓝ o·lee·o *oil*
лет ⓜ om·let *omelette*
ьоври ⓜ pl or·*dyo·*vree *entrées*
ехи ⓜ pl o·re·hee *walnuts*
из ⓜ o·reez *rice*
овни ястия ⓝ pl
·s·nov·nee yas·*tee·*ya *main courses*
люв ⓜ oh·*lyoov snail*
ет ⓜ o·tset *vinegar*
аф ⓜ o·*shaf stewed dried fruit*

ачинки ⓝ pl pa·la·cheen·kee
ancakes
ирана риба ⓕ pa·nee·ra·na *ree·*ba
eep-fried battered fish
ста ⓕ pas·ta *pastry*
стърва ⓕ pas·*tuhr·*va *mountain trout*
гатник ⓜ pa·*tat·*neek *hearty cheese &
otato omelette*
ешки сърца ⓝ pl
a·tesh·kee suhr·*tsa ducks' hearts*
гица ⓕ *pa·*tee·tsa *duck*
ладжан ⓜ pat·lad·*zhan
auberinge • eggplant*
ча ⓕ pa·cha
*ellied leg of pork with onion, carrots,
epper & pickled cucumbers*
чен pe·chen *baked • broiled • roasted*
чени чушки ⓕ pl
·e·che·nee *choosh·*kee *roasted peppers*
чени ядки ⓝ pl pe·che·nee *yad·*kee
oasted nuts
чено пиле с домати ⓝ
·che·no *pee·*le s do·*ma·*tee
*chicken with tomatoes roasted in the
wen & served with rice*

пилешка дроб-сарма ⓕ
pee·*lesh·*ka drob·*sar·*ma
chicken livers with rice & yogurt
пилешка супа (със зеленчуци) ⓕ
pee·*leesh·*ka *soo·*pa (suhs
ze·len·*choo·*tsee)
chicken soup (with vegetables)
пилешко ⓝ pee·lesh·ko *chicken (meat)*
пиле яхния ⓕ pee·le yah·*nee·*ya
chicken & onion stew
пипер ⓜ pee·per *pepper*
пирог ⓜ pee·rog *pie*
питка ⓕ *peet·*ka *bread roll*
пица ⓕ *pee·*tsa *pizza*
... плакия ⓕ ... *pla·*kee·ya
*a way of preparing fish by baking it in
an earthenware pot, usually in a rich
tomato sauce*
плод ⓜ plod *fruit*
плодов чай ⓜ *plo·*dov chai *fruit tea*
понички ⓕ pl po·*neech·*kee
*pastries similar in taste to doughnuts
but differently shaped*
попарен po·pa·ren *poached (egg)*
портокал ⓜ por·to·*kal orange*
портокалов сок ⓜ por·to·*ka·*lov sok
orange juice
праз ⓜ praz *leek*
прасковa ⓕ *pras·*ko·va *peach*
преварена вода ⓕ pre·va·*re·*na vo·*da
boiled water
предястия ⓝ pl pred·*yas·*tee·ya
appetisers • starters
препечен хляб ⓜ pre·pe·chen hlyab
toast • toasted sandwich
пресен *pre·*sen *fresh*
принцеса ⓕ preen·*tse·*sa *snack of
mincemeat paste served on toast*
пуйка ⓕ *pooy·*ka *turkey*
пушен *poo·*shen *cured • smoked*
пушена шунка ⓕ *poo·*she·na *shoon·*ka
smoked leg of ham
пушено сирене ⓝ *poo·*she·no *see·*re·ne
smoked cheese
пълнен *puhl·*nen *stuffed*
пълнена риба на фурна ⓕ
*puhl·*ne·na *ree·*ba na *foor·*na
*carp, sea bass or pike stuffed with rice,
hazelnuts, basil & rosemary, then baked*

menu decoder

185

пълнени гъби ① pl
puhl·ne·nee guh·bee stuffed mushrooms

пълнени пиперки с месо ① pl
puhl·ne·nee pee·per·kee s me·so
peppers stuffed with minced veal or
pork, paprika & rice, then cooked

пълнени тиквички ① pl *puhl·ne·nee*
teek·veech·kee zucchini stuffed with
cheese, vegetables and/or meat

пълнени чушки ① pl
puhl·ne·nee choosh·kee stuffed peppers

пълнен патладжан ⓜ
puhl·nen pat·lad·zhan
aubergine stuffed with meat & vegetables

пъпеш ⓜ *puh·pesh* melon

пържен *puhr·zhen*
deep-fried · fried · sautéed

пържени картофи ⓜ pl
puhr·zhe·nee kar·to·fee chips · French fries

пържени картофи по селски ⓜ pl
puhr·zhe·nee kar·to·fee po sel·skee
fried potatoes (country-style)

пържени филийки ① pl
puhr·zhe·nee fee·leey·kee French toast

пържоли ① pl *puhr·zho·lee* chops (meat)

пюре от чушки ⓜ *pyoo·re ot choosh·kee*
red pepper condiment used as a garnish
for broiled or barbecued meat

Р

ракия ① *ra·kee·ya*
brandy (usually made from grapes, but
also from plums or apricots)

репичка ① *re·peech·ka* radish

речен рак ⓜ *re·chen rak* crayfish

риба ① *ree·ba* fish

риба в плик *ree·ba v pleek* salted
fish covered with soft dough & cooked
between sheets of greaseproof paper

риба-плакия ① *ree·ba·pla·kee·ya*
baked fish (usually carp) with paprika &
tomato paste

риба тон ① *ree·ba ton* tuna

рогче ⓜ *rog·che* small horn-shaped
bread bun with a cheese filling

розе ① *ro·ze* rosé (wine)

ром ⓜ *rom* rum

рохък *ro·huhk* soft-boiled

ряпа ① *rya·pa* turnip

С

салам ⓜ *sa·lam* salami

салата ① *sa·la·ta* salad

салата от зеле и моркови ①
sa·la·ta ot ze·le ee mor·ko·vee
coleslaw (cabbage & carrot salad)

сандвич ⓜ *sand·veech* sandwich

сардина ① *sar·dee·na* sardine

сарми с лозов лист ① pl
sar·mee s lo·zov leest vine leaves stuff
with minced lamb or veal & rice, then
cooked in a sauce of tomatoes, served
with sour cream or yogurt

сарми със зелеви листа ① pl
sar·mee suhs ze·le·vee lees·ta
cabbage leaves stuffed with minced
meat & rice (can also be meatless)

сварен на пара *sva·ren na pa·ra* steam

свински кебап ⓜ *sveen·skee ke·bap*
pork shish kebab

свинско ① *sveen·sko* pork

свинско филе ① *sveen·sko fee·le*
pork fillet

сготвен *sgot·ven* cooked

сини боровинки ① pl
see·nee bo·ro·veen·kee blueberries

сирене ⓜ *see·re·ne* soft white cheese

сирене по шопски ⓜ
see·re·ne po shop·skee white cheese,
eggs & tomatoes baked in a clay pot

скара ① *ska·ra* grill

скарида ① *ska·ree·da* shrimp

скумрия ① *skoom·ree·ya* mackerel

сладолед ⓜ *sla·do·led* ice cream

слива ① *slee·va* plum

сливова ракия ① *slee·vo·va ra·kee·ya*
brandy made from plums

слънчогледови семки ① pl
sluhn·cho·gle·do·vee sem·kee
sunflower seeds

сметана ① *sme·ta·na* cream · sour crea

сметанова торта ① *sme·ta·no·va tor·*
cream cake

смокиня ① *smo·kee·nya* fig

снежанка ① *sne·zhan·ka*
salad of pickled cucumbers & plain yog

соев сос ⓜ *so·yev sos* soy sauce

сок ⓜ *sok* juice

ⓕ sol *salt*

...енка ⓕ so·len·ka *cracker*

ⓜ som *sheatfish (European catfish)*

ⓜ sos *sauce*

...нак ⓜ spa·nak *spinach*

...нак загора ⓜ spa·nak za·go·ra
...inach baked with sour cream, walnuts, ...armesan, garlic, onions & spices

...нак със сирене ⓜ
...ba·nak suhs see·re·ne
...inach purée with white cheese

...дно изпечен sred·no eez·pe·chen
...edium (of meat)

...фида ⓕ sta·fee·da *raisin · sultana*

...ида ⓕ stree·da *oyster*

...a ⓕ soo·pa *soup*

...a топчета ⓕ soo·pa top·che·ta
...eatball soup

...ов soo·rov *raw*

...ен soo·shen *dried*

...ени плодове ⓜ pl
...oo·she·nee plo·do·ve *dried fruit*

...мга ⓕ syom·ga *salmon*

...атор ⓜ ta·ra·tor
...hilled soup made with finely chopped ...ucumber, yogurt, walnuts & spices

...рдо сварен tvuhr·do sva·ren
...ard-boiled

...ила ⓕ te·kee·la *tequila*

...ешко ⓝ te·lesh·ko *beef · veal*

...ешко със сини сливи ⓝ te·lesh·ko
...uhs see·nee slee·vee *veal with prunes*

...ешко филе ⓝ te·lesh·ko fee·le
...eal fillet

...ва ⓕ teek·va *pumpkin*

...веник ⓜ teek·ve·neek *pumpkin pie*

...вени семки ⓕ pl
...eek·ve·nee sem·ke *pumpkin seeds*

...вички ⓕ pl teek·veech·ke
...ourgette · zucchini

...вички с кисело мляко и чесен ⓕ pl
...eek·veech·ke suhs kee·se·lo mlya·ko
...e che·sen *zucchini in yogurt sauce*

...ли напитки ⓕ pl top·lee na·peet·ke
...ot drinks

...та ⓕ tor·ta *cake*

...фу ⓝ to·foo *tofu*

турско кафе ⓝ toor·sko ka·fe
Turkish coffee

туршия ⓕ toor·shee·ya
pickled vegetables

тюрлюговеч ⓜ tyoor·lyoo·gyoo·vech
diced mutton stewed with tomatoes, peppers & potatoes in an earthenware pot

У

уиски ⓝ oo·ees·kee *whisky*

Ф

фасул ⓜ fa·sool *beans*

филе ⓝ fee·le *fillet*

фреш (от ...) ⓜ fresh (ot ...)
freshly squeezed juice (of ... fruit)

фурма ⓕ foor·ma *date*

фъстъци ⓜ pl fuh·stuh·tsee *peanuts*

Х

хайвер ⓜ hai·ver *roe*

халва ⓕ hal·va *dessert of melted butter, sugar & water, served with crushed walnuts & cinnamon*

хамбургер ⓜ ham·boor·ger *hamburger*

херинга ⓕ he·reen·ga *herring*

хлебче ⓝ hleb·che *bread roll*

хляб ⓜ hlyab *bread*

хотдог ⓜ hot·dog *hot dog*

Ц

царевица ⓕ tsa·re·vee·tsa
corn on the cob

Ч

чай ⓜ chai *tea*

чай без захар ⓜ chai bez za·har
tea without sugar

чай с лимон ⓜ chai s li·mon
tea with lemon

чай с мляко ⓜ chai s mlya·ko
tea with milk

червени боровинки ⓕ pl
cher·ve·nee bo·ro·veen·kee *cranberries*

червено вино ⓝ cher·ve·no vee·no
red wine

червено месо ⓝ cher·ve·no me·so
red meat
червен пипер ⓜ cher·ven pee·per
paprika • red pepper
черен дроб ⓜ che·ren drob liver
черен пипер ⓜ che·ren pee·per pepper
черен чай ⓜ che·ren chai black tea
череши ① pl che·re·shee sweet cherries
черно непресято брашно ⓝ cher·no
ne·pres·ya·to brash·no wholemeal flour
чесън ⓜ che·suhn garlic
чига ① chee·ga sterlet (fish)
чорба ① chor·ba soup
чорба от зрял фасул ①
chor·ba ot zryal fa·sool boiled beans
with tomato purée, paprika & mint
чорба от леща ① chor·ba ot lesh·ta
lentil stew
чорба от пиле ① chor·ba ot pee·le
soup made by cooking rice in chicken
stock, with yogurt, flour & egg yolks
чубрица ① choo·bree·tsa savory (a herb
with an aromatic flavour similar to thyme)

Ш

шампанско ⓝ sham·pan·sko
champagne
шам–фъстък ⓜ sham·fuhs·tuhk pistachio
шаран ⓜ sha·ran carp
шаран с орехов пълнеж ⓜ
sha·ran s o·re·hov puhl·nezh baked
carp stuffed with rice, onions, tomatoes,
peppers, walnuts & cinnamon

шардоне ⓝ shar·do·ne Chardonnay
шарена сол ① sha·re·na sol Balkan
mixed salt – a common condiment t
includes fenugreek & red pepper
шкембе ⓝ shkem·be tripe
шкембе чорба ① shkem·be chor·ba
tripe soup
шоколад ⓜ sho·ko·lad chocolate
шоколадова торта ①
sho·ko·la·do·va tor·ta chocolate cake
шопска салата ① shop·ska sa·la·ta
salad of fresh tomatoes, cucumbers,
sweet peppers & grated white cheese
шумящо вино ⓝ shoo·myash·to vee
sparkling wine
шунка ① shoon·ka ham

Щ

щука ① shtoo·ka pike

Я

ябълка ⓝ ya·buhl·ka apple
ягоди ① pl ya·go·dee strawberries
ядки ① pl yad·kee nuts
яйца ⓝ pl yai·tsa eggs
яйца по панагюрски ⓝ pl
yai·tsa po pa·nag·yoor·skee
'veiled' eggs – poached eggs served v
yogurt, melted butter & red pepper

Ю

юфка ① yoof·ka noodles

mergencies

спешни случаи

elp!	Помощ!	po·mosht
top!	Стоп!	stop
o away!	Махайте се!	ma·hai·te se
hief!	Крадец!	kra·dets
ire!	Пожар!	po·zhar
Vatch out!	Внимавайте!	vnee·ma·vai·te

all ...!	Повикайте ...! pol	po·vee·kai·te ...
	Повикай ...! inf	po·vee·kai ...
an ambulance	линейка	lee·ney·ka
a doctor	доктор	dok·tor
the police	полицията	po·lee·tsee·ya·ta

's an emergency.
Случаят е спешен.   sloo·cha·yuht e spe·shen

here's been an accident.
Стана катастрофа.   sta·na ka·tas·tro·fa

ould you please help?
Моля ви/те за помощ. pol/inf   mo·lyuh vee/te za po·mosht

an I use your phone?
Мога ли да използвам телефона?   mo·guh lee da eez·polz·vam te·le·fo·nuh

essentials

189

I'm lost.
Загубих се. za·*goo*·beeh se

Where are the toilets?
Къде са тоалетните? kuh·*de* suh to·a·*let*·nee·te

She's about to have a baby.
Тя всеки момент tya *vse*·kee mo·*ment*
ще роди. shte ro·*dee*

He/She is having Той/Тя има … toy/tya ee·ma …
a/an …
  allergic reaction алергична a·ler·*geech*·na
    реакция re·*ak*·tsee·ya
  asthma attack астматична ast·ma·*teech*·na
    криза *kree*·za
  epileptic fit епилептичен e·pee·lep·*tee*·chen
    припадък pree·*pa*·duhk
  heart attack сърдечен suhr·*de*·chen
    удар *oo*·dar

police

полиция

Where's the police station?
Къде е полицейският kuh·*de* e po·lee·*tsey*·skee·yuht
участък? oo·*chas*·tuhk

I want to report an offence.
Искам да съобщя за ees·kam da suh·obsh·*tyuh* za
едно нарушение. ed·*no* na·roo·*she*·nee·e

It was him/her.
Той/Тя беше. toy/tya *be*·she

I have insurance.
Имам застраховка. ee·mam za·stra·*hov*·ka

I've been … … ме. … me
He/She has … го/я. … go/ya
been …
  assaulted Нападнаха na·*pad*·na·ha
  raped Изнасилиха eez·na·*see*·lee·ha
  robbed Ограбиха o·*gra*·bee·ha

Вие сте	vee·e ste	You're charged
обвинени в …	ob·vee·ne·nee v …	with …
кражба	krazh·ba	shoplifting/ theft
липсата на виза	leep·sa·ta na vee·za	not having a visa
нападение	na·pa·de·nee·e	assault
нарушаване на реда	na·roo·sha·va·ne na re·duh	disturbing the peace
притежание на незаконни вещества	pree·te·zha·nee·e na ne·za·kon·nee vesh·test·va	possession of illegal substances
Имате глоба за …	ee·ma·te glo·ba za …	It's a … fine.
паркиране	par·kee·ra·ne	parking
превишаване на скоростта	pre·vee·sha·va·ne na sko·rost·ta	speeding

...e lost my ...	Изгубих си …	eez·goo·beeh see …
...y ... was/were ...olen.	Откраднаха ми …	ot·krad·na·ha mee …
backpack/ rucksack	раницата	ra·nee·tsa·ta
bags	чантите	chan·tee·te
credit card	кредитната карта	kre·deet·na·ta kar·ta
handbag	дамската чанта	dam·ska·ta chan·ta
jewellery	бижутата	bee·zhoo·ta·ta
money	парите	pa·ree·te
papers	документите	do·koo·men·tee·te
passport	паспорта	pas·por·tuh
travellers cheques	пътническите чекове	puht·nee·ches·kee·tee che·ko·ve
wallet	портмонето	port·mo·ne·to

essentials

191

What am I accused of?
В какво съм обвинен/
обвинена? **m/f**
v kak·*vo* suhm ob·vee·*nen*/
ob·vee·*ne*·na

I didn't realise I was doing anything wrong.
Не знаех, че правя
нещо нередно.
ne *zna*·eh che *prav*·yuh
nesh·to ne·*red*·no

I didn't do it.
Не съм го направил/
направила. **m/f**
ne suhm go na·*pra*·veel/
na·*pra*·vee·la

Can I pay an on-the-spot fine?
Мога ли да платя
глобата веднага?
mo·guh lee da plat·*yuh*
glo·ba·ta ved·*na*·ga

I want to contact my embassy.
Искам да се свържа
с нашето посолство.
ees·kam da se *svuhr*·zhuh
s *na*·she·to po·*sols*·tvo

Can I make a phone call?
Мога ли да се обадя
по телефона?
mo·guh lee da se o·*bad*·yuh
po te·le·*fo*·nuh

Can I have a lawyer (who speaks English)?
Моля за адвокат (който
говори английски).
mol·yuh za ad·vo·*kat* (*koy*·to
go·*vo*·ree an·*gleey*·skee)

This drug is for personal use.
Лекарството е за
лична употреба.
le·*kars*·tvo·to e za
leech·na oo·po·*tre*·ba

I have a prescription for this drug.
Имам рецепта за това
лекарство.
ee·mam re·*tsep*·ta za to·*va*
le·*kars*·tvo

---

lonely letters

The single consonants in the Bulgarian phrases and our coloured pronunciation guides represent some common prepositions. You'll see *в* v for 'at', 'in' or 'to', and *с* s for 'with'. In pronunciation they're usually run together with the following word. They're pronounced twice when the following word starts with a similar sound, and this is reflected in the written form, eg *във влака* vuhv *vla*·kuh (in the train), *със захар* suhs *za*·har (with sugar). For more on prepositions, see the **phrasebuilder**.

doctor

lways address doctors and dentists formally, with the title *октор dok·*tor (Dr) followed by their surname, or using the vocative *докторе dok·*to·re (the form of the noun used when ddressing someone). For more information on the vocative, ee the box **what's in a name?**, page 135.

/here's the earest ...?	Къде се намира най-близкият/ най-близката ...? m/f	kuh·de se na·mee·ra nai·bleez·kee·yuht/ nai·bleez·ka·ta ...
dentist	зъболекар m	zuh·bo·le·kar
doctor	лекар m	le·kar
emergency department	спешна помощ f	spesh·na po·mosht
health centre	клиника f	klee·nee·ka
hospital	болница f	bol·nee·tsa
optometrist	очен лекар m	o·chen le·kar
pharmacy	аптека f	ap·te·ka

need a doctor (who speaks English).
Трябва ми лекар (който говори английски).
tryab·va mee le·kar (koy·to go·vo·ree an·gleey·skee)

ould I see a female doctor?
Може ли да ме прегледа лекарка?
mo·zhe lee da me pre·gle·da le·kar·ka

ould the doctor come here?
Може ли лекарят да ме посети в къщи?
mo·zhe lee le·kar·yuht da me po·se·tee v kuhsh·tee

s there an after-hours emergency number?
Има ли номер за спешна помощ извън работното време?
ee·ma lee no·mer za spesh·na po·mosht eez·vuhn ra·bot·no·to vre·me

I've run out of my medication.

Свършиха ми се
лекарствата.

svuhr·shee·ha mee se
le·*kars*·tva·ta

This is my usual medicine.

Аз редовно взимам
това лекарство.

az re·dov·no vzee·mam
to·*va* le·*kars*·tvo

My child weighs (20 kilos).

Детето ми тежи
(двайсет килограма).

de·*te*·to mee te·*zhee*
(*dvai*·set kee·lo·*gra*·ma)

What's the correct dosage?

Каква е дозировката?

kak·*va* e do·zee·*rov*·ka·ta

I don't want a blood transfusion.

Не искам да ми
преливат кръв.

ne *ees*·kam da mee
pre·*lee*·vat kruhv

Please use a new syringe.

Моля, използвайте
нова спринцовка.

mol·yuh eez·*polz*·vai·te
no·va spreen·*tsov*·ka

I have my own syringe.

Нося си спринцовка.

nos·yuh see spreen·*tsov*·ka

I've been vaccinated against …	Аз съм ваксиниран/ ваксинирана против … m/f	az suhm vak·see·*nee*·ran/ vak·see·*ra*·na pro·*teev* …
encephalitis	енцефалит	en·tse·fa·*leet*
hepatitis A/B/C	хепатит A/B/C	he·pa·*teet* a/be/tse
tetanus	тетанус	*te*·ta·noos
typhoid	тиф	teef
I need new …	Трябват ми нови …	*tryab*·vat mee *no*·vee …
contact lenses	контактни лещи	kon·*takt*·nee *lesh*·tee
glasses	очила	o·chee·*la*

My prescription is …

Рецептата ми е …

re·*tsep*·ta·ta mee e …

How much will it cost?

Колко ще струва?

kol·ko shte *stroo*·va

an I have a receipt for my insurance?

Може ли да ми дадете
бележка за моята
страховтелна компания?

mo·zhe lee da mee da·*de*·te
be·*lezh*·ka za *mo*·ya·ta
stra·ho·*va*·tel·na kom·*pa*·nee·ya

the doctor may say ...

Какво ви боли? kak·vo vee bo·*lee*	**Where does it hurt?**
Имате ли температура? *ee*·ma·te lee tem·pe·ra·*too*·ra	**Do you have a temperature?**
Откога сте така? ot·ko·*ga* ste ta·*ka*	**How long have you been like this?**
Случвало ли ви се е преди? *slooch*·va·lo lee vee se e pre·*dee*	**Have you had this before?**
Алергичен/Алергична ли сте към нещо? m/f a·ler·*gee*·chen/a·ler·*geech*·na lee ste kuhm *nesh*·to	**Are you allergic to anything?**
Взимате ли лекарства? *vzee*·ma·te lee le·*kars*·tva	**Are you on medication?**
Водите ли сексуален живот? *vo*·dee·te lee sek·soo·*a*·len zhee·*vot*	**Are you sexually active?**
Имали ли сте секс без предпазни мерки? *ee*·ma·lee lee ste seks bez pred·*paz*·nee *mer*·kee	**Have you had unprotected sex?**
Пиете ли алкохол? *pee*·e·te lee al·ko·*hol*	**Do you drink?**
Пушите ли? *poo*·shee·te lee	**Do you smoke?**
Взимате ли наркотици? *vzee*·ma·te lee nar·ko·*tee*·tsee	**Do you take drugs?**
Колко време още ще сте на път? *kol*·ko *vre*·me *osh*·te shte ste na puht	**How long are you travelling for?**

Трябва да влезете в болница.
tryab·va da *vle*·ze·te
v *bol*·nee·tsa

You need to be admitted to hospital.

Трябва да се прегледате когато се върнете в къщи.
tryab·va da se pre·*gle*·da·te
ko·*ga*·to se *vuhr*·ne·te
v *kuhsh*·tee

You should have it checked when you go home.

Трябва да се приберете в къщи за лечение.
tryab·va da se pree·be·*re*·te
v *kuhsh*·tee za le·*che*·nee·e

You should return home for treatment.

Вие сте хипохондрик.
vee·e ste hee·po·hon·*dreek*

You're a hypochondriac.

symptoms & conditions

симптоми и състояни

I'm sick.
Аз съм болен/болна. m/f   az suhm *bo*·len/*bol*·na

My friend is (very) sick.
Приятелят ми е
(много) болен. m   pree·*ya*·tel·yuht mee e
                                 (*mno*·go) *bo*·len
Приятелката ми е
(много) болна. f   pree·*ya*·tel·ka·ta mee e
                                 (*mno*·go) *bol*·na

My child is (very) sick.
Детето ми е
(много) болно.   de·*te*·to mee e
                                 (*mno*·go) *bol*·no

I've been injured.
Аз съм ранен/ранена. m/f   az suhm *ra*·nen/*ra*·ne·na

He/She has been injured.
Той е ранен. m   toy e *ra*·nen
Тя е ранена. f   tya e *ra*·ne·na

I've been vomiting.
Аз повръщам вече от   az po·*vruhsh*·tam *ve*·che ot
известно време.   eez·*vest*·no *vre*·me

e/She has been vomiting.

Той/Тя повръща	toy/tya po·*vruhsh*·ta
вече от известно време.	*ve*·che ot eez·*vest*·no *vre*·me

feel weak.

Чувствам слабост.	*choovst*·vam *sla*·bost

feel better/worse.

По-добре/По-лошо ми е.	po·*do*·bre/*po*·lo·sho mee e

feel ... Чувствам се ... *choovst*·vam se ...

anxious	неспокоен m	ne·spo·*ko*·yen
	неспокойна f	ne·spo·*koy*·na
depressed	потиснат m	po·*tees*·nat
	потисната f	po·*tees*·na·ta
dizzy	замаян m	za·*ma*·yan
	замаяна f	za·*ma*·ya·na
strange	странно	*stran*·no

feel ...

hot and cold	Ту ми е горещо	too mee e go·*resh*·to
	ту ме тресе.	too me tre·*se*
nauseous	Гади ми се.	*ga*·dee mee se
shivery	Тресе ме.	tre·*se* me

under pressure

Whether or not they have cause for concern, nearly everyone in Bulgaria is obsessed with, and constantly checking,
their *кръвно налягане* kruhv·no na·*lya*·ga·ne (blood
pressure). If you share this obsession, the following phrases
might come in handy:

What's your blood pressure?

Колко ви/ти е кръвното	*kol*·ko vee/tee e *kruhv*·no·to
налягане? pol/inf	na·*lya*·ga·ne

Can you take my blood pressure?

Можете ли да ми	mo·*zhe*·te lee da mee
измерите кръвното	eez·*me*·ree·te *kruhv*·no·to
налягане? pol	na·*lya*·ga·ne
Можеш ли да ми	mo·zhesh lee da mee
измериш кръвното	eez·*me*·reesh *kruhv*·no·to
налягане? inf	na·*lya*·ga·ne

health

It hurts here.
　Боли ме тук.　　　　　　　　　bo·*lee* me took

I'm dehydrated.
　Аз съм обезводнен/　　　　　　az suhm o·bez·vod·*nen*/
　обезводнена. m/f　　　　　　　o·bez·vod·*ne*·na

I can't sleep.
　Не мога да спя.　　　　　　　　ne *mo*·guh da spyuh

I think it's the medication I'm on.
　Мисля, че е от　　　　　　　　　*mees*·lyuh che e ot
　лекарството,　　　　　　　　　le·*kars*·tvo·to
　което взимам.　　　　　　　　　ko·*ye*·to *vzee*·mam

I'm on medication for …
　Взимам лекарство за …　　　　*vzee*·mam le·*kars*·tvo za …

I have (a/an) …
　Имам …　　　　　　　　　　　*ee*·mam …

I've recently had (a/an) …
　Скоро имах …　　　　　　　　　*sko*·ro *ee*·mah …

cold n	простуда f	pro·*stoo*·da
constipation	запек m	*za*·pek
cough n	кашлица f	*kash*·lee·tsa
diabetes	диабет m	dee·a·*bet*
diarrhoea	разстройство n	raz·*stroys*·tvo
fever	температура f	tem·pe·ra·*too*·ra
headache	главоболие n	gla·vo·*bo*·lee·e
nausea	гадене n	*ga*·de·ne
pain n	болка f	*bol*·ka
sore throat	възпалено гърло n	vuhz·*pa*·le·no *guhr*·l

women's health

I think I'm pregnant.
　Мисля, че съм　　　　　　　　*mees*·lyuh che suhm
　бременна.　　　　　　　　　　*bre*·men·na

I'm pregnant.
　Бременна съм.　　　　　　　　*bre*·men·na suhm

Използвате ли противозачатъчни средства?
*eez·polz·va·te lee
pro·tee·vo·za·cha·tuhch·nee
sreds·tva*

**Are you using
contraception?**

Имате ли сега мензис?
ee·ma·te lee se·ga men·zees

Are you menstruating?

Кога беше последният ви мензис?
*ko·ga be·she po·sled·nee·yuht
vee men·zees*

**When did you last have
your period?**

Бременна ли сте?
bre·men·na lee ste

Are you pregnant?

Бременна сте.
bre·men·na ste

You're pregnant.

'm on the pill.

Взимам противо-
зачатъчни хапчета.

*vzee·mam pro·tee·vo·
za·cha·tuhch·nee hap·che·ta*

haven't had my period for (six) weeks.

(Шест) седмици не съм
имала мензис.

*(shest) sed·mee·tsee ne suhm
ee·ma·la men·zees*

've noticed a lump here.

Забелязах една
бучка тук.

*za·bel·ya·zah ed·na
booch·ka took*

Do you have something for (period pain)?

Имате ли нещо против
(болки при мензис)?

*ee·ma·te lee nesh·to pro·teev
(bol·kee pree men·zees)*

need (a/the) ... | Имам нужда
от ... | *ee·mam noozh·da
ot ...*
---|---|---
contraception | противо-
зачатъчни
средства | *pro·tee·vo·
za·cha·tuhch·nee
sreds·tva*
**morning-after
pill** | хапчето,
което се
взима сутрин
след секс | *hap·che·to,
ko·ye·to se
vzee·ma soo·treen
sled seks*
pregnancy test | тест за
бременност | *test za
bre·men·nost*

I have a ...	Имам ...	*ee*·mam ...
urinary tract infection	инфекция на пикочния канал	een·*fek*·tsee·ya na *pee*·koch·nee·yuh ka·*nal*
yeast infection	гъбички	*guh*·beech·kee

allergies

I have a skin allergy.
Имам кожна алергия.   *ee*·mam *kozh*·na a·*ler*·gee·y

I'm allergic to ...	Аз съм алергичен/ алергична към ... m/f	az suhm a·ler·*gee*·chen/ a·ler·*geech*·na kuhm ...
antibiotics	анти- биотици	an·tee· bee·o·tee·tsee
anti- inflammatories	противовъз- палителни средства	pro·tee·vo·*vuhz*· pa·*lee*·tel·nee *sreds*·tva
aspirin	аспирин	as·pee·*reen*
bees	пчели	pche·*lee*
codeine	кодеин	ko·de·*een*
penicillin	пеницилин	pe·nee·tsee·*leen*
pollen	полени	po·*le*·nee
sulphur-based drugs	лекарства в които има сяра	le·*kars*·tva v ko·*yee*·to ee·ma *sya*·ra
antihistamines	антихиста- мини m pl	an·tee·hees·ta· *mee*·nee
inhaler	инхалатор m	een·ha·*la*·tor
injection	инжекция f	een·*zhek*·tsee·ya

For food-related allergies, see **special diets & allergies**, page 180.

parts of the body

My ... hurts.
Боли ме ...

bo·lee me ...

I can't move my ...
Не мога да мръдна ...

ne mo·guh da mruhd·nuh ...

I have a cramp in my ...
Имам разтягане на
мускулите на ...

ee·mam raz·tya·ga·ne na
moos·koo·lee·te na ...

My ... is swollen.
... е подут/подута/
подуто. m/f/n
... са подути. pl

... e po·doot/po·doo·ta/
po·doo·to
... suh po·doo·tee

eye
око n
o·ko

nose
нос m
nos

mouth
уста f
oos·ta

ear
ухо n
oo·ho

head
глава f
gla·va

hand
ръка f
ruh·ka

arm
ръка f
ruh·ka

chest
гърди f pl
guhr·dee

stomach
стомах m
sto·mah

bum
дупе n
doo·pe

leg
крак m
krak

foot
крак m
krak

alternative treatments

алтернативна медицина

I don't use (Western medicine).

Не използвам (традиционната медицина).	ne eez·*polz*·vam (tra·dee·tsee·*on*·na·ta me·dee·*tsee*·na)

I prefer …	Предпочитам …	pred·po·*chee*·tam …
Can I see someone who practises …?	Може ли да отида при някого, който прави …?	*mo*·zhe lee da o·*tee*·duh pree *nya*·ko·go *koy*·to *pra*·vee …
acupuncture	акупунктура	a·koo·poonk·*too*·ra
naturopathy	екопатека	e·ko·*pa*·te·ka
reflexology	рефлексо-терапия	re·flek·so·te·*ra*·pee·ya

pharmacist

в аптеката

I need something for (a headache).

Трябва ми нещо против (главоболие).	*tryab*·va mee *nesh*·to pro·*teev* (gla·vo·*bo*·lee·e)

Do I need a prescription for (antihistamines)?

Трябва ли ми рецепта за (антихистамини)?	*tryab*·va lee mee re·*tsep*·ta za (an·tee·hees·ta·*mee*·nee)

have a prescription.
  Имам рецепта.   *ee*·mam re·*tsep*·ta

ow many times a day?
  Колко пъти на ден   *kol*·ko *puh*·tee na den
  се взима?   se *vzee*·ma

Vill it make me drowsy?
  Ще ме приспи ли?   shte me pree·*spee* lee

ntiseptic	антисептично n	an·tee·sep·*teech*·no
ontraceptives	контрацептиви m pl	kon·tra·tsep·*tee*·vee
ainkillers	обезболяващи pl	o·bez·bol·*ya*·vash·tee
ehydration	соли за	*so*·lee za
salts	оводняване f pl	o·vod·*nya*·va·ne
hermometer	термометър m	ter·mo·*me*·tuhr

or more pharmaceutical items, see the **dictionary**.

Два/Три пъти на ден. dva/tree *puh*·tee na den	Twice/Three times a day.
Преди/След ядене. pre·*dee*/sled *ya*·de·ne	Before/After meals.
По време на ядене. po *vre*·me na *ya*·de·ne	With meals.
Взимали ли сте го преди? *vzee*·ma·lee lee ste go pre·*dee*	Have you taken this before?
Трябва да ги вземете всичките. *tryab*·va da gee *vze*·me·te *vseech*·kee·te	You must complete the course.

health

203

dentist

I have a ...	Имам ...	ee·mam ...
broken tooth	счупен зъб	s·choo·pen zuhb
cavity	кариес	ka·ree·es
I need ...	Имам нужда	ee·mam noozh·da
	от ...	ot ...
an anaesthetic	упойка	oo·poy·ka
a filling	пломба	plom·ba

I have a toothache.
Боли ме зъбът. bo·lee me zuh·buht

I've lost a filling.
Падна ми пломбата. pad·na mee plom·ba·ta

My dentures are broken.
Протезата ми е счупена. pro·te·za·ta mee e s·choo·pe·na

My gums hurt.
Болят ми венците. bol·yuht mee ven·tsee·te

I don't want it extracted.
Не искам да го вадите. ne ees·kam da go va·dee·te

---

the dentist may say ...

Отворете устата широко.		
ot·vo·re·te oos·ta·ta shee·ro·ko		**Open wide.**
Няма да ви боли.		
nya·ma da vee bo·lee		**This won't hurt a bit.**
Захапете това.		
za·ha·pe·te to·va		**Bite down on this.**
Не мърдайте.		
ne muhr·dai·te		**Don't move.**
Изплакнете.		
eez·plak·ne·te		**Rinse.**
Върнете се, още не съм свършил/свършила. m/f		
vuhr·ne·te se osh·te ne suhm		**Come back, I haven't**
svuhr·sheel/svuhr·shee·la		**finished.**

DICTIONARY > english–bulgarian

ulgarian nouns in the dictionary have their gender indicated by ⓜ (masculine), ⓕ (feminine) or ⓝ (neuter). If it's a plural noun, you'll also see pl. For added clarity, ertain words are marked as nouns n, adjectives a, verbs v, adverbs adv, pronouns ⓟron or prepositions prep. The abbreviations sg (singular), pl (plural), inf (informal) nd pol (polite) are also used where necessary. Adjectives are given in the masculine ngular form only. Verbs are given in their present tense first person singular form. ost verbs are given in two aspects: perfective and imperfective. The two forms re separated by a slash with the perfective form given first. Note that if the verb is ollowed by the particle ce se – eg *обадя/обаждам се* o·*bad*·yuh/o·*bazh*·dam se (to all) – the particle is used both with the perfective (*обадя ce*) and imperfective (*баждам ce*). If only one verb form is given, it means that form can be used as both imperfective and perfective. For more information, refer to the **phrasebuilder**.

A

board на борда na *bor*·da
ortion аборт ⓜ a·*bort*
bout за za
bove над nad
broad в чужбина v choozh·*bee*·na
ccident злополука ⓕ zlo·po·*loo*·ka
ccommodation жилище ⓝ *zhee*·leesh·te
ccount (bill) сметка ⓕ *smet*·ka
cross през prez
ctivist n активист/активистка ⓜ/ⓕ
  ak·tee·*veest*/ak·tee·*veest*·ka
ctor актьор/актриса ⓜ/ⓕ
  ak·*tyor*/ak·*tree*·sa
cupuncture акупунктура ⓕ
  a·koo·poonk·*too*·ra
daptor адаптор ⓜ a·*dap*·tor
ddiction (drugs) наркомания ⓕ
  nar·ko·*ma*·nee·ya
ddress n адрес ⓜ a·*dres*
dministration администрация ⓕ
  ad·mee·nees·*tra*·tsee·ya
dmission price входна такса ⓕ
  vhod·na *tak*·sa
dmit (let in) пусна/пускам
  poos·nuh/*poos*·kam
dult n възрастен/възрастна ⓜ/ⓕ
  vuhz·ras·ten/*vuhz*·rast·na
dvertisement обява ⓕ o·*bya*·va

advice съвет ⓜ suh·*vet*
Aegean Sea Егейско море ⓝ
  e·*gey*·sko mo·*re*
Africa Африка ⓕ *a*·free·ka
after след sled
afternoon следобед ⓜ sle·*do*·bed
aftershave афтершейв ⓜ *af*·ter·sheyv
again отново ot·*no*·vo
age n възраст ⓕ *vuhz*·rast
(three days) ago преди (три дена)
  pre·*dee* (tree de·na)
agree съглася/съгласявам се
  suh·gla·*syuh*/suh·gla·*sya*·vam se
agriculture селско стопанство ⓝ
  sel·sko sto·*panst*·vo
ahead напред na·*pred*
AIDS СПИН ⓜ speen
air въздух ⓜ *vuhz*·dooh
air-conditioned с климатик
  s klee·ma·*teek*
air conditioning климатик ⓜ
  klee·ma·*teek*
airline самолетна компания ⓕ
  sa·mo·*let*·na kom·*pa*·nee·ya
airmail въздушна поща ⓕ
  vuhz·*doosh*·na *posh*·ta
airplane самолет ⓜ sa·mo·*let*
airport летище ⓝ le·*teesh*·te
airport tax летищна такса ⓕ
  le·*teesht*·na *tak*·sa
aisle (plane, etc) пътека ⓕ puh·*te*·ka

alarm clock будилник ⑩ boo-*deel*-neek
alcohol алкохол ⑩ *al*-ko-hol
all pron всичко *vseech*-ko
allergy алергия ① a-*ler*-gee-ya
almond бадем ⑩ ba-*dem*
almost почти poch-*tee*
alone сам sam
already вече *ve*-che
also също *suhsh*-to
altitude височина ① vee-so-chee-*na*
always винаги *vee*-na-gee
ambassador посланик/посланичка ⑩/①
po-*sla*-neek/po-*sla*-neech-ka
ambulance линейка ① lee-*ney*-ka
America Америка ① a-*me*-ree-ka
anaemia анемия ① a-*ne*-mee-ya
anarchist n анархист/анархистка ⑩/①
a-nar-*heest*/a-nar-*heest*-ka
ancient древен *dre*-ven
and и ee
angry ядосан ya-*do*-san
animal животно ⑩ zhee-*vot*-no
ankle глезен ⑩ *gle*-zen
another друг droog
answer n отговор ⑩ *ot*-go-vor
answer v отговоря/отговарям
ot-go-*vor*-yuh/ot-go-*var*-yam
ant мравка ① *mrav*-ka
antibiotics антибиотици ⑩ pl
an-tee-bee-o-*tee*-tsee
antinuclear противоядрен
pro-tee-vo-*ya*-dren
antique n антика ① an-*tee*-ka
antiseptic n антисептик ⑩ an-tee-sep-*teek*
any някакъв *nya*-ka-kuhv
apartment апартамент ⑩ a-par-ta-*ment*
appendix (body) апендикс ⑩ a-*pen*-deeks
apple ябълка ① *ya*-buhl-ka
appointment уговорена среща ①
oo-go-*vo*-re-na *sresh*-ta
apricot кайсия ① kai-*see*-ya
archaeological археологичен
ar-he-o-lo-*gee*-chen
architect архитект/архитектка ⑩/①
ar-hee-*tekt*/ar-hee-*tekt*-ka
architecture архитектура ①
ar-hee-tek-*too*-ra
argue споря *spo*-ryuh
arm (body) ръка ① ruh-*ka*

aromatherapy ароматерапия ①
a-ro-ma-te-*ra*-pee-ya
arrest v арестувам a-res-*too*-vam
arrivals (airport) пристигане ⑩
pree-*stee*-ga-ne
arrive пристигна/пристигам
pree-*steeg*-nuh/pree-*stee*-gam
art изкуство ⑩ eez-*koost*-vo
art gallery галерия ① ga-*le*-ree-ya
artist художник/художничка ⑩/①
hoo-*dozh*-neek/hoo-*dozh*-neech-ka
ashtray пепелник ⑩ pe-pel-*neek*
Asia Азия ① a-*zee*-ya
ask (a question) питам *pee*-tam
ask (for something) моля *mol*-yuh
asparagus аспержи ⑩ pl as-*per*-zhee
aspirin аспирин ⑩ as-pee-*reen*
asthma астма ① *ast*-ma
at на na
athletics лека атлетика ①
le-ka at-*le*-tee-ka
atmosphere атмосфера ① at-mos-*fe*-r
aunt леля ① *lel*-ya
ATM банкомат ⑩ ban-ko-*mat*
aubergine патладжан ⑩ pat-lad-*zhan*
Australia Австралия ① av-*stra*-lee-ya
autumn есен ① *e*-sen
avenue улица ① oo-lee-tsa
awful ужасен oo-*zha*-sen

B

B&W (film) черно-бял cher-no-*byal*
baby бебе ⑩ *be*-be
baby food бебешка храна ①
be-besh-ka hra-*na*
baby powder бебешка пудра ①
be-besh-ka *poo*-dra
babysitter бавачка ① ba-*vach*-ka
back (body) гръб ⑩ gruhb
back (position) задна част ①
zad-na chast
backpack раница ① *ra*-nee-tsa
bacon бекон ⑩ *be*-kon
bad лош losh
bag чанта ① *chan*-ta
baggage багаж ⑩ ba-*gazh*

ggage allowance
разрешено количество багаж ⓝ
az·re·she·no ko·lee·chest·vo ba·gazh
ggage claim получаване на багаж ⓝ
o·loo·cha·va·ne na ba·gazh
kery хлебарница ⓕ hle·bar·nee·tsa
lance (account) баланс ⓜ ba·lans
cony балкон ⓜ bal·kon
kan Peninsula
Балкански полуостров ⓜ
al·kan·skee po·loo·os·trov
ll (sport) топка ⓕ top·ka
llet балет ⓜ ba·let
ana банан ⓜ ba·nan
nd (music) оркестър ⓜ or·kes·tuhr
ndage превръзка ⓕ pre·vruhz·ka
nd-Aid лейкопласт ⓜ ley·ko·plast
nk банка ⓕ ban·ka
nk account банкова сметка ⓕ
ban·ko·va smet·ka
nknote банкнота ⓕ bank·no·ta
ptism кръщене ⓝ kruhsh·te·ne
r (pub) бар ⓜ bar
rber бръснар ⓜ bruhs·nar
r work работа като барман ⓕ
ra·bo·ta ka·to bar·man
seball бейзбол ⓜ beyz·bol
sket кошница ⓕ kosh·nee·tsa
sketball баскетбол ⓜ bas·ket·bol
th баня ⓕ ba·nya
thing suit бански костюм ⓜ
ban·skee kos·tyoom
throom баня ⓕ ba·nya
ttery батерия ⓕ ba·te·ree·ya
бъда buh·duh
ach плаж ⓜ plazh
ach volleyball плажен волейбол ⓜ
pla·zhen vo·ley·bol
ans фасул ⓜ fa·sool
autiful красив kra·seev
auty salon козметичен салон ⓜ
koz·me·tee·chen sa·lon
cause защото zash·to·to
ed легло ⓝ leg·lo
edding завивки ⓕ pl za·veev·kee
edroom спалня ⓕ spal·nya
ee пчела ⓕ pche·la
eef телешко ⓝ te·lesh·ko
eer бира ⓕ bee·ra
efore преди pre·dee

beggar просяк/просякиня ⓜ/ⓕ
pros·yak/pros·ya·kee·nya
behind зад zad
Belgium Белгия ⓕ bel·gee·ya
below под pod
berth спално място ⓝ spal·no myas·to
beside до do
best най-добър nai·do·buhr
bet n залог ⓜ za·log
bet v заложа/залагам
za·lo·zhuh/za·la·gam
better по-добър po·do·buhr
between между mezh·doo
Bible Библия ⓕ beeb·lee·ya
bicycle велосипед ⓜ ve·lo·see·ped
bicycle chain верига ⓕ ve·ree·ga
bicycle lock катинар ⓜ ka·tee·nar
bicycle path алея за велосипедисти ⓕ
a·le·ya za ve·lo·see·pe·dees·tee
bicycle shop магазин за велосипеди ⓜ
ma·ga·zeen za ve·lo·see·pe·dee
big голям go·lyam
bigger по-голям po·go·lyam
biggest най-голям nai·go·lyam
bike колело ⓝ ko·le·lo
bill (restaurant, etc) сметка ⓕ smet·ka
binoculars бинокъл ⓜ bee·no·kuhl
bird птица ⓕ ptee·tsa
birth certificate
свидетелство за раждане ⓝ
svee·de·telst·vo za razh·da·ne
birthday рожден ден ⓜ rozh·den den
biscuit бисквита ⓕ bees·kvee·ta
bite (dog) n ухапване от куче ⓝ
oo·hap·va·ne ot koo·che
bite (insect) n ужилване от насекомо ⓝ
oo·zheel·va·ne ot na·se·ko·mo
bitter горчив gor·cheev
black черен che·ren
black market черен пазар ⓜ
che·ren pa·zar
Black Sea Черно море ⓝ cher·no mo·re
bladder пикочен мехур ⓜ
pee·ko·chen me·hoor
blanket одеяло ⓝ o·de·ya·lo
blind a сляп slyap
blister мехур ⓜ me·hoor
blocked задръстен za·druhs·ten
blood кръв ⓕ kruhv

blood group кръвна група ①
kruhv·na *groo*·pa

blood pressure кръвно налягане ⑪
kruhv·no na·*lya*·ga·ne

blood test изследване на кръвта ①
eez·*sled*·va·ne na kruhv·*ta*

blue син seen

board (a plane, etc) кача/качвам се
ka·*chuh*/*kach*·vam se

boarding house пансион ⑪ pan·see·*on*

boarding pass бордна карта ①
bord·na *kar*·ta

boat кораб ⑪ *ko*·rab

body тяло ⑪ *tya*·lo

boiled варен va·*ren*

bone кост ① kost

book n книга ① *knee*·ga

book (reserve) v резервирам
re·zer·*vee*·ram

booked out разпродаден raz·pro·*da*·den

book shop книжарница ①
knee·*zhar*·nee·tsa

boots ботуши ① pl bo·*too*·shee

border (country) n граница ① *gra*·nee·tsa

bored отегчен o·teg·*chen*

boring досаден do·*sa*·den

borrow взема/взимам на заем
vze·muh/*vzee*·mam na *za*·em

botanic garden ботаническа градина ①
bo·ta·*nee*·ches·ka gra·*dee*·na

both и двата/двете ⑪/①&①
ee *dva*·ta/*dve*·te

bottle бутилка ① boo·*teel*·ka

bottle opener отварачка за бутилки ①
ot·va·*rach*·ka na boo·*teel*·kee

bottle shop
магазин за алкохолни напитки ⑪
ma·ga·*zeen* za al·ko·*hol*·nee na·*peet*·kee

bottom (body) дупе ① *doo*·pe

bottom (position) дъно ① *duh*·no

bowl n купа ① *koo*·pa

box n кутия ① *koo*·tee·ya

boxer shorts боксерки ① pl *bok*·ser·kee

boy момче ⑪ mom·*che*

boyfriend гадже ⑪ *gad*·zhe

bra сутиен ⑪ soo·tee·*en*

brakes спирачки ① pl spee·*rach*·kee

brandy ракия ① ra·*kee*·ya

brave храбър *hra*·buhr

bread хляб ⑪ hlyab

bread roll питка ① *peet*·ka

break v счупя/счупвам
s·*choop*·yuh/s·*choop*·vam

break down разваля/развалям се
raz·val·*yuh*/raz·*val*·yam se

breakfast закуска ① za·*koos*·ka

breasts гърди ① pl guhr·*dee*

breathe дишам dee·*sham*

bribe n подкуп ⑪ *pod*·koop

bridge n мост ⑪ most

briefcase дипломатическо куфарче ⑪
dee·plo·ma·*tee*·ches·ko *koo*·far·che

bring донеса/донасям
do·ne·*suh*/do·*nas*·yam

brochure брошура ① bro·*shoo*·ra

broken повреден po·vre·*den*

broken down развален raz·va·*len*

bronchitis бронхит ⑪ bron·*heet*

brother брат ⑪ brat

brown кафяв kaf·*yav*

bruise n натъртване ⑪ na·*turht*·va·ne

brush (hair) n четка ① *chet*·ka

bucket кофа ① *ko*·fa

budget бюджет ⑪ byood·*zhet*

buffet бюфет ⑪ byoo·*fet*

bug n буболечка ① boo·bo·*lech*·ka

build v построя/строя
po·stro·*yuh*/stro·*yuh*

builder строител ⑪ stroy·*ee*·tel

building сграда ① *sgra*·da

Bulgaria България ① buhl·*ga*·ree·ya

Bulgarian (language) n български ⑪
buhl·gar·skee

Bulgarian (person) n българин/
българка ⑪/① buhl·ga·reen/*buhl*·gar·

Bulgarian a български *buhl*·gar·skee

burn n изгаряне ① eez·*gar*·ya·ne

burnt изгорен eez·go·*ren*

bus (city) градски автобус ⑪
grad·skee av·to·*boos*

bus (intercity) автобус ⑪ av·to·*boos*

business търговия ① tuhr·go·*vee*·ya

business class бизнес класа ①
beez·nes *kla*·sa

businessperson бизнесмен/бизнесдам
⑪/① *beez*·nes·*men*/beez·nes·*da*·ma

business trip командировка ①
ko·man·dee·*rov*·ka

bus station автогара ① av·to·*ga*·ra

bus stop автобусна спирка ①
av-to-boos-na *speer*-ka
busy зает za-*et*
but но no
butcher касапин ⑩ ka-*sa*-peen
butcher's shop месарница ①
me-*sar*-nee-tsa
butter краве масло ⑩ *kra*-ve *mas*-lo
button n копче ⑩ *kop*-che
buy купя/купувам
koop-yuh/koo-*poo*-vam

C

cabbage зеле ⑩ *ze*-le
cable car кабинков лифт ⑩
ka-*been*-kov leeft
café кафене ⑩ ka-fe-*ne*
cake торта ① *tor*-ta
cake shop сладкарница ①
slad-*kar*-nee-tsa
calculator калкулатор ⑩ kal-koo-*la*-tor
calendar календар ⑩ ka-len-*dar*
call v обадя/обаждам се
o-*bad*-yuh/o-*bazh*-dam se
camera фотоапарат ⑩ fo-to-a-pa-*rat*
camera shop фотомагазин ⑩
fo-to-ma-ga-*zeen*
camp v лагерувам la-ge-*roo*-vam
camping ground къмпинг ⑩ *kuhm*-peeng
camping store магазин за
туристически стоки ⑩ ma-ga-*zeen* za
too-rees-*tee*-ches-kee *sto*-kee
camp site място за лагеруване ⑩
myas-to za la-ge-*roo*-va-ne
can (tin) консервна кутия ①
kon-*serv*-na koo-*tee*-ya
can мога *mo*-guh
Canada Канада ① ka-*na*-da
cancel анулирам a-noo-*lee*-ram
cancer рак ⑩ rak
candle свещ ① svesht
candy бонбон ⑩ bon-*bon*
can opener отварачка за консерви ①
ot-va-*rach*-ka za kon-*ser*-vee
car кола ① ko-*la*
caravan каравана ① ka-ra-*va*-na
cardiac arrest сърдечен удар ⑩
suhr-*de*-chen oo-dar

cards (playing) карти ① pl *kar*-tee
care (for someone) грижа се
gree-zhuh se
car hire наемане на кола ⑩
na-e-*ma*-ne na ko-*la*
car owner's title акт за собственост на
кола ⑩ akt za *sobst*-ve-nost na ko-*la*
car park паркинг ⑩ *par*-keeng
carpenter дърводелец ⑩ duhr-vo-*de*-lets
car registration регистрационен
талон на автомобил ⑩
re-gee-stra-tsee-*o*-nen ta-*lon* na
av-to-mo-*beel*
carrot морков ⑩ *mor*-kov
carry нося *nos*-yuh
carton картонена кутия ①
kar-*to*-ne-na koo-*tee*-ya
cash n пари в брой ① pl pa-*ree* v broy
cash (a cheque) v осребря/осребрявам
o-sreb-*ryuh*/o-sreb-*rya*-vam
cashew кашу ⑩ ka-*shoo*
cashier касиер/касиерка ⑩/①
ka-*see*-er/ka-see-*er*-ka
cash register каса ① *ka*-sa
casino казино ⑩ ka-*zee*-no
cassette касета ① ka-*set*-ka
castle замък ⑩ *za*-muhk
casual work временна работа ①
vre-men-na ra-*bo*-ta
cat котка ① *kot*-ka
cathedral катедрала ① ka-te-*dra*-la
cauliflower карфиол ⑩ *kar*-fee-ol
cave пещера ① pesh-te-*ra*
CD сиди ⑩ see-*dee*
celebration тържество ⑩ tuhr-zhest-*vo*
cell phone GSM ⑩ dzhee-es-*em*
cemetery гробище ⑩ *gro*-beesh-te
cent цент ⑩ tsent
centimetre сантиметър ⑩
san-tee-*me*-tuhr
centre n център ⑩ *tsen*-tuhr
ceramics керамика ① ke-*ra*-mee-ka
cereal (breakfast) овесени ядки ① pl
o-*ve*-se-nee *yad*-kee
certificate удостоверение ⑩
oo-dos-to-ve-*re*-nee-e
chain n верига ① ve-*ree*-ga
chair n стол ⑩ stol
chairlift (skiing) седалков лифт ⑩
se-*dal*-kov leeft

champagne шампанско ⓝ sham·*pan*·sko

championships шампионат ⓜ
sham·pee·o·*nat*

chance n случай ⓜ *sloo*·chai

change n промяна ① pro·*mya*·na

change (coins) n монети ① pl mo·*ne*·tee

change (money) v сменям *smen*·yam

changing room пробна ① *prob*·na

charming прелестен *pre*·les·ten

chat up заговоря/заговарям
za·go·vor·*yuh*/za·go·*var*·yam

cheap евтин *ev*·teen

cheat v излъжа/излъгвам
eez·*luh*·zhuh/eez·*luhg*·vam

check (banking) чек ⓜ *teen*

check (bill) сметка ① *smet*·ka

check v проверя/проверявам
pro·ver·*yuh*/pro·ver·*ya*·vam

check-in desk рецепция ① re·*tsep*·tsee·ya

checkpoint пропусквателен пункт ⓜ
pro·poosk·*va*·te·len poonkt

cheese (soft, white) сирене ⓝ *see*·re·ne

cheese (hard, yellow) кашкавал ⓜ
kash·ka·*val*

chef (man) главен готвач ⓜ
gla·ven got·*vach*

chef (woman) главна готвачка ①
glav·na got·*vach*·ka

chemist (pharmacist) аптекар/
аптекарка ⓜ/① ap·te·*kar*/ap·te·*kar*·ka

chemist (pharmacy) аптека ① ap·*te*·ka

cheque (banking) чек ⓜ chek

cherry (sour) вишня ① *veesh*·nya

cherry (sweet) череша ① che·*re*·sha

chess шах ⓜ shah

chessboard шахматна дъска ①
shah·*mat*·na duhs·*ka*

chest (body) гръден кош ⓜ
gruh·den kosh

chestnut кестен ⓜ *kes*·ten

chewing gum дъвка ① *duhv*·ka

chicken (meat) пилешко ⓝ *pee*·lesh·ko

chicken pox варицела ① va·ree·*tse*·la

child дете ⓝ de·*te*

children деца ⓝ pl de·*tsa*

child seat детска седалка ①
det·ska se·*dal*·ka

chilli лют чушки ① pl
lyoo·tee *choosh*·kee

China Китай ⓜ kee·*tai*

chiropractor мануален терапевт ⓜ
ma·noo·*a*·len te·ra·*pevt*

chocolate шоколад ⓜ sho·ko·*lad*

choose избера/избирам
eez·be·*ruh*/eez·*bee*·ram

chopping board дъска за рязане ①
duhs·*ka* za rya·za·ne

chopsticks пръчици за хранене ① pl
pruh·chee·tsee za *hra*·ne·ne

Christmas Коледа ① *ko*·le·da

Christmas Day Коледа ① *ko*·le·da

Christmas Eve Бъдни вечер ⓜ
buhd·nee *ve*·cher

church църква ① *tsuhr*·kva

cigar пура ① *poo*·ra

cigarette цигара ① tsee·*ga*·ra

cigarette lighter запалка ① za·*pal*·ka

cinema кино ⓝ *kee*·no

circus цирк ⓜ tseerk

citizenship гражданство ⓝ
grazh·danst·vo

city град ⓜ grad

city centre центърът на града ⓜ
tsen·tuh·ruht na gra·*duh*

civil rights граждански права ⓝ pl
grazh·dan·skee pra·*va*

class (category) класа ① *kla*·sa

classical класически kla·*see*·ches·kee

clean a чист cheest

clean v чистя *cheest*·yuh

cleaning чистене ⓝ *chees*·te·ne

client клиент/клиентка ⓜ/①
klee·*ent*/klee·*ent*·ka

cliff скала ① ska·*la*

climb v кача/качвам се
ka·*chuh*/*kach*·vam se

cloakroom гардероб ⓜ gar·de·*rob*

clock n часовник ⓜ cha·*sov*·neek

close a близък *blee*·zuhk

close v затворя/затварям
zat·vor·*yuh*/zat·*var*·yam

closed затворен zat·vo·ren

clothesline простор pro·*stor*

clothing дрехи ① pl *dre*·hee

clothing store магазин за облекло ⓜ
ma·ga·*zeen* za o·blek·*lo*

cloud n облак ⓜ o·*blak*

cloudy облачен o·bla·chen

clutch (car) съединител ⓜ
suh·e·dee·*nee*·tel

ch (bus) n междуградски автобус ⓜ
ı̯ezh-doo-*grad*-skee av-to-*boos*

ch (trainer) треньор ⓜ tren-*yor*

st крайбрежие ⓝ krai-*bre*-zhee-e

ıt палто ⓝ pal-*to*

kroach хлебарка ① hle-*bar*-ka

ktail коктейл ⓜ kok-*teyl*

oa какао ⓝ ka-*ka*-o

onut кокосов орех ⓜ *ko*-ko-sov o-reh

fee кафе ⓝ ka-*fe*

ıns монети ① pl mo-*ne*-tee

d (illness) n простуда ① pro-*stoo*-da

d а студен stoo-*den*

league колега ① ko-*le*-ga

lect call
ıбаждане за сметка на абоната
ı-*bazh*-da-ne za *smet*-ka na a-bo-*na*-tuh

lege колеж ⓜ ko-*lezh*

our n цвят ⓜ tsvyat

ıb n гребен ⓜ *gre*-ben

ıe дойда/идвам *doy*-duh/*eed*-vam

ımedy комедия ① ko-*me*-dee-ya

ımfortable удобен oo-*do*-ben

ımmission комисионна ①
ıo-mee-see-*on*-na

ımmunion причастие ⓝ pree-*chas*-tee-e

ımmunist n комунист ⓜ ko-moo-*neest*

ımmunist а комунистически
ıo-moo-nees-*tee*-ches-kee

ımpanion другар ⓜ droo-*gar*

ımpany компания ① kom-*pa*-nee-ya

ımpass компас ⓜ kom-*pas*

ımplain оплача/оплаквам се
ıo-*pla*-chuh/o-*plak*-vam se

ımplaint оплакване ⓝ o-*plak*-va-ne

ımplimentary (free) безплатен
ı̯ez-*pla*-ten

ımputer компютър ⓜ kom-*pyoo*-tuhr

ımputer game компютърна игра ①
kom-*pyoo*-tuhr-na ee-*gra*

ıncert концерт ⓜ kon-*tsert*

ıncussion мозъчно сътресение ⓝ
ımo-*zuhch*-no suh-*tre*-se-nee-e

ınditioner (hair) балсам ⓜ bal-*sam*

ındom презерватив ⓜ pre-zer-va-*teev*

conference (big) конференция ①
kon-fe-*ren*-tsee-ya

conference (small) събрание ⓝ
suh-*bra*-nee-e

confession (religious) изповед ①
eez-*po*-ved

confirm (a booking)
потвърдя/потвърждавам
pot-vuhr-*dyuh*/pot-vuhrzh-*da*-vam

congratulate поздравя/поздравявам
poz-drav-*yuh*/poz-drav-*ya*-vam

conjunctivitis конюнктивит ⓜ
kon-yoonk-tee-*veet*

connection (transport) връзка ①
vruhz-ka

conservative а консервативен
kon-ser-va-*tee*-ven

constipation запек ⓜ *za*-pek

consulate консулство ⓝ *kon*-soolst-vo

contact lenses контактни лещи ① pl
kon-*takt*-nee *lesh*-tee

contact lens solution
разтвор за контактни лещи ⓜ
raz-*tvor* za kon-*takt*-nee *lesh*-tee

contraceptives
противозачатъчни средства ⓝ pl
pro-tee-vo-za-*cha*-tuhch-nee *sreds*-tva

contract n договор ⓜ do-*go*-vor

convenience store денонощен магазин
ⓜ de-no-*nosh*-ten ma-ga-*zeen*

convent женски манастир ⓜ
zhen-skee ma-na-*steer*

cook n готвач/готвачка ⓜ/①
got-*vach*/got-*vach*-ka

cook v готвя got-*vyuh*

cookie бисквита ① beesk-*vee*-ta

cooking готвене ⓝ *got*-ve-ne

cool (groovy) страхотен stra-*ho*-ten

cool (temperature) хладен *hla*-den

corkscrew тирбушон ⓜ teer-boo-*shon*

corn царевица ① *tsa*-re-vee-tsa

corner ъгъл ⓜ *uh*-guhl

cornflakes корнфлейкс ⓜ pl *korn*-fleyks

corrupt а корумпиран ko-room-*pee*-ran

corruption корупция ① ko-*roop*-tsee-ya

cost n цена ① *tse*-na

cost v струвам *stroo*-vam

cotton n памук ⓜ pa-*mook*

cotton balls чист памук ⓜ
cheest pa-*mook*

cotton buds/swabs клечки за уши ① pl
klech-kee za oo-*shee*

cough n кашлица ① *kash*-lee-tsa

cough v кашлям *kash*-lyam

cough medicine сироп за кашлица ⓜ
see-*rop* za *kash*-lee-tsa
count v броя bro-*yuh*
counter (at bar) щанд ⓜ shtand
country държава ⓕ duhr-*zha*-va
countryside провинция ⓕ
pro-*veen*-tsee-ya
coupon купон ⓜ koo-*pon*
courgette тиквичка ⓕ *teek*-veech-ka
court (legal) съдебна зала ⓕ
suh-*deb*-na za-la
court (sport) игрище ⓝ ee-*greesh*-te
cover charge надценка ⓕ nad-*tsen*-ka
cow крава ⓕ *kra*-va
cracker соленка ⓕ so-*len*-ka
crafts занаяти ⓜ pl za-na-*ya*-tee
crash (accident) n катастрофа ⓕ
ka-tas-*tro*-fa
crazy луд lood
cream (lotion) крем ⓜ krem
crèche детска ясла ⓕ *det*-ska *yas*-la
credit n кредит ⓜ *kre*-deet
credit card кредитна карта ⓕ
kre-deet-na *kar*-ta
cross (religious) кръст ⓜ kruhst
crowded препълнен pre-*puhl*-nen
cucumber краставица ⓕ *kras*-ta-vee-tsa
cup чаша ⓕ *cha*-sha
cupboard шкаф ⓜ shkaf
currency exchange обмяна на валута ⓕ
ob-*mya*-na na va-*loo*-ta
current (electricity) ток ⓜ tok
current affairs текущи събития ⓝ pl
te-*koosh*-tee suh-*bee*-tee-ya
custom обичай ⓜ o-bee-*chai*
customs (immigration) митница ⓕ
meet-nee-tsa
cut n прорез ⓜ *pro*-rez
cut v режа *re*-zhuh
cutlery прибори за хранене ⓜ pl
pree-bo-ree za *hra*-ne-ne
CV автобиография ⓕ
av-to-bee-o-*gra*-fee-ya
cycle v карам велосипед
ka-ram ve-lo-see-*ped*
cycling колоездене ⓝ ko-lo-*ez*-de-ne
cyclist колоездач/колоездачка ⓜ/ⓕ
ko-lo-ez-*dach*/ko-lo-ez-*dach*-ka
cystitis цистит ⓜ tsees-*teet*

D

dad татко ⓜ *tat*-ko
daily adv ежедневно e-zhed-*nev*-no
dance n танц ⓜ tants
dance v танцувам tan-*tsoo*-vam
dancing танцуване ⓝ tan-*tsoo*-va-ne
dangerous опасен o-*pa*-sen
Danube Дунав ⓜ *doo*-nav
dark тъмен *tuh*-men
date (appointment) среща ⓕ *sresh*-t[a]
date (day) дата ⓕ *da*-ta
date (fruit) фурма ⓕ foor-*ma*
date (go out with) v изляза/излизам
eez-*lya*-zuh/eez-*lee*-zam s
date of birth дата на раждане ⓕ
da-ta na *razh*-da-ne
daughter дъщеря ⓕ duhsh-ter-*ya*
dawn зора ⓕ zo-*ra*
day ден ⓜ den
dead мъртъв *muhr*-tuhv
deaf глух glooh
deal (cards) v раздам/раздавам
raz-*dam*/raz-*da*-vam
decide реша/решавам re-*shuh*/re-*sha*-va[m]
deep дълбок duhl-*bok*
degrees (temperature) градуса ⓜ pl
gra-doo-sa
delay n закъснение ⓝ za-kuhs-*ne*-nee[e]
delicatessen магазин за деликатеси ⓜ
ma-ga-*zeen* za de-lee-ka-*te*-see
deliver доставя/доставям
do-*stav*-yuh/do-*stav*-yam
democracy демокрация ⓕ
de-mo-*kra*-tsee-ya
demonstration (display) демонстраци[я]
ⓕ de-mon-*stra*-tsee-ya
demonstration (rally) митинг ⓜ
mee-teeng
Denmark Дания ⓕ *da*-nee-ya
dental dam (safe sex) протеза ⓕ
pro-*te*-za
dental floss конец за зъби ⓜ
ko-*nets* za zuh-*bee*
dentist зъболекар/зъболекарка ⓜ/ⓕ
zuh-bo-le-*kar*/zuh-bo-le-*kar*-ka
deodorant дезодорант ⓜ de-zo-do-*ra*[nt]
depart замина/заминавам
za-*mee*-nuh/za-mee-*na*-vam

partment store универсален магазин ⓜ oo·nee·ver·*sa*·len ma·ga·*zeen*

parture заминаване ⓝ za·mee·*na*·va·ne

parture gate изход ⓜ *eez*·hod

posit n депозит ⓜ de·*po*·zeet

sert n пустиня ⓕ poos·*tee*·nya

sign n дизайн ⓜ dee·*zain*

ssert десерт ⓜ de·*sert*

stination дестинация ⓕ des·tee·*na*·tsee·ya

ails подробности ⓕ pl po·*drob*·nos·tee

betes диабет ⓜ dee·a·*bet*

l tone телефонен сигнал ⓜ te·le·*fo*·nen seeg·*nal*

per пелена ⓕ pe·le·*na*

phragm (contraceptive) спирала ⓕ spee·*ra*·la

rrhoea диария ⓕ dee·a·*ree*·a

ry дневник ⓜ dnev·*neek*

e n зарове ⓝ pl *za*·ro·ve

tionary речник ⓜ rech·*neek*

e умра/умирам oom·*ruh*/oo·*mee*·ram

et n диета ⓕ dee·*e*·ta

ferent различен raz·*lee*·chen

ficult труден *troo*·den

gital camera цифров фотоапарат ⓜ *tseef*·rov fo·to·a·pa·*rat*

ing car вагон-ресторант ⓜ va·gon·res·to·*rant*

nner вечеря ⓕ ve·*che*·rya

ect a пряк pryak

ection посока ⓕ po·*so*·ka

ty мръсен *mruh*·sen

abled инвалиден een·va·*lee*·den

co дискотека ⓕ dees·ko·*te*·ka

scount n намаление ⓝ na·ma·*le*·nee·e

crimination дискриминация ⓕ dees·kree·mee·*na*·tsee·ya

sease болест ⓕ *bo*·lest

sh ядене ⓝ *ya*·de·ne

sk (CD-ROM) диск ⓜ deesk

sk (floppy) дискета ⓕ dees·*ke*·ta

ving гмуркане ⓝ *gmoor*·ka·ne

ving equipment екипировка за гмуркане ⓕ e·kee·pee·*rov*·ka za *gmoor*·ka·ne

orced разведен raz·*ve*·den

zzy замаян za·*ma*·yan

правя *prav*·yuh

---

doctor лекар/лекарка ⓜ/ⓕ *le*·kar/*le*·kar·ka

documentary документален филм ⓜ do·koo·men·*ta*·len feelm

dog куче ⓝ *koo*·che

dole милостиня ⓕ mee·los·tee·nya

doll кукла ⓕ *kook*·la

dollar долар ⓜ *do*·lar

door врата ⓕ vra·*ta*

dope (drugs) марихуана ⓕ ma·ree·hoo·*a*·na

double a двоен *dvo*·yen

double bed двойно легло ⓝ *dvoy*·no leg·*lo*

double room стая с две легла ⓕ *sta*·ya s dve leg·*la*

down долу *do*·loo

downhill надолу na·*do*·loo

drama драма ⓕ *dra*·ma

dream n сън ⓜ suhn

dress n рокля ⓕ *rok*·lya

dried сушен soo·*shen*

dried fruit сушени плодове ⓜ pl soo·*she*·nee plo·*do*·ve

drink n напитка ⓕ na·*peet*·ka

drink v пия *pee*·yuh

drive v карам *ka*·ram

drivers licence шофьорска книжка ⓕ sho·*fyor*·ska *kneesh*·ka

drug (medication) лекарство ⓝ *le·karst*·vo

drug addiction наркомания ⓕ nar·ko·*ma*·nee·ya

drug dealer наркодилър ⓜ nar·ko·*dee*·luhr

drugs (illicit) наркотици ⓜ pl nar·ko·*tee*·tsee

drug trafficking трафик на наркотици ⓜ *tra*·feek na nar·ko·*tee*·tsee

drug user наркоман/наркоманка ⓜ/ⓕ nar·ko·*man*/nar·ko·*man*·ka

drum (instrument) барабан ⓜ ba·ra·*ban*

drums (kit) барабани ⓜ pl ba·ra·*ba*·nee

drunk пиян pee·*yan*

dry a сух sooh

dry (clothes) v изсуша/изсушавам eez·soo·*shuh*/eez·soo·*sha*·vam

dry (oneself) v избърша/избърсвам се eez·*buhr*·shuh/eez·*buhr*·svam se

---

duck патица ① *pa*·tee·tsa
dummy (pacifier) биберон ⓜ bee·be·*ron*
duty-free n безмитен магазин ⓜ
bez·*mee*·ten ma·ga·*zeen*
DVD дивиди ⓝ dee·vee·*dee*

E

each всеки *vse*·kee
ear ухо ⓝ oo·*ho*
early adv рано *ra*·no
earplugs тампони ⓜ pl tam·*po*·nee
earrings обици ① pl o·bee·*tsee*
Earth Земя ① zem·*ya*
earthquake земетресение ⓝ
ze·me·tre·*se*·nee·e
east n изток ⓜ *eez*·tok
Easter Великден ⓜ ve·*leek*·den
easy лесен *le*·sen
eat ям yam
economy class туристическа класа ①
too·rees·*tee*·ches·ka *kla*·sa
ecstasy (drug) екстази ⓝ *ek*·sta·zee
eczema екзема ① ek·*ze*·ma
education образование ⓝ
o·bra·zo·*va*·nee·e
egg яйце ⓝ *yai*·tse
eggplant патладжан ⓜ pat·lad·*zhan*
election избори ⓜ pl *eez*·bo·ree
electrical store
магазин за електроуреди ⓜ
ma·ga·*zeen* za e·lek·tro·oo·*re*·dee
electrician електротехник ⓜ
e·lek·tro·teh·*neek*
electricity електричество ⓝ
e·lek·*tree*·chest·vo
elevator асансьор ⓜ a·san·*syor*
email n и-мейл ⓜ ee·*meyl*
embarrassed притеснен pree·tes·*nen*
embassy посолство ⓝ po·*solst*·vo
emergency спешен случай ⓜ
spe·shen sloo·*chai*
emotional емоционален
e·mo·tsee·o·*na*·len
employee служител/служителка ⓜ/①
sloo·*zhee*·tel/sloo·*zhee*·tel·ka
employer работодател/работодателка
ⓜ/① ra·bo·to·*da*·tel/ra·bo·to·*da*·tel·ka

empty a празен *pra*·zen
end n край ⓜ krai
endangered species застрашен вид ⓜ
za·stra·*shen* veed
engaged (phone) зает za·*et*
engaged (to be married) сгоден sgo·
engagement (to marry) годеж ⓜ go·*de*
engine мотор ⓜ mo·*tor*
engineer инженер ⓜ een·zhe·*ner*
engineering инженерство ⓝ
een·zhe·*nerst*·vo
England Англия ① *an*·glee·ya
English (language) n английски ⓜ
an·*gleey*·skee
enjoy (oneself) забавлявам се
za·bav·*lya*·vam se
enough достатъчен do·*sta*·tuh·chen
enter влиза/влизам *vlya*·zuh/*vlee*·zam
entertainment guide развлекателна
програма ① raz·vle·*ka*·tel·na pro·*gra*·
entry вход ⓜ vhod
envelope плик за писмо ⓜ
pleek za pees·*mo*
environment околна среда ①
o·*kol*·na sre·*da*
epilepsy епилепсия ① e·pee·*lep*·see·y
equality равноправие ⓝ rav·no·*pra*·vee
equal opportunity равни възможнос
① *rav*·nee vuhz·*mozh*·nos·tee
equipment оборудване ⓝ
o·bo·*rood*·va·ne
escalator ескалатор ⓜ es·ka·*la*·tor
estate agency агенция за недвижими
имоти ① a·*gen*·tsee·ya za
ned·*vee*·zhee·mee ee·*mo*·tee
euro евро ⓝ *ev*·ro
Europe Европа ① ev·*ro*·pa
European Union Европейският съюз
ev·ro·*pey*·skee·yuht suh·*yooz*
euthanasia евтаназия ① ev·ta·*na*·zee·
evening вечер ① *ve*·cher
every всеки *vse*·kee
everyone всеки ⓜ *vse*·kee
everything всичко ⓝ *vseech*·ko
exactly точно *toch*·no
example пример ⓜ *pree*·mer
excellent отличен ot·*lee*·chen
excess baggage свръхбагаж ⓜ
svuhrh·ba·*gazh*

hange v размяна/разменям
az·men·yuh/raz·men·yam

hange rate
бменен курс на валутата ⓜ
o·me·nen koors na va·loo·ta·ta

luded изключен eez·klyoo·chen

aust (car) ауспух ⓜ a·oos·pooh

ibition изложба ⓕ eez·lozh·ba
ks·plo·a·ta·tsee·ya

: изход ⓜ eez·hod

ensive скъп skuhp

erience n опит ⓜ o·peet

loitation експлоатация ⓕ

ress a експресен eks·pre·sen

ress mail бърза поща ⓕ
uhr·za posh·ta

ension (visa) удължаване ⓝ
o·duhl·zha·va·ne

око o·ko

drops капки за очи ⓝ pl
ap·kee za o·chee

ric плат ⓜ plat

e n лице ⓝ lee·tse

e cloth кърпа за лице ⓕ
uhr·pa za lee·tse

tory фабрика ⓕ fa·bree·ka

(autumn) есен ⓕ e·sen

(down) v падна/падам
ad·nuh/pa·dam

ily семейство ⓝ se·meyst·vo

ily name фамилно име ⓜ
a·meel·no ee·me

ious известен eez·ves·ten

(machine) вентилатор ⓜ
en·tee·la·tor

(supporter) почитател/почитателка
ⓜ/ⓕ po·chee·ta·tel/po·chee·ta·tel·ka

belt ремък ⓜ re·muhk

adv далече da·le·che

e цена на билет ⓕ tse·na na bee·let

m n ферма ⓕ fer·ma

mer фермер/фермерка ⓜ/ⓕ
er·mer/fer·mer·ka

hion мода ⓕ mo·da

t a бърз buhrz

a тлъст tluhst

father баща ⓜ bash·ta
father-in-law (husband's father) свекър ⓜ sve·kuhr
father-in-law (wife's father) тъст ⓜ tuhst
faucet кран ⓜ kran
(someone's) fault грешка ⓕ gresh·ka
faulty дефектен de·fek·ten
fax факс ⓜ faks
feed v храня hran·yuh
feel (emotions) чувствам choovst·vam
feel (touch) пипам pee·pam
feeling (physical) чувство ⓝ choovst·vo
feelings чувства ⓝ pl choovst·va
female a женски zhen·skee
fence n ограда ⓕ o·gra·da
ferry n ферибот ⓜ fe·re·bot
festival фестивал ⓜ fes·tee·val
fever висока температура ⓕ
vee·so·ka tem·pe·ra·too·ra
few малко mal·ko
fiancé годеник ⓜ go·de·neek
fiancée годеница ⓕ go·de·nee·tsa
fiction художествена литература ⓕ
hoo·do·zhest·ve·na lee·te·ra·too·ra
fig смокиня ⓕ smo·kee·nya
fight n бой ⓜ boy
fill v пълня puhl·nyuh
fillet филе ⓝ fee·le
film (cinema/for camera) филм ⓜ feelm
film speed скорост ⓕ sko·rost
filtered филтриран feel·tree·ran
find v намеря/намирам
na·mer·yuh/na·mee·ram
fine a хубав hoo·bav
fine (payment) n глоба ⓕ glo·ba
finger пръст ⓜ pruhst
finish n край ⓜ krai
finish v завърша/завършвам
za·vuhr·shuh/za·vuhr·shvam
Finland Финландия ⓕ feen·lan·dee·ya
fire n огън ⓜ o·guhn
firewood дърва за огън ⓜ pl
duhr·va za o·guhn
first-aid kit аптечка ⓕ ap·tech·ka
first class първа класа ⓕ puhr·va kla·sa
first name собствено име ⓝ
sobst·ve·no ee·me
fish n риба ⓕ ree·ba
fishing риболов ⓜ ree·bo·lov

fish shop рибарски магазин ⓜ
ree-*bar*-skee ma-ga-*zeen*

flag n знаме ⓝ *zna*-me

flannel (face cloth) кърпа ⓕ *kuhr*-pa

flash (camera) светкавица ⓕ
svet-*ka*-vee-tsa

flashlight (torch) фенерче ⓝ fe-*ner*-che

flash memory флаш памет ⓕ flash pa-*met*

flat (apartment) апартамент ⓜ
a-par-ta-*ment*

flat a плосък *plo*-suhk

flea бълха ⓕ buhl-*ha*

fleamarket битпазар ⓜ beet-pa-*zar*

flight полет ⓜ *po*-let

flood n наводнение ⓝ na-vod-*ne*-nee-e

floor под ⓜ pod

floor (storey) етаж ⓜ e-*tazh*

florist (shop) цветарски магазин ⓜ
tsve-*tar*-skee ma-ga-*zeen*

flour брашно ⓝ *brash*-no

flower цвете ⓝ *tsve*-te

flu грип ⓜ greep

fly n муха ⓕ *moo*-ha

fly v летя let-*yuh*

foggy мъглив muhg-*leev*

follow следя/следвам sled-*yuh*/*sled*-vam

food храна ⓕ hra-*na*

foot (body) крак ⓜ krak

football (soccer) футбол ⓜ *foot*-bol

footpath пътека ⓕ puh-*te*-ka

foreign чуждестранен choozh-de-*stra*-nen

forest гора ⓕ go-*ra*

forever завинаги za-*vee*-na-gee

forget забравя/забравям
za-*brav*-yuh/za-*brav*-yam

forgive простя/прощавам
prost-*yuh*/prosh-*ta*-vam

fork вилица ⓕ *vee*-lee-tsa

fortnight две седмици ⓕ pl
dve *sed*-mee-tsee

fortune teller врачка ⓕ *vrach*-ka

foul (sport) нарушение ⓝ
na-roo-*she*-nee-e

foyer фойае ⓝ fo-a-*ye*

fragile чуплив choop-*leev*

France Франция ⓕ *fran*-tsee-ya

free (available/not bound) свободен
svo-*bo*-den

free (gratis) безплатен bez-*pla*-ten

freeze v замразя/замразявам
za-*mraz*-yuh/za-mraz-*ya*-vam

fresh пресен *pre*-sen

fridge хладилник ⓜ hla-*deel*-neek

fried пържен *puhr*-zhen

friend приятел/приятелка ⓜ/ⓕ
pree-*ya*-tel/pree-*ya*-tel-ka

from от ot

frost мраз ⓜ mraz

frozen замръзнал za-*mruhz*-nal

fruit плод ⓜ plod

fruit picking бране на плодове ⓝ
bra-*ne* na plo-do-*ve*

fry v пържа *puhr*-zhuh

frying pan тиган ⓜ tee-*gan*

full пълен puh-*len*

full-time на пълен работен ден
na *puh*-len ra-*bo*-ten den

fun a забавен za-*ba*-ven

funeral погребение ⓝ po-gre-*be*-nee

funny смешен *sme*-shen

furniture мебели ⓕ pl *me*-be-lee

future n бъдеще ⓝ *buh*-desh-te

G

game (sport) игра ⓕ ee-*gra*

garage гараж ⓜ ga-*razh*

garbage боклук ⓜ bok-*look*

garbage can кофа за боклук ⓕ
ko-fa za bok-*look*

garden n градина ⓕ gra-*dee*-na

gardener градинар/градинарка ⓜ/ⓕ
gra-dee-*nar*/gra-dee-*nar*-ka

gardening градинарство ⓝ
gra-dee-*narst*-vo

garlic чесън ⓜ *che*-suhn

gas (for cooking) газ ⓜ gaz

gas (petrol) бензин ⓜ ben-*zeen*

gas cartridge газова бутилка ⓕ
ga-zo-va boo-*teel*-ka

gastroenteritis гастроентерит ⓜ
gas-tro-en-te-*reet*

gate (airport, etc) изход ⓜ *eez*-hod

gauze марля ⓕ *mar*-lya

gay (homosexual) n&a гей ⓜ&ⓕ gey

gearbox скоростна кутия ⓕ
sko-rost-na koo-*tee*-ya

Germany Германия ⓕ ger-*ma*-nee-ya

получа/получавам
o-*loo*-chuh/po-*loo*-*cha*-vam

off (train, etc) слизам/слизам
ya-*zuh*/*slee*-zam

подарък ⓜ po-*da*-ruhk

концерт ⓜ kon-*tsert*

джин ⓜ dzheen

момиче ⓝ mo-*mee*-che

friend гадже ⓝ *gad*-zhe

дам/давам dam/*da*-vam

en name собствено име ⓝ
obst-ve-no *ee*-me

dular fever възпаление на
имфните възли ⓜ vuhz-pa-*le*-nee-e
a *leemf*-nee-te *vuhz*-lee

ss (drinking) чаша ① *cha*-sha

sses (spectacles) очила ① pl o-chee-*la*

ves (clothing) ръкавици ① pl
uh-ka-*vee*-tsee

ves (latex) гумени ръкавици ① pl
oo-me-nee ruh-ka-*vee*-tsee

e n лепило ⓝ le-*pee*-lo

отида/отивам o-*tee*-duh/o-*tee*-vam

l (sport) гол ⓜ gol

lkeeper вратар ⓜ vra-*tar*

t коза ① ko-*za*

d (general) бог ⓜ bog

ggles (skiing) скиорски очила ⓟ pl
kee-or-skee o-chee-*la*

ggles (swimming) очила за плуване
⓪ pl o-chee-*la* za *ploo*-va-ne

d n злато ⓝ *zla*-to

od добър do-*buhr*

out (with) излиза/излизам (с)
ez-*lya*-zuh/eez-*lee*-zam (s)

shopping пазаруваам pa-za-*roo*-vam

vernment правителство ⓝ
-ra-vee-*telst*-vo

m грам ⓜ gram

ndchild внуче ⓝ *vnoo*-che

ndfather дядо ⓜ *dya*-do

ndmother баба ① *ba*-ba

pes грозде ⓝ *groz*-de

ss трева ① tre-*va*

teful благодарен bla-go-*da*-ren

ve гроб ⓜ grob

at (fantastic) чудесен choo-*de*-sen

ece Гърция ① *guhr*-tsee-ya

en зелен ze-*len*

greengrocer
зарзаватчия/зарзаватчийка ⓜ/①
zar-za-vat-*chee*-ya/ zar-za-vat-*cheey*-ka

grey сив seev

groceries хранителни стоки ① pl
hra-*nee*-tel-nee *sto*-kee

grow раста ras-*tuh*

guarantee n гаранция ① ga-*ran*-tsee-ya

guess v отгатна/отгатвам
ot-*gat*-nuh/ot-*gat*-vam

guesthouse малък хотел ⓜ
ma-luhk ho-*tel*

guide (audio) аудио гид ⓜ
a-oo-dee-o geed

guide (person)
екскурзовод/екскурзоводка ⓜ/①
eks-koor-zo-*vod*/eks-koor-zo-*vod*-ka

guidebook пътеводител ⓜ
puh-te-vo-*dee*-tel

guide dog куче-водач ⓝ *koo*-che-vo-*dach*

guided tour екскурзия ① eks-*koor*-zee-ya

guilty виновен vee-*no*-ven

guitar китара ① kee-*ta*-ra

gums (mouth) венци ⓜ pl ven-*tsee*

gun оръжие ⓝ o-*ruh*-zhee-e

gym (place) фитнес център ⓜ
feet-nes tsen-*tuhr*

gynaecologist гинеколог/гинеколожка
ⓜ/① gee-ne-ko-*log*/gee-ne-ko-*lozh*-ka

H

hair коса ① ko-*sa*

hairbrush четка за коса ① *chet*-ka za ko-*sa*

haircut подстригване ⓝ pod-*streeg*-va-ne

hairdresser фризьор/фризьорка ⓜ/①
freez-*yor*/freez-*yor*-ka

half n половина ① po-lo-*vee*-na

hallucination халюцинация ①
ha-lyoo-tsee-*na*-tsee-ya

ham шунка ① *shoon*-ka

hammer n чук ⓜ chook

hammock хамак ⓜ ha-*mak*

hand ръка ① ruh-*ka*

handbag чанта ① *chan*-ta

handball хандбал ⓜ *hand*-bal

handicraft ръчна изработка ①
ruhch-na eez-ra-*bot*-ka

handkerchief носна кърпичка ⓕ
nos·na kuhr·*peech*·ka

handlebars кормило ⓝ kor·*mee*·lo

handmade ръчно изработен
ruhch·no eez·ra·*bo*·ten

handsome красив kra·*seev*

happy щастлив shtast·*leev*

harassment тормоз ⓜ tor·*moz*

harbour n пристанище ⓝ
pree·*sta*·neesh·te

hard (not soft) твърд tvuhrd

hardware store железария ⓕ
zhe·le·za·*ree*·ya

hat шапка ⓕ *shap*·ka

have имам ee·*mam*

have a cold настинал/настинала съм
ⓜ/ⓕ na·*stee*·nal/na·*stee*·na·la suhm

have fun забавлявам се
za·bav·*lya*·vam se

hay fever сенна хрема ⓕ *sen*·na *hre*·ma

hazelnut лешник ⓜ *lesh*·neek

he той toy

head глава ⓕ gla·*va*

headache главоболие ⓝ gla·vo·*bo*·lee·e

headlight фар ⓜ far

health здраве ⓝ *zdra*·ve

hear чуя/чувам *choo*·yuh/*choo*·vam

hearing aid слухов апарат ⓜ
sloo·hov a·pa·*rat*

heart сърце ⓝ suhr·*tse*

heart attack инфаркт ⓜ een·*farkt*

heart condition сърдечно заболяване ⓝ
suhr·*dech*·no za·bo·*lya*·va·ne

heat n горещина ⓕ go·resh·tee·*na*

heated затоплен za·*top*·len

heater радиатор ⓜ ra·dee·*a*·tor

heating отопление ⓝ o·top·*le*·nee·e

heavy тежък *te*·zhuhk

helmet каска ⓕ *kas*·ka

help n помощ ⓕ *po*·mosht

help v помогна/помагам
po·*mog*·nuh/po·*ma*·gam

hepatitis хепатит ⓜ he·pa·*teet*

her (possessive) неин *ne*·een

herbs билки ⓕ pl *beel*·kee

herbalist билкар/билкарка ⓜ/ⓕ
beel·*kar*/beel·*kar*·ka

here тука *too*·ka

herring херинга ⓕ *he*·reen·ga

high висок vee·*sok*

highchair детско столче ⓝ
det·sko *stol*·che

high school гимназия ⓕ geem·*na*·zee[...]

highway магистрала ⓕ ma·gees·*tra*·l[...]

hike v отида/отивам на поход
o·*tee*·duh/o·*tee*·vam na po·*hod*

hiking пешеходство ⓝ pe·she·*hod*·st[...]

hiking boots туристически обувки ⓕ
too·rees·*tee*·ches·kee o·*boov*·kee

hill хълм ⓜ huhlm

hire v наема/наемам na·e·muh/na·e·m[...]

his негов *ne*·gov

historical исторически ees·to·*ree*·ches·k[...]

history история ⓕ ees·*to*·ree·ya

hitchhike пътувам на автостоп
puh·*too*·vam na av·to·*stop*

HIV вирус на СПИН ⓜ *vee*·roos na sp[...]

holiday n празник ⓜ *praz*·neek

holidays ваканция ⓕ va·*kan*·tsee·ya

home дом ⓜ dom

homeless бездомен bez·*do*·men

homemaker домакиня ⓕ do·ma·*kee*·[...]

homesick обзет от носталгия
ob·*zet* ot nos·*tal*·gee·ya

homosexual a гей gey

honey мед ⓜ med

honeymoon меден месец ⓜ
me·den *me*·sets

horse кон ⓜ kon

horse racing надбягване с коне ⓝ
nad·*byag*·va·ne na ko·*ne*

horse riding конна езда ⓕ *kon*·na ez·[...]

hospital болница ⓕ *bol*·nee·tsa

hospitality гостоприемство ⓝ
gos·to·pree·*emst*·vo

hot (temperature) горещ go·*resht*

hotel хотел ⓜ ho·*tel*

hot water топла вода ⓕ *top*·la vo·*da*

hot water bottle грейка ⓕ *grey*·ka

hour час ⓜ chas

house къща ⓕ *kuhsh*·ta

housework домакинска работа ⓕ
do·ma·*keen*·ska *ra*·bo·ta

how как kak

how much колко *kol*·ko

hug v прегърна/прегръщам
pre·*guhr*·nuh/pre·*gruhsh*·tam

huge огромен o·*gro*·men

human rights човешки права ⓝ pl
cho·*vesh*·kee pra·*va*

ngry гладен *gla·den*
t v боли *bo·lee*
band мъж ⓜ muhzh

az
ed ⓜ led
cream сладолед ⓜ *sla·do·led*
hockey хокей на лед ⓜ *ho·key na led*
ntification лична карта ⓕ
ech·na kar·ta
t идиот ⓜ *ee·de·ot*
ko *a·ko*
olen *bo·len*
nigration имиграция ⓕ
e·mee·*gra·tsee·ya*
ortant важен *va·zhen*
ossible невъзможен ne·vuh·*zmo·zhen*
ⓕ

hurry набързо na·*buhr·zo*
uded включен *vklyoo·chen*
ome tax данък общ доход ⓜ
a·nuhk obsht do·hod
ia Индия ⓕ *een·dee·ya*
icator показател ⓜ *po·ka·za·*tel
gestion лошо храносмилане
·sho hra·no·*smee·la·ne*
oor на закрито na *za·kree·*to
v
ustry промишленост ⓕ
·ro·*meesh·le·nost*
ection инфекция ⓕ een·*fek·tsee·ya*
ammation възпаление ⓜ
uhz·pa·*le·nee·e*
uenza грип ⓜ greep
ormation информация ⓕ
·en·for·*ma·tsee·ya*
ront of пред pred
redient съставка ⓕ *suh·stav·ka*
ect инжектирам een·zhek·*tee·ram*
ection инфекция ⓕ een·*zhek·tsee·ya*
ured ранен ra·*nen*
ury контузия ⓕ kon·*too·zee·ya*
ocent невинен ne·*vee·nen*
ect насекомо ⓜ na·se·*ko·mo*
ect repellent репелент ⓜ re·pe·*lent*
de adv вътре *vuh·tre*
tructor инструктор/инструкторка
ⓕ een·*strook·tor*/een·*strook·tor·ka*

insurance застраховка ⓕ za·stra·*hov·ka*
interesting интересен *een·te·re·sen*
intermission пауза ⓕ *pa·oo·za*
international международен
mezh·doo·na·*ro·den*
internet Интернет ⓜ *een·ter·net*
internet café Интернет кафе ⓜ
een·ter·net ka·fe
interpreter преводач/преводачка ⓜ/ⓕ
pre·vo·*dach*/pre·vo·*dach·ka*
interview n интервю ⓜ een·ter·*vyoo*
invite v каня *kan·yuh*
iron (for clothes) n ютия ⓕ yoo·*tee·ya*
Ireland Ирландия ⓕ eer·*lan·dee·ya*
island остров ⓜ *os·trov*
Israel Израел ⓜ eez·ra·*el*
it то to
IT информационни технологии ⓕ pl
een·for·ma·tsee·o·nee teh·no·lo·*gee·ee*
Italy Италия ⓕ ee·*ta·lee·ya*
itch n сърбеж ⓜ suhr·*bezh*
itemised описан точка по точка
o·pee·san *toch·ka* po *toch·ka*
itinerary маршрут ⓜ marsh·*root*
IUD вътрематочен контрацептив ⓜ
vuh·tre·ma·to·chen kon·tra·tsep·*teev*

J

jacket яке ⓜ *ya·ke*
jail n затвор ⓜ zat·*vor*
jam конфитюр ⓜ kon·fee·*tyoor*
Japan Япония ⓕ ya·*po·nee·ya*
jar буркан ⓜ boor·*kan*
jaw челюст ⓕ *chel·yoost*
jealous ревнив rev·*neev*
jewellery бижута ⓕ bee·*zhoo·ta*
job работа ⓕ *ra·bo·ta*
jogging джогинг ⓜ *dzho·geeng*
joke n шега ⓕ she·*ga*
journalist журналист/журналистка ⓜ/ⓕ
zhoor·na·*leest*/zhoor·na·*leest·ka*
journey n пътуване ⓜ puh·*too·va·ne*
judge n съдия/съдийка ⓜ/ⓕ
suh·dee·*ya*/suh·*deey·ka*
juice сок ⓜ sok
jump v скоча/скачам *sko·chuh*/*ska·cham*
jumper (sweater) пуловер ⓜ *poo·lo·ver*

english–bulgarian

K

ketchup кетчуп ⓜ *ket*-choop
key n ключ ⓜ klyooch
keyboard клавиатура ⓕ kla·vee·a·*too*·ra
kick v ритна/ритам *reet*·nuh/*ree*·tam
kidney бъбрек ⓜ *buh*·brek
kill v убия/убивам oo·*bee*·yuh/oo·*bee*·vam
kilogram килограм ⓜ *kee*·lo·*gram*
kilometre километър ⓜ kee·lo·*me*·tuhr
kind (nice) любезен lyoo·*be*·zen
kindergarten детска градина ⓕ
  det·ska gra·*dee*·na
king крал ⓜ kral
kiosk будка ⓕ *bood*·ka
kiss n целувка ⓕ tse·*loov*·ka
kiss v целуна/целувам
  tse·*loo*·nuh/tse·*loo*·vam
kitchen кухня ⓕ *kooh*·nya
knee коляно ⓝ ko·*lya*·no
knife нож ⓜ nozh
know зная *zna*·yuh
kosher кашер *ka*·sher

L

labourer работник/работничка ⓜ/ⓕ
  ra·*bot*·neek/ra·*bot*·neech·ka
lace n дантела ⓕ dan·*te*·la
lake езеро ⓝ e·ze·ro
lamb (meat) агнешко ⓝ *ag*·nesh·ko
land n земя ⓕ zem·ya
landlady хазайка ⓕ ha·*zai*·ka
landlord хазаин ⓜ ha·*za*·een
landslide свличане ⓝ *svlee*·cha·ne
language език ⓜ e·*zeek*
laptop лаптоп ⓜ *lap*·top
large голям go·*lyam*
last (final) последен po·*sle*·den
last (previous) минал *mee*·nal
late adv късно *kuhs*·no
later adv по-късно po·*kuhs*·no
laugh v смея се *sme*·yuh se
laundrette обществена пералня на
  самообслужване ⓕ *obsh*·*test*·ve·na
  pe·*ral*·nya na sa·mo·ob·*sloozh*·va·ne
laundry (clothes) пране ⓝ *pra*·ne
laundry (room) пералня ⓕ pe·*ral*·nya
law (rule) закон ⓜ *za*·kon

law (study/profession) право ⓝ *pra*◁
lawyer адвокат ⓜ ad·vo·*kat*
laxative n очистително ⓝ
  o·chees·*tee*·tel·no
lazy мързелив muhr·ze·*leev*
leaf листо ⓝ lees·*to*
learn уча oo·*chuh*
leather n кожа ⓕ *ko*·zha
ledge полица ⓕ po·*lee*·tsa
left (direction) ляв lyav
left-luggage office гардероб ⓜ
  gar·de·*rob*
left-wing ляв lyav
leg (body) крак ⓜ krak
legal законен za·*ko*·nen
legislation законодателство ⓝ
  za·ko·no·*da*·telst·vo
legume бобово растение ⓝ
  bo·bo·vo ras·*te*·nee·e
lemon лимон ⓜ lee·*mon*
lemonade лимонада ⓕ lee·mo·*na*·da
lens (camera) обектив ⓜ o·bek·*teev*
lentils леща ⓕ pl *lesh*·ta
lesbian a гей gey
less по-малко po·*mal*·ko
letter (mail) писмо ⓝ pees·*mo*
lettuce маруля ⓕ ma·*roo*·lya
liar лъжец/лъжкиня ⓜ/ⓕ
  luh·*zhets*/luhzh·*kee*·nya
librarian
  библиотекар/библиотекарка ⓜ/ⓕ
  bee·blee·o·te·*kar*/bee·blee·o·te·*kar*·k◁
library библиотека ⓕ bee·blee·o·*te*·ka◁
lice въшки ⓕ pl *vuhsh*·kee
licence n разрешение ⓝ raz·re·*she*·ne◁
license plate number номер на кола
  no·mer na ko·la
lie (down) v легна/лягам *leg*·nuh/*lya*·g◁
lie (to someone) v лъжа *luh*·zhuh
life живот ⓜ zhee·*vot*
life jacket спасителна жилетка ⓕ
  spa·*see*·tel·na zhee·*let*·ka
lift (elevator) асансьор ⓜ a·san·*syor*
light n светлина ⓕ svet·lee·*na*
light (colour) a светъл *sve*·tuhl
light (weight) a лек lek
light bulb електрическа крушка ⓕ
  e·lek·*tree*·ches·ka *kroosh*·ka
lighter (cigarette) запалка ⓕ za·*pal*·k◁
light meter светломер ⓜ svet·lo·*mer*

v харесам/харесвам
a-re-sam/ha-res-vam
e лайм m laim
n (fabric) лен m len
n (sheets) спално бельо n
pal-no bel-yo
palm гланц за устни m
ants za oost-nee
устни f pl oost-nee
or store
магазин за алкохолни напитки m
na-ga-zeen za al-ko-hol-nee na-peet-kee
en слушам sloo-sham
e (quantity) малко mal-ko
e (size) малък ma-luhk
живея zhee-ve-yuh
r черен дроб m che-ren drob
al а местен mes-ten
k n ключалка f klyoo-chal-ka
k v заключа/заключвам
a-klyoo-chuh/za-klyooch-vam
ked заключен za-klyoo-chen
es бонбони m pl bon-bo-nee
k дълъг duh-luhg
k v гледам gle-dam
k after грижа се за gree-zhuh se za
k for търся tuhr-syuh
se наблюдателен пост
ab-lyoo-da-te-len post
se (clothing) широк shee-rok
t губя goob-yuh
t изгубен eez-goo-ben
x-property office
юро за изгубени вещи n
yoo-ro za eez-goo-be-nee vesh-tee
lot много mno-go
d шумен shoo-men
e n обич f o-beech
e v обичам o-bee-cham
er любовник/любовница m/f
yoo-bov-neek/lyoo-bov-nee-tsa
нисък nee-suhk
ricant смазочно масло n
ma-zoch-no mas-lo
k късмет m kuhs-met
ky късметлия kuhs-met-lee-ya
gage багаж m ba-gazh
gage locker гардероб m gar-de-rob
gage tag етикет за багаж m
-tee-ket za ba-gazh

lump буца f boo-tsa
lunch обед m o-bed
lung бял дроб m byal drob
luxury разкош m ras-kosh

M

Macedonian Македония f ma-ke-don-ski
machine машина f ma-shee-na
magazine списание n spee-sa-nee-e
mail (letters/postal system) n поща f posh-ta
mail v пратя/пращам по пощата prat-yuh/prash-tam po posh-ta-ta
mailbox пощенска кутия f posh-ten-ska koo-tee-ya
main главен gla-ven
main road главен път m gla-ven puht
make направя/правя na-prav-yuh/prav-yuh
make-up n грим m greem
mammogram мамограма f ma-mo-gra-ma
man човек m cho-vek
manager (business) директор/директорка m/f dee-rek-tor/dee-rek-tor-ka
manager (sport) мениджър/мениджърка m/f me-need-zhuhr/me-need-zhuhr-ka
mandarin мандарина f man-da-ree-na
manual worker работник m ra-bot-neek
many много mno-go
map (of country) карта f kar-ta
map (of town) план m plan
margarine маргарин m mar-ga-reen
marijuana марихуана f ma-ree-hoo-a-na
marital status семейно положение n se-mey-no po-lo-zhe-nee-e
market n пазар m pa-zar
marriage брак m brak
married женен/омъжена m/f zhe-nen/o-muh-zhe-na
marry (by man/woman) v оженя/омъжа се o-zhen-yuh/o-muh-zhuh se
martial arts бойни изкуства n pl boy-nee eez-koost-va

english–bulgarian

mass (Catholic) католическа литургия ⓕ
　ka·to·lee·ches·ka lee·toor·ge·ya
massage n масаж ⓜ ma·sazh
masseur масажист ⓜ ma·sa·zheest
masseuse масажистка ⓕ ma·sa·zheest·ka
mat подложка ⓕ pod·lozh·ka
match (sports) мач ⓜ mach
matches (for lighting) кибрит ⓜ kee·breet
mattress матрак ⓜ mat·rak
maybe може би mo·zhe bee
mayonnaise майонеза ⓕ ma·yo·ne·za
mayor кмет ⓜ kmet
me мене me·ne
meal ядене ⓝ ya·de·ne
measles шарка ⓕ shar·ka
meat месо ⓝ me·so
mechanic механик ⓜ me·ha·neek
media медии ⓕ pl me·dee·ee
medicine (medication) лекарство ⓝ
　le·karst·vo
medicine (study/profession) медицина ⓕ
　me·dee·tsee·na
meditation медитация ⓕ
　me·dee·ta·tsee·ya
meet (first time)
　запозная/запознавам се
　za·poz·na·yuh/za·poz·na·vam se
meet (get together) срещна/срещам
　sresht·nuh/sresh·tam
melon пъпеш ⓜ puh·pesh
member член ⓜ chlen
memory card/stick флаш памет ⓜ
　flash pa·met
menstruation менструация ⓕ
　mens·troo·a·tsee·ya
menu меню ⓝ men·yoo
message съобщение ⓝ
　suh·ob·shte·nee·e
metal n метал ⓜ me·tal
metre метър ⓜ me·tuhr
microwave oven микровълнова печка ⓕ
　mee·kro·vuhl·no·va pech·ka
midday обяд ⓝ ob·yad
midnight полунощ ⓕ po·loo·nosht
migraine мигрена ⓕ mee·gre·na
military n военните ⓜ pl vo·en·nee·te
military service военна служба ⓕ
　vo·en·na sloozh·ba
milk мляко ⓝ mlya·ko
millimetre милиметър ⓜ mee·lee·me·tuhr

mincemeat кайма ⓕ kai·ma
mineral water минерална вода ⓕ
　mee·ne·ral·na vo·da
minute минута ⓕ mee·noo·ta
mirror n огледало ⓝ o·gle·da·lo
miscarriage спонтанен аборт ⓜ
　spon·ta·nen a·bort
miss (feel absence of …) … ми липсе
　… mee leep·sva
miss (train, etc) изпусна/изпускам
　ees·poos·nuh/ees·poos·kam
mistake n грешка ⓕ gresh·ka
mix v смеся/смесвам smes·yuh/smes·
mobile phone GSM ⓜ dzhee·es·em
modem модем ⓜ mo·dem
modern съвременен suh·vre·me·nen
moisturiser овлажнител ⓜ o·vlazh·nee
monastery манастир ⓜ ma·nas·teer
money пари ⓜ pl pa·ree
monk монах ⓜ mo·nah
month месец ⓜ me·sets
monument паметник ⓜ pa·met·neek
moon луна ⓕ loo·na
more повече po·ve·che
morning утро ⓝ oo·tro
mosque джамия ⓕ dzha·mee·ya
mosquito комар ⓜ ko·mar
mosquito net комарник ⓜ ko·mar·ne
motel мотел ⓜ mo·tel
mother майка ⓕ mai·ka
mother-in-law (husband's mother)
　свекърва ⓕ sve·kuhr·va
mother-in-law (wife's mother)
　тъща ⓕ tuhsh·ta
motorbike мотоциклет ⓜ mo·to·tsee·
motorboat моторница ⓕ mo·tor·nee
motorway магистрала ⓕ ma·gees·tra
mountain планина ⓕ pla·nee·na
mountain bike планински велосипед
　pla·neen·skee ve·lo·see·ped
mountaineering планинарство ⓝ
　pla·nee·narst·vo
mountain path пътека по планините
　puh·te·ka po pla·nee·nee·te
mountain range планинска верига ⓕ
　pla·neen·ska ve·ree·ga
mouse (animal/computer) мишка ⓕ
　meesh·ka
mouth уста ⓕ oos·ta
movie кино ⓝ kee·no

d кал ① kal
esli мюсли ⑩ myoos·lee
m мама ① ma·ma
mps заушки ① pl za·oosh·kee
rder n убийство ⑩ oo·beeys·tvo
rder v убия/убивам
o·bee·yuh/oo·bee·vam
scle мускул ⑩ moos·kool
seum музей ⑩ moo·zey
shroom гъба ① guh·ba
sic музика ① moo·zee·ka
sician музикант/музикантка ⑩/①
moo·zee·kant/moo·zee·kant·ka
sic shop музикален магазин ⑩
moo·zee·ka·len ma·ga·zeen
ssel мида ① mee·da
stard горчица ① gor·chee·tsa
te ням nyam
мой moy

l clippers нокторезачка ①
ok·to·re·zach·ka
me n име ⑩ ee·me
pkin салфетка ① sal·fet·ka
ppy пелена ① pe·le·na
ppy rash подсичане ⑩ pod·see·cha·ne
rionality националност ①
na·tsee·o·nal·nost
tional park национален парк ⑩
na·tsee·o·na·len park
ture природа ① pree·ro·da
turopath екопатевт ⑩ e·ko·pa·tevt
ar prep близо до blee·zo do
arby adv наблизо na·blee·zo
arest най-близкият nai·bleez·kee·yuht
cessary необходим ne·ob·ho·deem
ck шия ① shee·ya
cklace огърлица ① o·guhr·lee·tsa
ctarine гола праскова ①
go·la pras·ko·va
ed v нуждая се от noozh·da·yuh se ot
edle (sewing) игла ① eeg·la
edle (syringe) спринцовка ①
preen·tsov·ka
gative a отрицателен ot·ree·tsa·te·len
gatives (photos) негатив ⑩ ne·ga·teev

neither adv нито ... нито nee·to ... nee·to
net мрежа ① mre·zha
Netherlands Холандия ① ho·lan·dee·ya
network (phone) мрежа ① mre·zha
never никога nee·ko·ga
new нов nov
news новина ① no·vee·na
newsagency информационна агенция ①
een·for·ma·tsee·on·na a·gen·tsee·ya
newspaper вестник ⑩ vest·neek
newsstand вестникарска будка ①
vest·nee·kar·ska bood·ka
New Year's Day Нова година ①
no·va go·dee·na
New Year's Eve Новогодишна нощ ①
no·vo·go·deesh·na nosht
New Zealand Нова Зеландия ①
no·va ze·lan·dee·ya
next (following) следващ sled·vasht
nice приятен pree·ya·ten
nickname прякор ⑩ prya·kor
night нощ ① nosht
nightclub нощен клуб ⑩ nosh·ten kloob
night out нощ на открито
nosht na ot·kree·to
no не ne
noisy шумен shoo·men
none никакъв nee·ka·kuhv
nonsmoking за непушачи
za ne·poo·sha·chee
noodles юфка ① yoof·ka
noon обяд ⑩ ob·yad
north n север ⑩ se·ver
North Macedonia Северна Македония
① se·ver·na ma·ke·do·nee·ya
Norway Норвегия ① nor·ve·gee·ya
nose нос ⑩ nos
not не ne
notebook тетрадка ① tet·rad·ka
nothing нищо neesh·to
now сега se·ga
nuclear energy атомна енергия ①
a·tom·na e·ner·gee·ya
nuclear test ядрени опити ⑩ pl
ya·dre·nee o·pee·tee
nuclear waste
радиоактивни отпадъци ⑩ pl
ra·dee·o·ak·teev·nee ot·pa·duh·tsee
number n число ⑩ chees·lo

numberplate номер на кола ⓜ
no-mer na ko-*la*

nun монахиня ① mo-na-*hee*-nya

nurse n медицинска сестра ①
me-dee-*tseen*-ska ses-*tra*

nut ядка ① *yad*-ka

O

oatmeal овесени ядки ① pl
o-*ve*-se-nee *yad*-kee

ocean океан ⓜ o-ke-*an*

off (power) изключен eesk-*lyoo*-chen

off (spoiled) развален raz-va-*len*

office офис ⓜ o-fees

office worker служител/служителка ⓜ/①
sloo-*zhee*-tel/sloo-zhee-tel-ka

often често *ches*-to

oil (cooking) олио ① o-lee-o

oil (petrol) нефт ⓜ neft

old стар star

olive маслина ① mas-*lee*-na

olive oil зехтин ⓜ zeh-*teen*

omelette омлет ⓜ om-*let*

on на na

on (power) включен *vklyoo*-chen

once веднъж ved-*nuhzh*

one-way ticket еднопосочен билет ⓜ
ed-no-po-*so*-chen bee-*let*

onion лук ⓜ look

only само *sa*-mo

on time навреме na-*vre*-me

open (business) a отворен ot-*vo*-ren

open v отворя/отварям
ot-*vor*-yuh/ot-*var*-yam

opening hours работно време ⓝ
ra-*bot*-no *vre*-me

opera опера ① o-*pe*-ra

opera house опера ① o-*pe*-ra

operation (medical) операция ①
o-pe-*ra*-tsee-ya

operator (telephone)
телефонист/телефонистка ⓜ/①
te-le-fo-*neest*/te-le-fo-*neest*-ka

opinion мнение ⓝ *mne*-nee-e

opposite prep срещу sresh-*too*

optometrist оптик ⓜ op-*teek*

or или ee-*lee*

orange (colour) оранжев o-*ran*-zhev

orange (fruit) портокал ⓜ por-to-*kal*

orange juice портокалов сок ⓜ
por-to-*ka*-lov sok

orchestra оркестър ⓜ or-*kes*-tuhr

order n ред ⓜ red

order v поръчам/поръчвам
po-*ruh*-cham/po-*ruhch*-vam

ordinary обикновен o-beek-no-*ven*

orgasm оргазъм ⓜ or-*ga*-zuhm

original a първоначален
puhr-vo-na-*cha*-len

other друг droog

our наш nash

out of order повреден po-*vre*-den

outside adv навън na-*vuhn*

ovarian cyst киста на яйчниците ①
kees-ta na yaich-nee-tsee-te

ovary яйчник ⓜ *yaich*-neek

oven фурна ① *foor*-na

overcoat палто ⓝ pal-*to*

overdose n свръхдоза ① svruh-do-za

overnight adv за една нощ za ed-*na* nо

overseas adv в чужбина v choozh-*bee*

owe дължа duhl-*zhuh*

owner собственик/собственичка ⓜ/
sobst-ve-neek/*sobst*-ve-neech-ka

oxygen кислород ⓜ kees-lo-*rod*

oyster стрида ① *stree*-da

ozone layer озонов слой ⓜ o-*zo*-nov s

P

pacemaker пейсмейкър ⓜ *peys*-mey-k

pacifier (dummy) биберон ⓜ bee-be-*r*

package пакет ⓜ pa-*ket*

packet пакет ⓜ pa-*ket*

padlock катинар ⓜ ka-tee-*nar*

page страница ① *stra*-nee-tsa

pain болка ① *bol*-ka

painful болезнен bo-*lez*-nen

painkillers
болкоуспокоителни лекарства ①
bol-ko-oos-po-ko-ee-tel-nee le-*karst*-v

painter (artist)
художник/художничка ⓜ/①
hoo-*dozh*-neek/hoo-*dozh*-neech-ka

painter (tradesperson) бояджия ⓜ
bo-yad-*zhee*-ya

painting (a work) картина ① kar-*tee*-r

inting (the art)
изобразително изкуство ⓝ
eezo·bra·zee·tel·no eez·koost·vo
ir (couple) двойка ⓕ dvoy·ka
lace дворец ⓜ dvo·rets
nts тенджера ⓕ tend·zhe·ra
nts (trousers) панталони ⓜ pl
pan·ta·lo·nee
ntyhose чорапогащник ⓜ
cho·ra·po·gasht·neek
nty liners дамски превръзки ⓕ pl
dam·skee pre·vruhz·kee
per n хартия ⓕ har·tee·ya
perwork попълване на документи ⓝ
po·puhl·va·ne na do·koo·men·tee
raplegic а параплегичен
pa·ra·ple·gee·chen
rcel колет ⓜ ko·let
rents родители ⓜ pl ro·dee·te·lee
rk n парк ⓜ park
rk (a car) v паркирам par·kee·ram
rliament парламент ⓜ par·la·ment
rt (component) част ⓕ chast
rt-time на непълен работен ден
na ne·puh·len ra·bo·ten den
rty (entertainment) купон ⓜ koo·pon
rty (politics) партия ⓕ par·tee·ya
ss (go by) мина/минавам
mee·nuh/mee·na·vam
ss (in sport) v подам/подавам
po·dam/po·da·vam
ssenger пътник/пътничка ⓜ/ⓕ
puht·neek/puht·neech·ka
ssport паспорт ⓜ pas·port
ssport number номер на паспорта ⓜ
no·mer na pas·por·ta
st n минало ⓝ mee·na·lo
sta макарони ⓜ pl ma·ka·ro·nee
stry паста ⓕ pas·ta
th пътека ⓕ puh·te·ka
y v платя/плащам plat·yuh/plash·tam
yment плащане ⓝ plash·ta·ne
ace мир ⓜ meer
ach праскова ⓕ pras·ko·va
ak (mountain) връх ⓜ vruhh
anut фъстък ⓜ fuhs·tuhk
ar круша ⓕ kroo·sha
as грах ⓜ grah
dal n педал ⓜ pe·dal

pedestrian n пешеходец/пешеходка
ⓜ/ⓕ pe·she·ho·dets/pe·she·hod·ka
pen писалка ⓕ pee·sal·ka
pencil молив ⓜ mo·leev
penis пенис ⓜ pe·nees
penknife джобно ножче ⓝ
dzhob·no nozh·che
pensioner пенсионер/пенсионерка
ⓜ/ⓕ pen·see·o·ner/pen·see·o·ner·ka
people хора pl ho·ra
pepper пипер ⓜ pee·per
per (day, etc) на na
per cent процент pro·tsent
perfect а съвършен suh·vuhr·shen
performance представление ⓝ
pred·stav·le·nee·e
perfume парфюм ⓜ par·fyoom
period pain менструална болка ⓕ
mens·troo·al·na bol·ka
permission позволение ⓝ poz·vo·le·nee·e
permit n разрешително ⓝ
raz·re·shee·tel·no
person човек ⓜ cho·vek
petition молба ⓕ mol·ba
petrol бензин ⓜ ben·zeen
petrol station бензиностанция ⓕ
ben·zee·no·stan·tsee·ya
pharmacist аптекар/аптекарка ⓜ/ⓕ
ap·te·kar/ap·te·kar·ka
pharmacy аптека ⓕ ap·te·ka
phone book телефонен указател ⓜ
te·le·fo·nen oo·ka·za·tel
phone box телефонна кабина ⓕ
te·le·fon·na ka·bee·na
phonecard фонокарта ⓕ fo·no·kar·ta
photo снимка ⓕ sneem·ka
photograph v снимам snee·mam
photographer фотограф ⓜ fo·to·graf
photography фотография ⓕ
fo·to·gra·fee·ya
phrasebook разговорник ⓜ
raz·go·vor·neek
piano пиано ⓝ pee·a·no
pickles туршия ⓕ toor·shee·ya
picnic пикник ⓜ peek·neek
pie пирог ⓜ pee·rog
piece парче ⓝ par·che
pig свиня ⓕ svee·nya
pill таблетка ⓕ tab·let·ka

225

(the) pill противозачатъчно ⑩
pro-tee-vo-za-*cha*-tuhch-no
pillow възглавница ① vuhz-*glav*-nee-tsa
pillowcase калъфка за възглавница ①
ka-*luhf*-ka za vuhz-*glav*-nee-tsa
pineapple ананас ⑩ a-na-*nas*
pink розов *ro*-zov
pistachio шам-фъстък ⑩ *sham*-fuhs-tuhk
place n място ⑩ *myas*-to
place of birth място на раждане ⑩
myas-to na *razh*-da-ne
plane самолет ⑩ sa-mo-*let*
planet планета ① pla-*ne*-ta
plant n растение ⑩ ras-*te*-nee-e
plastic a пластмасов plast-*ma*-sov
plate чиния ① chee-*nee*-ya
plateau плато ⑩ pla-*to*
platform трибуна ① tree-*boo*-na
play (game) v играя ee-*gra*-yuh
play (instrument) v свиря *sveer*-yuh
play (theatre) n пиеса ① pee-*e*-sa
plug (bath) запушалка ① za-*poo*-shal-ka
plug (electricity) щепсел ⑩ *shtep*-sel
plum слива ① *slee*-va
plumber водопроводчик ⑩
vo-do-pro-*vod*-cheek
poached (egg) попарен po-*pa*-ren
pocket n джоб ⑩ dzhob
pocket knife джобно ножче ⑩
dzhob-no *nozh*-che
poetry поезия ① po-e-*zee*-ya
point v соча *so*-chuh
poisonous отровен o-*tro*-ven
police полиция ① po-*lee*-tsee-ya
police officer полицай/полицайка ⑩/①
po-lee-*tsai*/po-lee-*tsai*-ka
police station полицейски участък ⑩
po-lee-*tsey*-skee oo-*chas*-tuhk
policy политика ① po-*lee*-tee-ka
politician политик ⑩ po-*lee*-teek
politics политика ① po-*lee*-tee-ka
pollen цветен прашец ⑩
tsve-ten pra-*shets*
pollution замърсяване ⑩
za-muhr-*sya*-va-ne
pool (game) билярд ⑩ beel-*yard*
pool (swimming) плувен басейн ⑩
ploo-ven ba-*seyn*
poor (wealth) беден *be*-den
popular популярен po-poo-*lya*-ren

pork свинско ⑩ *sveen*-sko
port (river/sea) пристанище ⑩
pree-*sta*-neesh-te
positive положителен po-lo-*zhee*-te-ler
possible възможен vuhz-*mo*-zhen
post n поща ① *posh*-ta
post v изпратя/изпращам по пощата
eez-*prat*-yuh/eez-*prash*-tam po *posh*-tai
postage пощенски разноски ① pl
posh-ten-skee raz-*nos*-kee
postcard пощенска картичка ①
posh-ten-ska *kar*-teech-ka
postcode пощенски код ⑩
posh-ten-skee kod
poster плакат ⑩ pla-*kat*
post office поща ① *posh*-ta
pot (ceramics) гърне ⑩ guhr-*ne*
pot (cooking) тенджера ① *tend*-zhe-ra
potato картоф ⑩ kar-*tof*
pottery керамика ① ke-ra-mee-ka
pound (money) лира ① *lee*-ra
pound (weight) фунт ⑩ foont
poverty бедност ① *bed*-nost
powder n пудра ① *pood*-ra
power (political) n власт ① vlast
prawn едра скарида ① *ed*-ra ska-*ree*-d
prayer молитва ① mo-*leet*-va
prayer book молитвеник ⑩
mo-*leet*-ve-neek
prefer предпочета/предпочитам
pred-po-che-*tuh*/pred-po-*chee*-tam
pregnancy test kit тест за бременност ⑩
test za *bre*-men-nost
pregnant бременна *bre*-men-na
premenstrual syndrome
предменструален синдром ⑩
pred-mens-troo-a-len seen-*drom*
prepare подготвя/подготвям
pod-*got*-vyuh/pod-*got*-vyam
prescription рецепта ① re-*tsep*-ta
present (gift) подарък ⑩ po-da-ruhk
present (time) настоящ момент ⑩
na-sto-*yasht* mo-ment
president председател/председателк
⑩/① pred-se-da-tel/pred-se-da-tel-ka
pressure (tyre) налягане ⑩ na-*lya*-ga-ne
pretty хубав *hoo*-bav
price n цена ① tse-*na*
priest свещеник ⑩ svesh-*te*-neek
printer (computer) принтер ⑩ *preen*-tu

son затвор ⓜ zat·vor
soner затворник/затворничка ⓜ/ⓕ
at·vor·neek/zat·vor·neech·ka
vate а частен chas·ten
duce v произведа/произвеждам
pro·eez·ve·duh/pro·eez·vezh·dam
ofit n печалба ⓕ pe·chal·ba
gramme n програма ⓕ pro·gra·ma
jector прожекционен апарат ⓜ
pro·zhek·tsee·o·nen a·pa·rat
mise v обещая/обещавам
o·besh·ta·ya/o·besh·ta·vam
ostitute n проститутка ⓕ
pros·tee·toot·ka
otect защита/защитавам
zash·tee·tyuh/zash·tee·ta·vam
otected (species, etc) защитен
zash·tee·ten
otest n протест ⓜ pro·test
otest v протестирам pro·tes·tee·ram
b (bar) кръчма ⓕ kruch·ma
blic gardens парк ⓜ park
blic phone уличен телефон ⓜ
oo·lee·chen te·le·fon
blic relations
връзки с обществеността ⓕ pl
vruhz·kee s obsh·test·ve·nost·ta
blic toilet обществена тоалетна ⓕ
obsh·test·ve·na to·a·let·na
ll дърпам duhr·pam
mp n помпа ⓕ pom·pa
mpkin тиква ⓕ teek·va
ncture спукана гума ⓕ
spoo·ka·na goo·ma
re чист cheest
rple лилав цвят lee·lav tsvyat
rse дамска чанта ⓕ dam·ska chan·ta
sh v бутам boo·tam
t сложа/слагам slo·zhuh/sla·gam

adriplegic а парализиран на
всички крайници pa·ra·lee·zee·ran na
vseech·kee krai·nee·tsee
alifications умения ⓝ pl oo·me·nee·ya
ality n качество ⓝ ka·chest·vo
arantine карантина ⓕ ka·ran·tee·na
arter n четвърт ⓕ chet·vuhrt

queen кралица ⓕ kra·lee·tsa
question n въпрос ⓜ vuh·pros
queue n опашка ⓕ o·pash·ka
quick бърз buhrz
quiet тих teeh
quit откажа/отказвам се
ot·ka·zhuh/ot·kaz·vam se

R

rabbit (meat) заешко ⓝ za·esh·ko
race (sport) n състезание ⓝ
suhs·te·za·nee·e
racetrack писта ⓕ pees·ta
racing bike състезателен велосипед ⓜ
suhs·te·za·te·len ve·lo·see·ped
racism расизъм ⓜ ra·see·zuhm
radish репичка ⓕ re·peech·ka
racquet ракета ⓕ ra·ke·ta
radiator (car) радиатор ⓜ ra·dee·a·tor
radio радио ⓝ ra·dee·o
railway station гара ⓕ ga·ra
rain n дъжд ⓜ duhzhd
raincoat дъждобран ⓜ duhzh·do·bran
raisin стафида ⓕ sta·fee·da
rally (protest) n митинг ⓜ mee·teeng
rape n изнасилване ⓝ eez·na·seel·va·ne
rape v изнасиля/изнасилвам
eez·na·seel·yuh/eez·na·seel·vam
rare (uncommon) рядък rya·duhk
rash обрив ⓜ ob·reev
raspberry малина ⓕ ma·lee·na
rat плъх ⓜ pluhh
rave party рейв парти ⓜ reyv par·tee
raw суров soo·rov
razor самобръсначка ⓕ
sa·mo·bruhs·nach·ka
razor blade ножче за бръснене ⓝ
nozh·che za bruhs·ne·ne
read v чета che·tuh
reading четене ⓝ che·te·ne
ready готов go·tov
real estate agent
агент за недвижими имоти ⓜ
a·gent za ned·vee·zhee·mee e·mo·tee
realistic реалистичен re·a·lees·tee·chen
rear (location) n задна част ⓕ
zad·na chast
reason n причина ⓕ pree·chee·na

receipt разписка ① *raz*-pees-ka
recently неотдавна ne-ot-*dav*-na
recommend
препоръчам/препоръчвам
pre-po-*ruh*-cham/pre-po-*ruhch*-vam
record v записва/записвам
za-*pee*-shuh/za-*pees*-vam
recording запис ⓜ za-pees
recyclable годен за рециклиране
go-den za re-tsee-*klee*-ra-ne
recycle рециклирам re-tsee-*klee*-ram
red червен cher-*ven*
red wine червено вино ⓝ
cher-*ve*-no *vee*-no
referee n съдия ① suh-dee-*ya*
reference n справка ① *sprav*-ka
refrigerator хладилник ⓜ hla-*deel*-neek
refugee бежанец/бежанка ⓜ/①
be-zha-*nets*/be-*zhan*-ka
refund n връщане на парите ⓝ
vruhsh-ta-ne na pa-*ree*-te
refuse v откажа/отказвам
ot-*ka*-zhuh/ot-*kaz*-vam
regional регионален re-gee-o-*na*-len
registered mail препоръчана поща ①
pre-po-*ruh*-cha-na *posh*-ta
rehydration salts соли за оводняване
① pl *so*-lee za o-vod-*nya*-va-ne
relationship връзка ① *vruhz*-ka
relax v отпусна/отпускам се
ot-*poos*-nuh/ot-*poos*-kam se
relic останка ① o-*stan*-ka
religion религия ① re-*lee*-gee-ya
religious религиозен re-lee-gee-*o*-zen
remote далечен da-*le*-chen
remote control
дистанционно управление ⓝ
dees-tan-tsee-*o*-no oo-*prav*-*le*-nee-e
rent n наем ⓜ *na*-em
rent v взема/взимам под наем
vze-muh/*vzee*-mam pod *na*-em
repair v поправя/поправям
po-*prav*-yuh/po-*prav*-yam
republic република ① re-*poob*-lee-ka
reservation (booking) резервация ①
re-zer-*va*-tsee-ya
rest n почивка ① po-*cheev*-ka
restaurant ресторант ⓜ res-to-*rant*
résumé (CV) автобиография ①
av-to-bee-o-*gra*-fee-ya

retired пенсиониран pen-see-o-*nee*-ra…
return v върна/връщам се
vuhr-na/*vruhsh*-tam se
return ticket двупосочен билет ⓜ
dvoo-po-*so*-chen bee-*let*
review n преглед ⓜ *pre*-gled
rhythm ритъм ⓜ *ree*-tuhm
rib (body) ребро ⓝ reb-*ro*
rice ориз ⓜ o-*reez*
rich (wealthy) богат bo-*gat*
ride n езда ① ez-*da*
ride (bike) v карам колело *ka*-ram ko-le…
ride (horse) v яздя кон *yaz*-dyuh kon
right (correct) правилен *pra*-vee-len
right (direction) десен de-sen
right-wing десен *de*-sen
ring (jewellery) пръстен ⓜ *pruhs*-ten
ring (phone) v звъня zvuh-*nyuh*
rip-off n измама ① eez-*ma*-ma
risk v рискувам rees-*koo*-vam
river река ① re-*ka*
road път ⓜ puht
road map пътна карта ① *puht*-na *kar*-…
rob обера/обирам o-be-*ruh*/o-*bee*-ram…
rock n скала ① ska-*la*
rock (music) рок ⓜ rok
rock climbing скалнокатерене ⓝ
skal-no-ka-*te*-re-ne
rock group рокгрупа ① rok-*groo*-pa
roll (bread) хлебче ⓝ *hleb*-che
rollerblading каране на ролкови кънк…
ⓝ *ka*-ra-ne na *rol*-ko-vee kuhn-kee
Romania Румъния ① roo-*muh*-nee-ya
romantic a романтичен ro-man-*tee*-ch…
room стая ① *sta*-ya
room number номер на стаята ⓜ
no-mer na *sta*-ya-ta
rope въже ⓝ *vuh*-zhe
round (drinks) n по едно питие за всеки…
ⓝ po ed-*no* pee-tee-e za *vse*-kee
round a кръгъл *kruh*-guhl
route n маршрут ⓜ marsh-*root*
rowing гребане ⓝ *gre*-ba-ne
rubbish боклук ⓜ bok-*look*
rubella рубеола ① roo-be-o-la
rug килим ⓜ kee-*leem*
rugby ръгби ⓜ *ruhg*-bee
ruins останки ⓝ pl o-*stan*-kee
rule n правило ⓝ *pra*-vee-lo
rum ром ① rom

run v тичам *tee*-cham
running бягане ⓝ *bya*-ga-ne
runny nose хрема ⓕ *hre*-ma
Russia Русия ⓕ roo-*see*-ya

S

sad тъжен *tuh*-zhen
safe n сейф ⓜ seyf
safe a безопасен bez-*o*-*pa*-sen
safe sex безопасен секс ⓜ
  bez-*o*-*pa*-sen seks
sailboarding каране на уинд ⓝ
  ka-ra-ne na oo-*eend*
saint n светец/светица ⓜ/ⓕ
  sve-*tets*/sve-*tee*-tsa
salad салата ⓕ *sa*-la-ta
salami салам ⓜ sa-*lam*
salary заплата ⓕ za-*pla*-ta
sale n разпродажба ⓕ raz-pro-*dazh*-ba
sales assistant продавач/продавачка
  ⓜ/ⓕ pro-da-*vach*/pro-da-*vach*-ka
sales tax данък добавена стойност ⓜ
  da-nuhk do-*ba*-ve-na *stoy*-nost
salmon сьомга ⓕ *syom*-ga
salt n сол ⓕ sol
same същият *suhsh*-tee-yuht
sand пясък ⓜ *pya*-suhk
sandals сандали ⓜ pl san-*da*-lee
sanitary napkin дамска превръзка ⓕ
  dam-ska pre-*vruhz*-ka
sardine сардина ⓕ sar-*dee*-na
sauce сос ⓜ sos
saucepan тенджера ⓕ *tend*-zhe-ra
sauna сауна ⓕ *sa*-oo-na
sausage наденица ⓕ *na*-de-nee-tsa
say кажа/казвам *ka*-zhuh/*kaz*-vam
scalp скалп ⓜ skalp
scarf шал ⓜ shal
school училище ⓝ oo-*chee*-leesh-te
science наука ⓕ *na*-oo-ka
scientist учен ⓜ *oo*-chen
scissors ножица ⓕ *no*-zhee-tsa
score v отбележа/отбелязвам
  ot-be-*le*-zhuh/ot-be-*lyaz*-vam
scoreboard табло за резултатите ⓝ
  tab-lo za re-*zool*-ta-tee-te
Scotland Шотландия ⓕ shot-*lan*-dee-ya
scrambled бъркан *buhr*-kan

sculpture скулптура ⓕ skoolp-*too*-ra
sea море ⓝ mo-*re*
seasick болен от морска болест
  bo-len ot *mor*-ska *bo*-lest
seaside n морски бряг ⓜ *mor*-skee bryag
season n сезон ⓜ se-*zon*
seat (chair, etc) седалка ⓕ se-*dal*-ka
seatbelt предпазен колан ⓜ
  pred-*pa*-zen ko-*lan*
second (time unit) n секунда ⓕ
  se-*koon*-da
second a втори *vto*-ree
second class втора класа ⓕ *vto*-ra *kla*-sa
secondhand от втора употреба
  ot *vto*-ra oo-po-*tre*-ba
secondhand shop магазин за стоки
  втора употреба ⓜ ma-ga-*zeen* za
  sto-kee *vto*-ra oo-po-*tre*-ba
secretary секретар/секретарка ⓜ/ⓕ
  se-kre-*tar*/se-kre-*tar*-ka
see видя/виждам *veed*-yuh/*veezh*-dam
self-employed на свободна практика
  na svo-*bod*-na *prak*-tee-ka
selfish егоистичен e-go-ees-*tee*-chen
self-service на самообслужване
  na sa-mo-ob-*sloozh*-va-ne
sell продам/продавам
  pro-*dam*/pro-*da*-vam
send изпратя/изпращам
  eez-*prat*-yuh/eez-*prash*-tam
sensible разумен ra-*zoo*-men
sensual чувствен *choovs*-tven
separate a отделен ot-*de*-len
Serbia Сърбия ⓕ *suhr*-bee-ya
serious сериозен se-ree-*o*-zen
service n обслужване ⓝ ob-*sloozh*-va-ne
service charge процент за обслужване ⓜ
  pro-*tsent* za ob-*sloozh*-va-ne
serviette салфетка ⓕ sal-*fet*-ka
several няколко *nya*-kol-ko
sew шия *shee*-yuh
sex (gender) пол ⓜ pol
sex (intercourse) секс ⓜ seks
sexism сексизъм ⓜ sek-*see*-zuhm
sexually transmitted infection
  венерическа болест ⓕ
  ve-ne-*ree*-ches-ka *bo*-lest
sexy сексапилен sek-*sa*-pee-len
shade n сянка ⓕ *syan*-ka
shadow n сянка ⓕ *syan*-ka

shampoo шампоан ⓜ sham·po·*an*

shape n форма ① for·ma

share (a room, etc) v споделя/споделям
spo·*del*·yuh/spo·*del*·yam

shave v бръсна се *bruhs*·nuh se

shaving cream крем за бръснене ⓜ
krem za *bruhs*·ne·ne

she тя tya

sheep овца ① ov·*tsa*

sheet (bed) чаршаф ⓜ char·*shaf*

shelf полица ① po·lee·tsa

shiatsu шиатсу ⓜ shee·*at*·soo

shingles (illness) херпес ⓜ *her*·pes

ship n кораб ⓜ *ko*·rab

shirt риза ① *ree*·za

shoes обувки ① pl o·*boov*·kee

shoelace връзка за обувки ①
vruhz·ka za o·*boov*·kee

shoe shop магазин за обувки ⓜ
ma·ga·*zeen* za o·*boov*·kee

shoot v стрелям *strel*·yam

shop n магазин ⓜ ma·ga·*zeen*

shop v пазарувам pa·za·*roo*·vam

shopping пазаруване ① pa·za·*roo*·va·ne

shopping centre търговски център ⓜ
tuhr·*gov*·skee *tsen*·tuhr

short (height) нисък *nee*·suhk

short (length) къс kuhs

shortage недостиг ⓜ ne·*dos*·teeg

shorts шорти ① pl *shor*·tee

shoulder рамо ① *ra*·mo

shout v викам *vee*·kam

show n представление ⓝ
pred·stav·*le*·nee·e

show v покажа/показвам
po·*ka*·zhuh/po·*kaz*·vam

shower n душ ⓜ doosh

shrine светилище ① sve·*tee*·leesh·te

shut a затворен zat·*vo*·ren

shut v затворя/затварям
zat·*vor*·yuh/zat·*var*·yam

shy срамежлив sra·*mezh*·leev

sick болен *bo*·len

side n страна ① stra·*na*

sign n знак ⓜ znak

sign v подпиша/подписвам
pod·*pee*·shuh/pod·*pees*·vam

signature подпис ⓜ *pod*·pees

silk n коприна ① ko·*pree*·na

silver n сребро ⓝ sreb·*ro*

SIM card сим-карта ① *seem*·kar·ta

similar подобен po·*do*·ben

simple прост prost

since (time) от от

sing пея *pe*·yuh

singer певец/певица ⓜ/①
pe·*vets*/pe·*vee*·tsa

single (person) а неженен/неомъжена
ⓜ/① ne·*zhe*·nen/ne·o·*muh*·zhe·na

single room единична стая ①
e·dee·*neech*·na *sta*·ya

singlet потник ⓜ *pot*·neek

sister сестра ① ses·*tra*

sit седна/сядам sed·*nuh*/*sya*·dam

size номер ⓜ *no*·mer

skate v пързалям се на кънки
puhr·*zal*·yam se na *kuhn*·kee

skateboarding каране на скейтборд ⓝ
ka·ra·ne na *skeyt*·bord

ski v карам ски *ka*·ram skee

skiing каране на ски ⓝ *ka*·ra·ne na skee

skim milk обезмаслено мляко ⓝ
o·bez·*mas*·le·no *mlya*·ko

skin кожа ① *ko*·zha

skirt пола ① po·*la*

skull череп ⓜ *che*·rep

sky небе ⓝ ne·*be*

sleep n сън ⓜ suhn

sleep v спя spyuh

sleeping bag спален чувал ⓜ
spa·len choo·*val*

sleeping berth легло ⓝ leg·*lo*

sleeping car спален вагон ⓜ
spa·len va·*gon*

sleeping pills приспивателно ⓝ
pree·spee·*va*·tel·no

sleepy сънлив suhn·*leev*

slice n филия ① fee·*lee*·ya

slide film диапозитивен филм ⓜ
dee·a·po·zee·*tee*·ven feelm

slow бавен *ba*·ven

slowly бавно *bav*·no

small малък *ma*·luhk

smaller по-малък po·*ma*·luhk

smallest най-малкият *nai*·mal·kee·yuht

smell v мириазма ① mee·*reez*·ma

smile v усмихна/усмихвам се
oo·*smeeh*·nuh/oo·*smeeh*·vam se

smoke v пуша *poo*·shuh

snack n закуска ① za·*koos*·ka

snail охлюв ⓜ *oh-lyoov*

snake змия ① *zmee-ya*

snorkelling плуване със шнорхел ⓜ
ploo-va-ne suhs shnor-hel

snow n сняг ⓜ *snyag*

snowboarding
пързаляне със сноуборд ⓝ
puhr-za-lya-ne suhs sno-oo-bord

soap сапун ⓜ *sa-poon*

soap opera сапунена опера ①
sa-poo-ne-na o-pe-ra

soccer футбол ⓜ *foot-bol*

socialist n социалист ⓜ *so-tsee-a-leest*

socialist a социалистически
so-tsee-a-lees-tee-ches-kee

social welfare социално подпомагане ⓝ
so-tsee-al-no pod-po-ma-ga-ne

socks чорапи ⓜ pl *cho-ra-pee*

Sofia София ① *so-fee-ya*

soft drink безалкохолна напитка ①
bez-al-ko-hol-na na-peet-ka

soldier войник ⓜ *voy-neek*

some някакъв *nya-ka-kuhv*

someone някой *nya-koy*

something нещо *nesh-to*

sometimes понякога *po-nya-ko-ga*

son син ⓜ *seen*

song песен ① *pe-sen*

soon скоро *sko-ro*

sore a болезнен *bo-lez-nen*

soup супа ① *soo-pa*

south n юг ⓜ *yoog*

souvenir сувенир ⓜ *soo-ve-neer*

souvenir shop магазин за сувенири ⓜ
ma-ga-zeen za soo-ve-nee-ree

soy milk мляко от соя ⓝ *mlya-ko ot so-ya*

soy sauce соев сос ⓜ *so-yev sos*

space (area) място ⓝ *myas-to*

Spain Испания ① *ees-pa-nee-ya*

sparkling wine шумящо вино ⓝ
shoom-yash-to vee-no

speak говоря *go-vor-yuh*

special a особен *o-so-ben*

specialist n специалист/специалистка
ⓜ/① *spe-tsee-a-leest/spe-tsee-a-leest-ka*

speed (drug) амфетамин ⓜ
am-fe-ta-meen

speed (travel) n скорост ① *sko-rost*

speed limit
максимална позволена скорост ①
mak-see-mal-na poz-vo-le-na sko-rost

speedometer скоростомер ⓜ
sko-ros-to-mer

spider паяк ⓜ *pa-yak*

spinach спанак ⓜ *spa-nak*

spoilt (food) развален *raz-va-len*

spoke спица ① *spee-tsa*

spoon лъжица ① *luh-zhee-tsa*

sport спорт ⓜ *sport*

sportsperson спортист/спортистка ⓜ/①
spor-teest/spor-teest-ka

sports store спортен магазин ⓜ
spor-ten ma-ga-zeen

sprain n навяхване ⓝ *nav-yah-va-ne*

spring (coil) пружинка ① *proo-zheen-ka*

spring (season) пролет ① *pro-let*

square (town) площад ⓜ *plosh-tad*

stadium стадион ⓜ *sta-dee-on*

stairway стълбище ⓝ *stuhl-beesh-te*

stale стар *star*

stamp (postage) n марка ① *mar-ka*

star n звезда ① *zvez-da*

(four-)star с (четири) звезди
s (che-tee-ree) zvez-dee

start n начало ⓝ *na-cha-lo*

start v започна/започвам
za-poch-nuh/za-poch-vam

station гара ① *ga-ra*

statue статуя ① *sta-too-a*

stay (at a hotel) отседна/отсядам
ot-sed-nuh/ot-sya-dam

stay (in one place) остана/оставам
o-sta-nuh/o-sta-vam

steak бифтек ⓜ *beef-tek*

steal v открадна/открадвам
ot-krad-nuh/ot-krad-vam

steep стръмен *struh-men*

step n стъпка ① *stuhp-ka*

stereo n стерео ⓝ *ste-re-o*

stockings чорапи ⓜ pl *cho-ra-pee*

stolen откраднат *ot-krad-nat*

stomach стомах ⓜ *sto-mah*

stomachache болки в стомаха ① pl
bol-kee v sto-ma-huh

stone n камък ⓜ *ka-muhk*

stoned (drugged) дрогиран *dro-gee-ran*

stop (bus, tram) n спирка ① *speer-ka*

stop (cease) спра/спирам
spruh/*spee*·ram

stop (prevent) попреча/попречвам
po·*pre*·chuh/po·*prech*·vam

storm n буря ⓕ *boor*·ya

story разказ ⓜ *raz*·kaz

stove печка ⓕ *pech*·ka

straight прав prav

strange странен *stra*·nen

stranger непознат човек ⓜ
ne·poz·*nat* cho·*vek*

strawberry ягода ⓕ *ya*·go·da

stream n поток ⓜ po·*tok*

street улица ⓕ oo·*lee*·tsa

street market уличен пазар ⓜ
oo·lee·chen pa·*zar*

strike n стачка ⓕ *stach*·ka

string n връв ⓕ vruhv

stroke (health) удар ⓜ oo·*dar*

stroller (pram) бебешка количка ⓕ
be·*besh*·ka ko·*leech*·ka

strong силен *see*·len

stubborn упорит oo·po·*reet*

student студент/студентка ⓜ/ⓕ
stoo·*dent*/stoo·*dent*·ka

studio ателие ⓝ a·te·lee·*e*

stupid глупав *gloo*·pav

style n стил ⓜ steel

subtitles субтитри ⓕ pl soob·*teet*·ree

suburb предградие ⓝ pred·*gra*·dee·e

subway (train) метро ⓝ *met*·ro

sugar захар ⓜ *za*·har

suitcase куфар ⓜ *koo*·far

sultana стафида ⓕ sta·*fee*·da

summer лято ⓝ *lya*·to

sun слънце ⓝ *sluhn*·tse

sunblock слънцезащитен крем ⓜ
sluhn·tse·zash·*tee*·ten krem

sunburn слънчево изгаряне ⓝ
sluhn·che·vo eez·*gar*·ya·ne

sunglasses слънчеви очила ⓝ pl
sluhn·che·vee o·chee·*la*

sunny слънчев *sluhn*·chev

sunrise изгрев слънце ⓜ
eez·grev *sluhn*·tse

sunset залез слънце ⓜ *za*·lez *sluhn*·tse

sunstroke слънчев удар ⓜ
sluhn·chev oo·*dar*

supermarket супермаркет ⓜ
soo·per·mar·*ket*

superstition суеверие ⓝ soo·e·*ve*·ree·e

supporter (politics)
поддръжник/поддръжница ⓜ/ⓕ
pod·*druhzh*·neek/pod·*druhzh*·nee·tsa

supporter (sport) запалянко ⓜ
za·pa·*lyan*·ko

surf v сърфирам suhr·*fee*·ram

surface mail (land/sea) обикновена поща
ⓕ o·beek·no·*ve*·na *posh*·ta

surfboard сърф ⓜ suhrf

surfing сърфиране ⓝ suhr·*fee*·ra·ne

surname фамилно име ⓝ
fa·*meel*·no ee·me

surprise n изненада ⓕ eez·ne·*na*·da

sweater пуловер ⓜ poo·*lo*·ver

Sweden Швеция ⓕ *shve*·tsee·ya

sweet сладък *sla*·duhk

sweets сладкиши ⓜ pl slad·*kee*·shee

swelling подутина ⓕ po·doo·tee·*na*

swim v плувам *ploo*·vam

swimming плуване ⓝ *ploo*·va·ne

swimming pool плувен басейн ⓜ
ploo·ven ba·*seyn*

swimsuit бански костюм ⓜ
ban·skee kos·*tyoom*

Switzerland Швейцария ⓕ
shvey·*tsa*·ree·ya

synagogue синагога ⓕ see·na·*go*·ga

synthetic a синтетичен seen·te·*tee*·chen

syringe спринцовка ⓕ spreen·*tsov*·ka

T

table маса ⓕ *ma*·sa

tablecloth покривка ⓕ po·*kreev*·ka

table tennis тенис на маса ⓜ
te·nees na *ma*·sa

tail n опашка ⓕ o·*pash*·ka

tailor n шивач/шивачка ⓜ/ⓕ
shee·*vach*/shee·*vach*·ka

take v взема/взимам vze·muh/*vzee*·ma

take a photo снимам *snee*·mam

talk v говоря go·*vor*·yuh

tall висок vee·*sok*

tampon тампон ⓜ tam·*pon*

tanning lotion плажно масло ⓝ
plazh·no *mas*·lo

tap n кран ⓜ kran

tap water течаща вода ①
te-*chash*-ta vo-*da*

tasty вкусен *vkoo*-sen

tax n данък ⑩ *da*-nuhk

taxi такси ⑪ tak-*see*

taxi stand/rank таксиметрова стоянка ①
tak-*see*-me-tro-va sto-*yan*-ka

tea чай ⑩ chai

teacher учител/учителка ⑩/①
oo-*chee*-tel/oo-*chee*-tel-ka

team отбор ⑩ ot-*bor*

teaspoon чаена лъжичка ①
cha-e-na luh-*zheech*-ka

technique техника ① *teh*-nee-ka

teeth зъби ⑩ pl *zuh*-bee

telegram телеграма ① te-le-*gra*-ma

telephone n телефон ⑩ te-le-*fon*

telephone v обадя/обаждам се
o-*bad*-yuh/o-*bazh*-dam se

telephone centre телефонна централа ①
te-le-*fon*-na tsen-*tra*-la

telescope телескоп ⑩ te-le-*skop*

television телевизия ① te-le-*vee*-zee-ya

tell кажа/казвам *ka*-zhuh/*kaz*-vam

temperature (fever/weather)
температура ① tem-pe-ra-*too*-ra

tennis тенис ⑩ *te*-nees

tennis court тенискорт ⑩ te-nees-*kort*

tent палатка ① pa-*lat*-ka

tent peg копче на опъване на палатка ⑩
kop-che za o-*puh*-va-ne na pa-*lat*-ka

terrible ужасен oo-*zha*-sen

terrorism тероризъм ⑩ te-ro-*ree*-zuhm

terrorist терорист/терористка ⑩/①
te-ro-*reest*/te-ro-*reest*-ka

test n изпит ⑩ *eez*-peet

thank благодаря bla-go-dar-*yuh*

that а онзи *on*-zee

that (one) pron онзи *on*-zee

theatre театър ⑩ te-*a*-tuhr

their техен *te*-hen

there там tam

they те te

thick ръст guhst

thief крадец/крадка ⑩/①
kra-dets/*krad*-ka

thin тънък *tuh*-nuhk

think мисля *mees*-lyuh

thirsty жаден *zha*-den

this а този *to*-zee

this (one) pron този *to*-zee

thread n конец ⑩ ko-*nets*

throat гърло ⑩ *guhr*-lo

thrush (illness) стоматомикоза ①
sto-ma-to-mee-*ko*-za

thunder гръмотевица ①
gruh-mo-*te*-vee-tsa

ticket билет ⑩ bee-*let*

ticket collector кондуктор ⑩ kon-*dook*-tor

ticket machine
автомат за продаване на билети ⑩
av-to-*mat* za pro-*da*-va-ne na bee-*le*-tee

ticket office билетен център ⑩
bee-*le*-ten tsen-*tuhr*

(high/low) tide прилив/отлив ⑩
pree-leev/*ot*-leev

tight тесен *te*-sen

time n време ⑩ *vre*-me

time difference часова разлика ①
cha-so-va *raz*-lee-ka

timetable разписание ⑩ raz-pee-*sa*-nee-e

tin (can) консервна кутия ①
kon-*serv*-na koo-*tee*-ya

tin opener отварачка за консерви ①
ot-va-*rach*-ka za kon-*ser*-vee

tiny мъничък *muh*-nee-chuhk

tip (gratuity) n бакшиш ⑩ bak-*sheesh*

tire (car) гума ① *goo*-ma

tired уморен oo-*mo*-ren

tissues хартиени кърпички ① pl
har-*tee*-e-nee *kuhr*-peech-kee

to за za

toast препечен хляб ⑩ pre-*pe*-chen hlyab

toaster тостер ⑩ *tos*-ter

tobacco тютюн ⑩ tyoo-*tyoon*

tobacconist продавач на цигари ⑩
pro-*da*-vach za tsee-*ga*-ree

tobogganing спускане с тобоган ⑩
spoos-ka-ne s to-*bo*-gan

today днес dnes

toe пръст на крака ⑩ pruhst na kra-*kuh*

tofu тофу ⑩ *to*-foo

together заедно *za*-ed-no

toilet тоалетна ① to-a-*let*-na

toilet paper тоалетна хартия ①
to-a-*let*-na har-*tee*-ya

tomato домат ⑩ do-*mat*

tomorrow утре oo-*tre*

tonight довечера do-*ve*-che-ra

too (also) също *suhsh*-to

too (much) прекалено pre·ka·le·no

tooth зъб Ⓜ zuhb

toothache зъбобол Ⓜ zuh·bo·bol

toothbrush четка за зъби Ⓕ chet·ka za zuh·bee

toothpaste паста за зъби Ⓕ pas·ta za zuh·bee

toothpick клечка за зъби Ⓕ klech·ka za zuh·bee

torch (flashlight) фенерче Ⓝ fe·ner·che

touch v пипам pee·pam

tour n обиколка Ⓕ o·bee·kol·ka

tourist n турист/туристка Ⓜ/Ⓕ too·reest/too·reest·ka

tourist office туристическо бюро Ⓝ too·rees·tee·ches·ko byoo·ro

towards към kuhm

towel кърпа Ⓕ kuhr·pa

tower кула Ⓕ koo·la

toxic waste токсични отпадъци Ⓜ pl tok·seech·nee ot·pa·duh·tsee

toy shop магазин за играчки Ⓜ ma·ga·zeen za ee·grach·kee

track (path) пътека Ⓕ puh·te·ka

track (sport) писта Ⓕ pees·ta

trade n търговия Ⓕ tuhr·go·vee·ya

tradesperson търговец/търговка Ⓜ/Ⓕ tuhr·go·vets/tuhr·gov·ka

traffic n движение Ⓝ dvee·zhe·nee·e

traffic light светофар Ⓜ sve·to·far

trail n пътека Ⓕ puh·te·ka

train n влак Ⓜ vlak

train station гара Ⓕ ga·ra

tram трамвай Ⓜ tram·vai

transit lounge зала за транзитни пътници Ⓕ za·la za tran·zeet·nee puht·nee·tsee

translate преведа/превеждам pre·ve·duh/pre·vezh·dam

translator преводач/преводачка Ⓜ/Ⓕ pre·vo·dach/pre·vo·dach·ka

transport n транспорт Ⓜ trans·port

trash (garbage) боклук Ⓜ bok·look

travel v пътувам v puh·too·va·ne

travel agency пътническа агенция Ⓕ puht·nee·ches·ka a·gen·tsee·ya

travellers cheque пътнически чек Ⓜ puht·nee·ches·kee chek

travel sickness прилошаване по време на пътуване Ⓝ pree·lo·sha·va·ne po vre·me na puh·too·va·ne

tree дърво Ⓝ duhr·vo

trip (journey) пътуване Ⓝ puh·too·va·ne

trolley тролейбус Ⓜ tro·ley·boos

trousers панталони Ⓜ pl pan·ta·lo·nee

truck камион Ⓜ ka·mee·on

trust v доверя/доверявам се do·ver·yuh/do·ver·ya·vam se

try (attempt) опитам/опитвам се o·pee·tam/o·peet·vam se

try (taste) опитам/опитвам o·pee·tam/o·peet·vam

T-shirt тениска Ⓕ te·nees·ka

tube (tyre) вътрешна гума Ⓕ vuh·tresh·na goo·ma

tumour тумор Ⓜ too·mor

tuna риба тон Ⓕ ree·ba ton

tune n мелодия Ⓕ me·lo·dee·ya

turkey пуйка Ⓕ pooy·ka

Turkey Турция Ⓕ toor·tsee·ya

turn v завия/завивам za·vee·yuh/za·vee·vam

TV (set) телевизор Ⓜ te·le·vee·zor

tweezers пинцета Ⓕ peen·tse·ta

twice два пъти dva puh·tee

twin beds две единични легла Ⓝ pl dve e·dee·neech·nee leg·la

twins близнаци Ⓜ pl bleez·na·tsee

type n вид Ⓜ veed

typical типичен tee·pee·chen

tyre гума Ⓕ goo·ma

U

ultrasound ултразвук Ⓜ ool·tra·zvook

umbrella чадър Ⓜ cha·duhr

uncomfortable неудобен ne·oo·do·ben

understand разбера/разбирам raz·be·ruh/raz·bee·ram

underwear бельо Ⓝ bel·yo

unemployed безработен bez·ra·bo·ten

unfair несправедлив ne·spra·ved·leev

uniform n униформа Ⓕ oo·nee·for·ma

universe вселена Ⓕ vse·le·na

university университет Ⓜ oo·nee·ver·see·tet

unleaded petrol безоловен бензин ⓜ
bez-o-*lo*-ven ben-*zeen*

unsafe неосигурен ne-o-see-goo-*ren*

until до do

unusual необикновен ne-o-beek-no-*ven*

up горе *go*-re

uphill нагоре na-*go*-re

urgent спешен *spe*-shen

urinary tract infection инфекция на
пикочните канали ⓕ een-*fek*-tsee-ya
na *pee*-koch-nee-te ka-*na*-lee

USA САЩ sasht

useful полезен po-*le*-zen

V

vacancy свободни стаи ⓕ pl
svo-*bod*-nee sta-*yee*

vacant свободен svo-*bo*-den

vacation ваканция ⓕ va-*kan*-tsee-ya

vaccination ваксинация ⓕ
vak-see-*na*-tsee-ya

vagina влагалище ⓝ vla-*ga*-leesh-te

validate потвърдя/потвърждавам
pot-vuhr-*dyuh*/pot-vuhrzh-*da*-vam

valley долина ⓕ do-lee-*na*

valuable скъпоценен skuh-po-*tse*-nen

value (price) стойност ⓕ *stoy*-nost

van микробус ⓜ mee-kro-*boos*

veal телешко ⓝ *te*-lesh-ko

vegetable n зеленчук ⓜ ze-len-*chook*

vegetarian n
вегетарианец/вегетарианка ⓜ/ⓕ
ve-ge-ta-ree-*a*-nets/ve-ge-ta-ree-*an*-ka

vegetarian a вегетариански
ve-ge-ta-ree-*an*-skee

vein вена ⓕ *ve*-na

venue място ⓝ *myas*-to

very много *mno*-go

video camera видеокамера ⓕ
vee-de-o-*ka*-me-ra

video recorder видеомагнетофон ⓜ
vee-de-o-mag-ne-to-*fon*

video tape видеокасета ⓕ
vee-de-o-ka-*se*-ta

view n гледка ⓕ *gled*-ka

village село ⓝ *se*-lo

vine лоза ⓕ *lo*-za

vinegar оцет ⓜ *o*-tset

vineyard лозе ⓝ *lo*-ze

violin цигулка ⓕ tsee-*gool*-ka

virus вирус ⓜ *vee*-roos

visa виза ⓕ *vee*-za

visit v посетя/посещавам
po-set-*yuh*/po-sesh-*ta*-vam

visually impaired с увредено зрение
s oo-vre-de-no zre-nee-e

vitamin витамин ⓜ vee-ta-*meen*

vodka водка ⓕ *vod*-ka

voice n глас ⓜ glas

volleyball (sport) волейбол ⓜ *vo*-ley-bol

volume обем ⓜ o-*bem*

vote v гласувам gla-*soo*-vam

W

wage n заплата ⓕ za-*pla*-ta

wait чакам *cha*-kam

waiter сервитьор/сервитьорка ⓜ/ⓕ
ser-veet-*yor*/ser-veet-*yor*-ka

waiting room чакалня ⓕ cha-*kal*-nya

wake (someone) up събудя/събуждам
suh-*bood*-yuh/suh-*boozh*-dam

Wales Уелс ⓜ oo-*els*

walk v вървя vuhr-*vyuh*

wall (inner) зид ⓜ zeed

wall (outer) стена ⓕ ste-*na*

want искам *ees*-kam

war n война ⓕ voy-*na*

wardrobe гардероб ⓜ gar-de-*rob*

warm a топъл *to*-puhl

warn предупредя/предупреждавам
pre-doo-pre-*dyuh*/pre-doo-prezh-*da*-vam

wash (oneself) мия се *mee*-yuh se

wash (something) мия *mee*-yuh

washcloth (flannel) парцал за миене ⓜ
par-*tsal* za mee-e-ne

washing machine перална машина ⓕ
pe-*ral*-na ma-*shee*-na

wasp оса ⓕ o-*sa*

watch n часовник ⓜ cha-*sov*-neek

watch v гледам *gle*-dam

water n вода ⓕ vo-*da*

water bottle бутилка за вода ⓕ
boo-*teel*-ka za vo-*da*

waterfall водопад ⓜ vo-do-*pad*

watermelon диня ⓕ *deen*-ya

waterproof водонепромокаем
vo-do-ne-pro-mo-*ka*-em

water-skiing каране на водни ски ⓝ
ka-ra-ne na *vod*-nee skee

wave (ocean) вълна ⓕ vuhl-*na*

V

way (road) път ⓜ puht
way (manner) начин ⓜ na-cheen
we ние nee-e
weak слаб slab
wealthy богат bo-gat
wear v нося nos-yuh
weather n време ⓝ vre-me
wedding сватба ⓕ svat-ba
week седмица ⓕ sed-mee-tsa
weekend уикенд ⓜ oo-ee-kend
weigh тежа te-zhuh
weight тежест ⓕ te-zhest
weights (gym) тежести ⓕ pl te-zhes-tee
welcome v посрещна/посрещам
    po-sresht-nuh/po-sresh-tam
welfare n благосъстояние ⓝ
    bla-go-suhs-to-ya-nee-e
well adv добре do-bre
west запад ⓜ za-pad
wet a мокър mo-kuhr
what какво kak-vo
wheel колело ⓝ ko-le-lo
wheelchair инвалидна количка ⓕ
    een-va-leed-na ko-leech-ka
when кога ko-ga
where къде kuh-de
which кой koy
whisky уиски ⓝ oo-ees-kee
white бял byal
white wine бяло вино ⓝ bya-lo vee-no
who кой koy
why защо zash-to
wide широк shee-rok
wife жена ⓕ zhe-na
win v печеля pe-chel-yuh
wind n вятър ⓜ vya-tuhr
window прозорец ⓜ pro-zo-rets
windscreen предно стъкло ⓝ
    pred-no stuhk-lo
wine вино ⓝ vee-no
wings крила ⓝ pl kree-la
winner победител/победителка ⓜ/ⓕ
    po-be-dee-tel/po-be-dee-tel-ka
winter зима ⓕ zee-ma
wire n жица ⓕ zhee-tsa
wish v желая zhe-la-yuh
with c s
within (time) в рамките на v ram-kee-te na
without без bez
woman жена ⓕ zhe-na
wonderful чудесен choo-de-sen

wood дървен материал ⓜ
    duhr-ven ma-te-ree-al
wool вълна ⓕ vuhl-na
word дума ⓕ doo-ma
work n работа ⓕ ra-bo-ta
work v работя ra-bot-yuh
work experience професионален опит ⓜ
    pro-fe-see-o-na-len o-peet
work out v тренирам tre-nee-ram
work permit разрешително за работа ⓝ
    raz-re-shee-tel-no za ra-bo-ta
workshop семинар ⓜ se-mee-nar
world n свят ⓜ svyat
worms (intestinal) глисти ⓕ pl glees-tee
worried притеснен pree-tes-nen
worship v практикувам религия
    prak-tee-koo-vam re-lee-gee-ya
wrist китка ⓕ keet-ka
write пиша pee-shuh
writer писател/писателка ⓜ/ⓕ
    pee-sa-tel/pee-sa-tel-ka
wrong a погрешен po-gre-shen

Y

year година ⓕ go-dee-na
yellow жълт zhuhlt
yes да da
yesterday вчера vche-ra
(not) yet още (не) osh-te (ne)
yoga йога ⓕ yo-ga
yogurt кисело мляко ⓝ kee-se-lo mlya-ko
you inf sg ти tee
you pol sg вие vee-e
you pl вие vee-e
young млад mlad
your inf sg твой tvoy
your pol sg ваш vash
your pl ваш vash
youth hostel хостел ⓜ hos-tel

Z

zip/zipper цип ⓜ tseep
zodiac зодиак ⓜ zo-dee-ak
zoo зоопарк ⓜ zo-o-park
zoom lens вариообектив ⓜ
    va-ree-o-ob-ek-teev
zucchini тиквички ⓕ pl teek-veech-kee

bulgarian–english

Bulgarian nouns in the dictionary have their gender indicated by ⓜ (masculine), ⓕ (feminine) or ⓝ (neuter). If it's a plural noun, you'll also see pl. For added clarity, certain words are marked as nouns n, adjectives a, verbs v, adverbs adv, pronouns pron or prepositions prep. The abbreviations sg (singular), pl (plural), inf (informal) and pol (polite) are also used where necessary. Adjectives are given in the masculine singular form only. Verbs are given in their present tense first person singular form. Most verbs are given in two aspects: perfective and imperfective. The two forms are separated by a slash with the perfective form given first. Note that if the verb is followed by the particle **ce** se – eg *обадя/обаждам се* o-*bad*-yuh/o-*bazh*-dam se (to call) – the particle is used both with the perfective (*обадя се*) and imperfective form (*обаждам се*). If only one verb form is given, it means that form can be used as both imperfective and perfective. For more information, refer to the phrasebuilder.

The **bulgarian–english** dictionary has been ordered according to the Cyrillic alphabet, shown below in both roman and italic text:

Аа Бб Вв Гг Дд Ее Жж Зз Ии Йй Кк Лл Мм Нн Оо Пп
Аа Бб Вв Гг Дд Ее Жж Зз Ии Йй Кк Лл Мм Нн Оо Пп

Рр Сс Тт Уу Фф Хх Цц Чч Шш Щщ Ъъ ь Юю Яя
Рр Сс Тт Уу Фф Хх Цц Чч Шш Щщ Ъъ ь Юю Яя

А

Австралия ⓕ av-*stra*-lee-ya Australia
автобус ⓜ av-to-*boos* bus
автобусна спирка ⓕ
av-to-*boos*-na *speer*-ka bus stop
автогара ⓕ av-to-*ga*-ra bus station
агенция за недвижими имоти ⓕ
a-*gen*-tsee-ya za ned-*vee*-zhee-mee
ee-*mo*-tee estate agency
адаптор ⓜ a-*dap*-tor adaptor
адвокат ⓜ ad-vo-*kat* lawyer
адрес ⓜ a-*dres* address n
аз az I
Азия ⓕ *a*-zee-ya Asia
актьор/актриса ⓜ/ⓕ
ak-*tyor*/ak-*tree*-sa actor
алергия ⓕ a-*ler*-gee-ya allergy
алкохол ⓜ al-ko-*hol* alcohol
Америка ⓕ a-*me*-ree-ka America
английски ⓜ an-*gleey*-skee
English (language) n
Англия ⓕ *an*-glee-ya England

антибиотици ⓜ pl an-tee-bee-o-*tee*-tsee
antibiotics
антика ⓕ an-*tee*-ka antique n
антисептик ⓜ an-tee-sep-*teek*
antiseptic n
анулирам a-noo-*lee*-ram cancel
апартамент ⓜ a-par-ta-*ment* apartment
аптека ⓕ ap-*te*-ka chemist · pharmacy
аптекар/аптекарка ⓜ/ⓕ ap-te-*kar*/
ap-te-*kar*-ka chemist · pharmacist
аптечка ⓕ ap-*tech*-ka first-aid kit
архитект/архитектка ⓜ/ⓕ
ar-hee-*tekt*/ar-hee-*tekt*-ka architect
архитектура ⓕ ar-hee-tek-*too*-ra
architecture
асансьор ⓜ a-san-*syor* elevator · lift
аспирин ⓜ as-pee-*reen* aspirin
Африка ⓕ *a*-free-ka Africa
афтершейв ⓜ *af*-ter-sheyv aftershave

Б

баба ⓕ *ba*-ba grandmother
бавачка ⓕ ba-*vach*-ka babysitter

бавно bav·no slowly

багаж ⓜ ba·gazh baggage · luggage

бакшиш ⓜ bak·sheesh tip (gratuity)

Балкански полуостров ⓜ bal·kan·skee po·loo·os·trov Balkan Peninsula

балсам ⓜ bal·sam hair conditioner

банка ⓕ ban·ka bank

банкнота ⓕ bank·no·ta banknote

банкова сметка ⓕ ban·ko·va smet·ka bank account

банкомат ⓜ ban·ko·mat ATM

бански костюм ⓜ ban·skee kos·tyoom swimsuit

баня ⓕ ba·nya bath · bathroom

бар ⓜ bar bar

батерия ⓕ ba·te·ree·ya battery

баща ⓜ bash·ta father

бебе ⓝ be·be baby

бебешка количка ⓕ be·besh·ka ko·leech·ka pram · stroller

бебешка храна ⓕ be·besh·ka hra·na baby food

без bez without

безмитен магазин ⓜ bez·mee·ten ma·ga·zeen duty-free shop

безопасен секс ⓜ bez·o·pa·sen seks safe sex

безплатен bez·pla·ten complimentary (free)

бельо ⓝ bel·yo underwear

бензин ⓜ ben·zeen gas · petrol

бензиностанция ⓕ ben·zee·no·stan·tsee·ya petrol station

биберон ⓜ bee·be·ron dummy · pacifier

библиотека ⓕ bee·blee·o·te·ka library

бижута ⓕ bee·zhoo·ta jewellery

бизнес класа ⓕ beez·nes kla·sa business class

билет ⓜ bee·let ticket

билетен център ⓜ bee·le·ten tsen·tuhr ticket office

битпазар ⓜ beet·pa·zar fleamarket

благодарен bla·go·da·ren grateful

близо до blee·zo do near prep

близък blee·zuhk close a

болезнен bo·lez·nen painful

болен bo·len sick

болка ⓕ bol·ka pain

болки в стомаха ⓕ pl bol·kee v sto·ma·huh stomach ache

болкоуспокоителни лекарства ⓝ pl bol·ko·oos·po·ko·ee·tel·nee le·karst·va painkillers

болница ⓕ bol·nee·tsa hospital

бордна карта ⓕ bord·na kar·ta boarding pass

брат ⓜ brat brother

бременна bre·men·na pregnant

брошура ⓕ bro·shoo·ra brochure

бръсна се bruhs·nuh se shave v

будилник ⓜ boo·deel·neek alarm clock

будка ⓕ bood·ka kiosk

бутилка ⓕ boo·teel·ka bottle

българин/българка ⓜ/ⓕ buhl·ga·reen/buhl·gar·ka Bulgarian (person) n

България ⓕ buhl·ga·ree·ya Bulgaria

български buhl·gar·skee Bulgarian (language) n

български buhl·gar·skee Bulgarian a

бърз buhrz fast a

бърза поща ⓕ buhr·za posh·ta express mail

бюджет ⓜ byood·zhet budget n

бюфет ⓜ byoo·fet buffet

бял byal white

В

вагон-ресторант ⓜ va·gon·res·to·rant dining car

важен va·zhen important

ваканция ⓕ va·kan·tsee·ya vacation

ваксинация ⓕ vak·see·na·tsee·ya vaccination

ваш vash your sg pol&pl

вегетарианец/вегетарианка ⓜ/ⓕ ve·ge·ta·ree·a·nets/ve·ge·ta·ree·an·ka vegetarian n

вегетариански ve·ge·ta·ree·an·skee vegetarian a

Великден ⓜ ve·leek·den Easter

велосипед ⓜ ve·lo·see·ped bicycle

вентилатор ⓜ ven·tee·la·tor fan (machine)

вестник ⓜ vest·neek newspaper

вечер ⓕ ve·cher evening

вечеря ⓕ ve·che·rya dinner

взема/взимам под наем vze·muh/vze·mam pod na·em rent v

видеокамера ⓕ vee·de·o·*ka*·me·ra
video camera

видеокасета ⓕ vee·de·o·ka·*se*·ta
video tape

видеомагнетофон ⓜ
vee·de·o·mag·ne·to·*fon* video recorder

вие *vee*·e you sg pol&pl

виза ⓕ *vee*·za visa

вилица ⓕ *vee*·lee·tsa fork

висока температура ⓕ
vee·*so*·ka tem·pe·ra·*too*·ra fever

вкусен *vkoo*·sen tasty

влак ⓜ vlak train n

вляза/влизам *vlya*·zuh/*vlee*·zam enter

внуче ⓝ *vnoo*·che grandchild

вода ⓕ vo·*da* water n

връщане на парите ⓝ
vrush·ta·ne na pa·*ree*·te refund n

всеки *vse*·kee each • every • everyone

всичко *vseech*·ko all pron • everything

втора класа ⓕ *vto*·ra *kla*·sa second class

ход ⓜ vhod entry

входна такса ⓕ *vhod*·na *tak*·sa
admission price

вчера *vche*·ra yesterday

чужбина v choozh·*bee*·na overseas

възглавница ⓕ vuhz·*glav*·nee·tsa pillow

въздушна поща ⓕ
vuhz·*doosh*·na *posh*·ta airmail

вълна ⓕ *vuhl*·na wool

вървя vuhr·*vyuh* walk v

връна/връщам се
vuhr·na/*vrush*·tam se return v

вътрешна гума ⓕ *vuh*·tresh·na *goo*·ma
tyre

Г

гадене ⓝ *ga*·de·ne nausea

гадже ⓝ *gad*·zhe boyfriend • girlfriend

газ ⓜ gaz gas (for cooking)

галерия ⓕ ga·*le*·ree·ya art gallery

гара ⓕ *ga*·ra railway station

гаранция ⓕ ga·*ran*·tsee·ya guarantee n

гардероб ⓜ gar·de·*rob* cloakroom •
left-luggage office • luggage locker

гастроентерит ⓜ gas·tro·en·te·*reet*
gastroenteritis

гей ⓜ&ⓕ gey gay (homosexual) n&a

глава ⓕ gla·*va* head

главен готвач ⓜ *gla*·ven got·*vach*
chef (man)

главна готвачка ⓕ *glav*·na got·*vach*·ka
chef (woman)

главоболие ⓝ gla·vo·bo·*lee*·e headache

гладен *gla*·den hungry

гледам *gle*·dam look v • watch v

гледка ⓕ *gled*·ka view n

глезен ⓜ *gle*·zen ankle

глоба ⓕ *glo*·ba fine (payment) n

говоря go·*vor*·yuh speak

годеж ⓜ go·*dezh* engagement (to marry)

годеник ⓜ go·de·*neek* fiancé

годеница ⓕ go·de·*nee*·tsa fiancée

година ⓕ go·*dee*·na year

голям go·*lyam* big

гора ⓕ go·*ra* forest

горе *go*·re up

горещ go·*resht* hot (temperature)

горещина ⓕ go·resh·tee·*na* heat n

горчив gor·*cheev* bitter

готвач/готвачка ⓜ/ⓕ
got·*vach*/got·*vach*·ka cook n

готвя *got*·vyuh cook v

град ⓜ grad city

градина ⓕ gra·*dee*·na garden n

градски автобус ⓜ
grad·skee av·to·*boos* city bus

грам ⓜ gram gram

граница ⓕ *gra*·nee·tsa border (country)

гребен ⓜ *gre*·ben comb n

грейка ⓕ *grey*·ka hot water bottle

грим ⓜ greem make-up

грип ⓜ greep flu

гробище ⓝ *gro*·beesh·te cemetery

гръб ⓜ gruhb back (body)

гръден кош ⓜ *gruh*·den kosh chest (body)

гума ⓕ *goo*·ma tyre

гърло ⓝ *guhr*·lo throat

Гърция ⓕ *guhr*·tsee·ya Greece

Д

да da yes

далече da·*le*·che far adv

дамска превръзка ⓕ
dam·ska pre·*vruhz*·ka
panty liner • sanitary napkin

дамска чанта ① *dam*·ska *chan*·ta *purse*
дата ① *da*·ta *date (day)*
дата на раждане ① *da*·ta na *razh*·da·ne *date of birth*
две седмици ① pl dve *sed*·mee·tsee *fortnight*
двойно легло ⑩ *dvoy*·no *leg*·lo *double bed*
дворец ⑩ *dvo*·rets *palace*
двупосочен билет ⑩ dvoo·po·*so*·chen bee·*let* *return ticket*
дезодорант ⑩ de·zo·do·*rant* *deodorant*
ден ⑩ den *day*
денонощен магазин ⑩ de·no·*nosh*·ten ma·ga·*zeen* *convenience store*
депозит ⑩ de·po·*zeet* *deposit* n
десен de·sen *right (direction)* a
дестинация ① des·tee·*na*·tsee·ya *destination*
дете ⑩ de·*te* *child*
детска седалка ① *det*·ska se·*dal*·ka *child seat (car)*
дефектен de·*fek*·ten *faulty*
деца ⑩ pl de·*tsa* *children*
джобно ножче ⑩ *dzhob*·no *nozh*·che *penknife*
диабет ⑩ dee·a·*bet* *diabetes*
диапозитивен филм ⑩ dee·a·po·zee·*tee*·ven feelm *slide film*
диария ① dee·a·*ree*·a *diarrhoea*
дипломатическо куфарче ⑩ dee·plo·ma·*tee*·ches·ko *koo*·far·che *briefcase*
директор/директорка ⑩/① dee·*rek*·tor/dee·*rek*·tor·ka *manager (business)*
диск ⑩ deesk *disk (CD-ROM)*
дискета ① dees·*ke*·ta *floppy disk*
дистанционно управление ⑩ dees·tan·tsee·o·no oo·prav·*le*·nee·e *remote control*
дневник ⑩ *dnev*·neek *diary*
днес dnes *today*
до do *beside* • *until*
добър do·*buhr* *good*
довечера do·ve·che·ra *tonight*
долар ⑩ *do*·lar *dollar*
долу *do*·loo *down*
дом ⑩ dom *home*
досаден do·*sa*·den *boring*

доставя/доставям do·*stav*·yuh/do·*stav*·yam *deliver*
достатъчен do·*sta*·tuh·chen *enough*
дрехи ① pl *dre*·hee *clothing*
друг droog *another* • *other*
другар ⑩ droo·*gar* *companion*
Дунав ⑩ *doo*·nav *Danube*
душ ⑩ doosh *shower* n
дъжд ⑩ duhzhd *rain* n
дъждобран ⑩ duhzh·do·*bran* *raincoat*
дълъг *duh*·luhg *long*
дъщеря ① duhsh·ter·*ya* *daughter*
дядо ⑩ *dya*·do *grandfather*

Е

евро ⑩ *ev*·ro *euro*
Европа ① *ev*·ro·pa *Europe*
Европейският съюз ⑩ ev·ro·*pey*·skee·yuht suh·*yooz* *European Union*
евтин *ev*·teen *cheap*
Егейско море ⑩ e·*gey*·sko mo·re *Aegean Sea*
единична стая ① e·dee·*neech*·na *sta*·ya *single room*
еднопосочен билет ⑩ ed·no·po·*so*·chen bee·*let* *one-way ticket*
ежедневно e·zhed·*nev*·no *daily* adv
езеро ⑩ *e*·ze·ro *lake*
език ⑩ e·*zeek* *language*
екскурзия ① eks·*koor*·zee·ya *guided tour*
екскурзовод/екскурзоводка ⑩/① eks·koor·zo·*vod*/eks·koor·zo·*vod*·ka *guide (person)*
електричество ⑩ e·lek·*tree*·chest·vo *electricity*
ескалатор ⑩ es·ka·*la*·tor *escalator*
етаж ⑩ e·*tazh* *floor (storey)*

Ж

жаден *zha*·den *thirsty*
жена ① zhe·*na* *wife* • *woman*
женен ⑩ *zhe*·nen *married (man)*
женски *zhen*·skee *female* a
жилище ⑩ *zhee*·leesh·te *accommodation*

журналист/журналистка ⓜ/ⓕ
zhoor·na·*leest*/zhoor·na·*leest*·ka
journalist
кълт zhuhlt *yellow*

З

за za *about* • *to*
зад zad *behind*
задръстен za·*druhs*·ten *blocked*
за една нощ za ed·*na* nosht
overnight adv
заедно za·*ed*·no *together*
заключен za·*klyoo*·chen *locked*
закуска ⓕ za·*koos*·ka *breakfast* • *snack*
закъснение ⓝ za·kuhs·*ne*·nee·e *delay* n
залез слънце za·*lez* sluhn·tse *sunset*
замина/заминавам
za·mee·*nuh*/za·mee·*na*·vam *depart*
заминаване ⓝ za·mee·*na*·va·ne
departure
замръзнал za·*mruhz*·nal *frozen*
замък ⓜ *za*·muhk *castle*
занаяти ⓜ pl za·na·*ya*·tee *crafts*
за непушачи za ne·poo·*sha*·chee
nonsmoking
запад ⓜ *za*·pad *west*
запалка ⓕ za·*pal*·ka *cigarette lighter*
запек ⓜ *za*·pek *constipation*
запушалка ⓕ za·poo·*shal*·ka
plug (bath)
застраховка ⓕ za·stra·*hov*·ka *insurance*
затворен zat·*vo*·ren *closed* • *shut*
затворя/затварям
zat·*vor*·yuh/zat·*var*·yam *close* v • *shut* v
затоплен za·*top*·len *heated*
защо zash·*to* *why*
зелен ze·*len* *green*
зеленчук ⓜ ze·len·*chook* *vegetable* n
зима ⓕ *zee*·ma *winter*
злато ⓝ *zla*·to *gold* n
злополука ⓕ zlo·po·*loo*·ka *accident*
зоопарк ⓜ zo·o·*park* *zoo*
зора ⓕ *zo*·ra *dawn*
зъбобол ⓜ zuh·bo·*bol* *toothache*
зъболекар/зъболекарка ⓜ/ⓕ
zuh·bo·*le*·kar/zuh·bo·*le*·kar·ka *dentist*

И

и ee *and*
игла ⓕ eeg·*la* *needle (sewing)*
игрище ⓝ ee·*greesh*·te *sports court*
и двата/двете ⓜ/ⓕ&ⓝ
ee *dva*·ta/*dve*·te *both*
изгаряне ⓝ eez·*gar*·ya·ne *burn* n
изгрев слънце ⓜ eez·grev sluhn·tse
sunrise
изгубен eez·*goo*·ben *lost*
изкуство ⓝ eez·*koost*·vo *art*
изложба ⓕ eez·*lozh*·ba *exhibition*
изляза/излизам (с)
eez·*lya*·zuh/eez·*lee*·zam (s) *go out (with)*
изпусна/изпускам eez·*poos*·nuh/
ees·*poos*·kam *miss (train, etc)* v
изсуша/изсушавам eez·soo·*shuh*/
eez·soo·*sha*·vam *dry (clothes)* v
изток ⓜ *eez*·tok *east* n
изход ⓜ *eez*·hod *exit*
имам *ee*·mam *have*
име ⓝ *ee*·me *name* n
и-мейл ⓜ *ee*·meyl *email* n
инвалиден een·va·*lee*·den *disabled*
инвалидна количка ⓕ
een·va·*leed*·na ko·*leech*·ka *wheelchair*
инжекция ⓕ een·*zhek*·tsee·ya *injection*
инженер ⓜ een·zhe·*ner* *engineer*
инженерство ⓝ een·zhe·*nerst*·vo
engineering
Интернет ⓜ een·ter·*net* *internet*
Интернет кафе ⓝ een·ter·net ka·*fe*
internet café
инфекция ⓕ een·*fek*·tsee·ya *infection*
информационна агенция ⓕ
een·for·ma·tsee·*on*·na a·*gen*·tsee·ya
newsagency
информационни технологии ⓕ pl
een·for·ma·tsee·o·nee teh·no·*lo*·gee·ee
IT (information technology)
информация ⓕ een·for·*ma*·tsee·ya
information

К

калкулатор ⓜ kal·koo·*la*·tor *calculator*
калъфка за възглавница ⓕ ka·*luhf*·ka
za vuhz·*glav*·nee·tsa *pillowcase*

Канада ⓕ *ka·na·da Canada*
карам *ka·ram drive* v
каране на ски ⓝ *ka·ra·ne na skee skiing*
карта ⓕ *kar·ta map (of country)*
каса ⓕ *ka·sa cash register*
касетка ⓕ *ka·set·ka cassette*
касиер/касиерка ⓜ/ⓕ
  ka·see·er/ka·see·er·ka cashier
катедрала ⓕ *ka·te·dra·la cathedral*
катинар ⓜ *ka·tee·nar padlock*
кафене ⓝ *ka·fe·ne café*
кафяв *kaf·yav brown*
кача/качвам се *ka·chuh/kach·vam se*
  board (a plane, etc)
кашлям *kash·lyam cough* v
кибрит ⓜ *kee·breet*
  matches (for lighting)
килограм ⓜ *kee·lo·gram kilogram*
километър ⓜ *kee·lo·me·tuhr kilometre*
кино ⓝ *kee·no cinema • movie*
класически *kla·see·ches·kee classical*
клиент/клиентка ⓜ/ⓕ
  klee·ent/klee·ent·ka client
ключ ⓜ *klyooch key* n
ключалка ⓕ *klyoo·chal·ka lock* n
книга ⓕ *knee·ga book* n
книжарница ⓕ *knee·zhar·nee·tsa*
  book shop
кога *ko·ga when*
кожа ⓕ *ko·zha leather* n
козметичен салон ⓜ
  koz·me·tee·chen sa·lon beauty salon
кой *koy which • who*
кола ⓕ *ko·la car*
колега ⓕ *ko·le·ga colleague*
колет ⓜ *ko·let parcel*
коляно ⓝ *ko·lya·no knee*
командировка ⓕ *ko·man·dee·rov·ka*
  business trip
комисионна ⓕ *ko·mee·see·on·na*
  commission
компания ⓕ *kom·pa·nee·ya company*
компютър ⓜ *kom·pyoo·tuhr computer*
комунистически
  ko·moo·nees·tee·ches·kee communist a
конец за зъби ⓜ *ko·nets za zuh·bee*
  dental floss
конна езда ⓕ *kon·na ez·da horse riding*
консервна кутия ⓕ
  kon·serv·na koo·tee·ya can • tin

консулство ⓝ *kon·soolst·vo consulate*
контактни лещи ⓕ pl
  kon·takt·nee lesh·tee contact lenses
контузия ⓕ *kon·too·zee·ya injury*
конференция ⓕ *kon·fe·ren·tsee·ya*
  big conference
концерт ⓜ *kon·tsert concert • gig*
коприна ⓕ *ko·pree·na silk* n
копче ⓝ *kop·che button* n
кораб ⓜ *ko·rab boat*
кофа за боклук ⓕ *ko·fa za bok·look*
  garbage can
край ⓜ *krai end* n
крак ⓜ *krak foot (body) • leg (body)*
кран ⓜ *kran faucet • tap*
красив *kra·seev beautiful • handsome*
кредит ⓜ *kre·deet credit* n
кредитна карта ⓕ *kre·deet·na kar·ta*
  credit card
крем за бръснене ⓜ
  krem za bruhs·ne·ne shaving cream
кръв ⓕ *kruhv blood*
кръвна група ⓕ *kruhv·na groo·pa*
  blood group
кръчма ⓕ *kruhch·ma bar • pub*
купа ⓕ *koo·pa bowl* n
купон ⓜ *koo·pon party (entertainment)*
купя/купувам *koop·yuh/koo·poo·vam*
  buy
кутия ⓕ *koo·tee·ya box* n
куфар ⓜ *koo·far suitcase*
кухня ⓕ *kooh·nya kitchen*
куче ⓝ *koo·che dog*
къде *kuh·de where*
къмпинг ⓜ *kuhm·peeng*
  camping ground
кърпа ⓕ *kuhr·pa towel*
кърпа за лице ⓕ *kuhr·pa za lee·tse*
  face cloth
късно *kuhs·no late* adv

Л

лаптоп ⓜ *lap·top laptop*
лед ⓜ *led ice*
лейкопласт ⓜ *ley·ko·plast Band-Aid*
лек *lek light (weight)* a
лекар/лекарка ⓜ/ⓕ *le·kar/le·kar·ka*
  doctor

лекарство ⓝ le·karst·vo
drug (medication)
леля ⓕ lel·ya *aunt*
лен ⓜ len *linen (fabric)*
летище ⓝ le·teesh·te *airport*
летищна такса ⓕ le·teesht·na tak·sa
airport tax
лилав цвят lee·lav tsvyat *purple*
линейка ⓕ lee·ney·ka *ambulance*
лице ⓝ lee·tse *face* n
лична карта ⓕ leech·na kar·ta
identification
лош losh *bad*
лошо храносмилане ⓜ
lo·sho hra·no·smee·la·ne *indigestion*
лъжица ⓕ luh·zhee·tsa *spoon*
любезен lyoo·be·zen *kind (nice)*
ляв lyav *left (direction)*
лято ⓝ lya·to *summer*

М

магазин ⓜ ma·ga·zeen *shop* n
магазин за деликатеси ⓜ ma·ga·zeen
za de·lee·ka·te·see *delicatessen*
магазин за електроуреди ⓜ
ma·ga·zeen za e·lek·tro·oo·re·dee
electrical store
магазин за облекло ⓜ
ma·ga·zeen za o·blek·lo *clothing store*
магазин за обувки ⓜ
ma·ga·zeen za o·boov·kee *shoe shop*
магазин за сувенири ⓜ ma·ga·zeen za
soo·ve·nee·ree *souvenir shop*
магистрала ⓕ ma·gees·tra·la
highway • motorway
майка ⓕ mai·ka *mother*
македония ⓕ ma·ke·don·ski
Macedonian
малък ma·luhk *small*
малък хотел ⓜ ma·luhk ho·tel *guesthouse*
мама ⓕ ma·ma *mum*
марка ⓕ mar·ka *postage stamp*
маршрут ⓜ marsh·root *itinerary*
масаж ⓜ ma·sazh *massage* n
масажист ⓜ ma·sa·zheest *masseur*
масажистка ⓕ ma·sa·zheest·ka
masseuse
матрак ⓜ mat·rak *mattress*

мач ⓜ mach *sports match*
мебели ⓜ pl me·be·lee *furniture*
меден месец ⓜ me·den me·sets
honeymoon
медицина ⓕ me·dee·tsee·na
medicine (study/profession)
медицинска сестра ⓕ
me·dee·tseen·ska ses·tra *nurse* n
междуградски автобус ⓜ
mezh·doo·grad·skee av·to·boos
coach (bus)
мене me·ne *me*
меню ⓝ men·yoo *menu*
месарница ⓕ me·sar·nee·tsa
butcher's shop
месец ⓜ me·sets *month*
месо ⓝ me·so *meat*
местен mes·ten *local* a
метър ⓜ me·tuhr *metre*
мехур ⓜ me·hoor *blister*
микровълнова печка ⓕ
mee·kro·vuhl·no·va pech·ka
microwave oven
милиметър ⓜ mee·lee·me·tuhr
millimetre
минал mee·nal *last (previous)*
минута ⓕ mee·noo·ta *minute*
миризма ⓕ mee·reez·ma *smell* n
митница ⓕ meet·nee·tsa
customs (immigration)
мия mee·yuh *wash (something)*
мляко ⓝ mlya·ko *milk*
мода ⓕ mo·da *fashion*
модем ⓜ mo·dem *modem*
мозъчно сътресение ⓝ mo·zuhch·no
suh·tre·se·nee·e *concussion*
мой moy *my*
молив ⓜ mo·leev *pencil*
момиче ⓝ mo·mee·che *girl*
момче ⓝ mom·che *boy*
монети ⓕ pl mo·ne·tee *change (coins)* n
море ⓝ mo·re *sea*
мост ⓜ most *bridge* n
мотел ⓜ mo·tel *motel*
мотор ⓜ mo·tor *engine*
мръсен mruh·sen *dirty*
музей ⓜ moo·zey *museum*
музика ⓕ moo·zee·ka *music*
музикален магазин ⓜ
moo·zee·ka·len ma·ga·zeen *music shop*

bulgarian–english

муха ① moo·ha fly n
мъж ⓜ muhzh husband

Н

на na at • on • per (day, etc)
наблизо na·blee·zo nearby adv
на борда na bor·da aboard
набързо na·buhr·zo in a hurry
навреме na·vre·me on time
навън na·vuhn outside adv
навяхване ⓝ nav·yah·va·ne sprain n
надценка ① nad·tsen·ka cover charge
наем ⓜ na·em rent n
наема/наемам na·e·muh/na·e·mam hire v
наемане на кола na·e·ma·ne na ko·la
    car hire
най-близкият nai·bleez·kee·yuht nearest
най-голям nai·go·lyam biggest
най-добър nai·do·buhr best
най-малкият nai·mal·kee·yuht smallest
намаление ⓝ na·ma·lee·nee·e discount n
напитка ① na·peet·ka drink n
наркотик ⓜ nar·ko·teek dope (drugs)
наркотици ⓜ pl nar·ko·tee·tsee
    illicit drugs
на самообслужване
    na sa·mo·ob·sloozh·va·ne self-service
наука ① na·oo·ka science
наш nash our
не ne no
негов ne·gov his
неженен ⓜ ne·zhe·nen single (man) a
неин ne·een her (possessive)
неомъжена ① ne·o·muh·zhe·na
    single (woman) a
неудобен ne·oo·do·ben uncomfortable
нефт ⓜ neft oil (petrol)
нисък nee·suhk short (height)
нищо neesh·to nothing
нов nov new
Нова година ① no·va go·dee·na
    New Year's Day
Нова Зеландия ① no·va ze·lan·dee·ya
    New Zealand
новина ① no·vee·na news
Новогодишна нощ ①
    no·vo·go·deesh·na nosht New Year's Eve
нож ⓜ nozh knife

ножица ① no·zhee·tsa scissors
ножче за бръснене ⓝ
    nozh·che za bruhs·ne·ne razor blade
нокторезачка ① nok·to·re·zach·ka
    nail clippers
номер ⓜ no·mer size
номер на паспорта ⓜ
    no·mer na pas·por·ta passport number
номер на стаята ① no·mer na sta·ya·ta
    room number
нос ⓜ nos nose
носна кърпичка ①
    nos·na kuhr·peech·ka handkerchief
нощ ① nosht night
нощен клуб ⓜ nosh·ten kloob nightclub
нощ на открито ① nosht na ot·kree·to
    night out

О

обадя/обаждам се o·bad·yuh/
    o·bazh·dam se call v • telephone v
обед ⓜ o·bed lunch
обектив ⓜ o·bek·teev lens (camera)
обикновена поща ① o·beek·no·ve·na
    posh·ta surface mail (land/sea)
обиколка ① o·bee·kol·ka tour n
обици ① pl o·bee·tsee earrings
обич ① o·beech love n
обичай ⓜ o·bee·chai custom
обичам o·bee·cham love v
обменен курс на валутата ⓜ
    ob·me·nen koors na va·loo·ta·ta
    exchange rate
обмяна на валута ① ob·mya·na na
    va·loo·ta currency exchange
обслужване ⓝ ob·sloozh·va·ne service
обувки ① pl o·boov·kee shoes
обществена тоалетна ①
    obsh·test·ve·na to·a·let·na public toilet
обяд ⓜ ob·yad midday
огледало ⓝ o·gle·da·lo mirror n
огърлица ① o·guhr·lee·tsa necklace
одеяло ⓝ o·de·ya·lo blanket
око ⓝ o·ko eye
олио ⓝ o·lee·o oil (cooking)
омъжена ① o·muh·zhe·na
    married (woman)
онзи on·zee that a • that one pron

опасен o·pa·sen dangerous
опитам/опитвам o·pee·tam/o·peet·vam try (taste)
опитам/опитвам се o·pee·tam/o·peet·vam se try (attempt)
оплакване ⓝ o·plak·va·ne complaint
оранжев o·ran·zhev orange (colour)
осребря/осребрявам o·sreb·ryuh/o·sreb·rya·vam cash (a cheque) v
останки ⓝ pl o·stan·kee ruins
остров os·trov island
от ot from
отварачка за бутилки ⓕ ot·va·rach·ka na boo·teel·kee bottle opener
отварачка за консерви ⓕ ot·va·rach·ka za kon·ser·vee can opener • tin opener
отида/отивам o·tee·duh/o·tee·vam go
отида/отивам на поход o·tee·duh/o·tee·vam na po·hod hike v
откраднат ot·krad·nat stolen
отново ot·no·vo again
очила ⓝ pl o·chee·la glasses (spectacles)
очистително ⓝ o·chees·tee·tel·no laxative n

П

пазар pa·zar market n
пазарувам pa·za·roo·vam shop v
пакет pa·ket package • packet
палто pal·to coat
памук pa·mook cotton n
пансион pan·see·on boarding house
панталони ⓝ pl pan·ta·lo·nee pants • trousers
пари ⓕ pl pa·ree money
пари в брой ⓕ pl pa·ree v broy cash n
паркирам par·kee·ram park (a car) v
парфюм par·fyoom perfume
паспорт pas·port passport
паста за зъби pas·ta za zuh·bee toothpaste
пауза ⓕ pa·oo·za intermission
пелена pe·le·na diaper • nappy
пенсионер/пенсионерка ⓜ/ⓕ pen·see·o·ner/pen·see·o·ner·ka pensioner
пепелник ⓜ pe·pel·neek ashtray

перална машина ⓕ pe·ral·na ma·shee·na washing machine
пешеходство ⓝ pe·she·hod·stvo hiking
пиеса ⓕ pee·e·sa play (theatre) n
пикник ⓜ peek·neek picnic
пинцета ⓕ peen·tse·ta tweezers
писалка ⓕ pee·sal·ka pen
писмо pees·mo letter (mail)
пиша pee·shuh write
пия pee·yuh drink v
пиян pee·yan drunk
плаж ⓜ plazh beach
плажно масло ⓝ plazh·no mas·lo tanning lotion
план ⓜ plan map (of town)
планина ⓕ pla·nee·na mountain
плащане ⓝ plash·ta·ne payment
плик за писмо ⓜ pleek za pees·mo envelope
плод ⓜ plod fruit
плосък plo·suhk flat a
площад ⓜ plo·shtad town square
плувам ploo·vam swim v
плувен басейн ⓜ ploo·ven ba·seyn swimming pool
повече po·ve·che more
повреден po·vre·den broken • out of order
по-голям po·go·lyam bigger
подарък ⓜ po·da·ruhk gift
по-добър po·do·buhr better
подстригване ⓝ pod·streeg·va·ne haircut
поздравя/поздравявам poz·drav·yuh/poz·drav·ya·vam congratulate
покажа/показвам po·ka·zhuh/po·kaz·vam show v
по-късно po·kuhs·no later adv
пол pol sex (gender)
пола ⓕ po·la skirt
полет ⓜ po·let flight
полицай/полицайка ⓜ/ⓕ po·lee·tsai/po·lee·tsai·ka police officer
полицейски участък ⓜ po·lee·tsey·skee oo·chas·tuhk police station
полиция ⓕ po·lee·tsee·ya police
половина po·lo·vee·na half n
полунощ ⓕ po·loo·nosht midnight
получаване на багаж po·loo·cha·va·ne na ba·gazh baggage claim

по-малко po-mal-ko less

по-малък po-ma-luhk smaller

помогна/помагам
po-mog-nuh/po-ma-gam help v

помощ ① po-mosht help n

поправя/поправям
po-prav-yuh/po-prav-yam repair v

последен po-sle-den last (final)

посока ① po-so-ka direction

посолство ⑩ po-solst-vo embassy

потвърдя/потвърждавам
pot-vuhr-dyuh/pot-vuhrzh-da-vam
confirm (a booking) • validate

почивка ① po-cheev-ka rest n

поща ① posh-ta mail • post office

пощенска картичка ①
posh-ten-ska kar-teech-ka postcard

пощенска кутия ①
posh-ten-ska koo-tee-ya mailbox

пощенски код ⑩ posh-ten-skee kod
postcode

право ⑩ pra-vo law (study/profession)

празен pra-zen empty a

празник ⑩ praz-neek holiday

пране ⑩ pra-ne laundry (clothes)

преведа/превеждам
pre-ve-duh/pre-vezh-dam translate

превръзка ① pre-vruhz-ka bandage

преди pre-dee before

предпазен колан ⑩ pred-pa-zen ko-lan
seatbelt

представление ⑩ pred-stav-le-nee-e
show n

презерватив ⑩ pre-zer-va-teev condom

препоръчам/препоръчвам
pre-po-ruh-cham/pre-po-ruhch-vam
recommend

препоръчана поща ①
pre-po-ruh-cha-na posh-ta
registered mail

прибори за хранене ⑩ pl
pree-bo-ree za hra-ne-ne cutlery

принтър ⑩ preen-tuhr
printer (computer)

пристигане ⑩ pree-stee-ga-ne
arrivals (airport)

приятел/приятелка ⑩/①
pree-ya-tel/pree-ya-tel-ka friend

пробна ① prob-na changing room

провинция ① pro-veen-tsee-ya
countryside

прозорец ⑩ pro-zo-rets window

пролет ① pro-let spring (season)

промяна ① pro-mya-na change n

проститутка ① pros-tee-toot-ka
prostitute n

процент за обслужване ⑩ pro-tsent za
ob-sloozh-va-ne service charge

пръст ⑩ pruhst finger

пръстен ⑩ pruhs-ten ring (jewellery)

пряк pryak direct a

пуловер ⑩ poo-lo-ver jumper • sweater

пура ① poo-ra cigar

пуша poo-shuh smoke v

пълен puh-len full

първа класа ① puhr-va kla-sa first class

път ⑩ puht road • way

пътеводител ⑩ puh-te-vo-dee-tel
guidebook

пътека ① puh-te-ka
aisle (plane, etc) • footpath • path

пътник/пътничка ⑩/①
puht-neek/puht-neech-ka passenger

пътническа агенция ①
puht-nee-ches-ka a-gen-tsee-ya
travel agency

пътнически чек ⑩ puht-nee-ches-kee
chek travellers cheque

пътувам на автостоп
puh-too-vam na av-to-stop hitchhike

пътуване ① puh-too-va-ne journey n

Р

работа ① ra-bo-ta job

работно време ⑩ ra-bot-no vre-me
opening hours

радио ⑩ ra-dee-o radio

развален raz-va-len broken down

разведен raz-ve-den divorced

развлекателна програма ①
raz-vle-ka-tel-na pro-gra-ma
entertainment guide

разговорник ⑩ raz-go-vor-neek
phrasebook

разкош ⑩ ras-kosh luxury

различен raz-lee-chen different

разменя/разменям
raz-men-yuh/raz-men-yam *exchange* v

азписание ⓝ raz-pee-sa-nee-e
timetable

азписка ⓕ raz-pees-ka *receipt*

амо ⓝ ra-mo *shoulder*

анен ra-nen *injured*

аница ⓕ ra-nee-tsa *backpack*

ано ra-no *early* adv

ежа re-zhuh *cut* v

езервация ⓕ re-zer-va-tsee-ya
booking • reservation

езервирам re-zer-vee-ram
book v • *reserve*

ейв парти ⓜ reyv par-tee *rave party*

ека ⓕ re-ka *river*

есторант ⓜ res-to-rant *restaurant*

ецепта ⓕ re-tsep-ta *prescription*

ецепция ⓕ re-tsep-tsee-ya
check-in desk

чник ⓜ rech-neek *dictionary*

барски магазин ⓜ
ree-bar-skee ma-ga-zeen *fish shop*

болов ⓜ ree-bo-lov *fishing*

за ⓕ ree-za *shirt*

дители ⓜ pl ro-dee-te-lee *parents*

жден ден ⓜ rozh-den den *birthday*

зов ro-zov *pink*

к ⓜ rok *rock music*

кля ⓕ rok-lya *dress* n

мантичен ro-man-tee-chen *romantic* a

мъния ⓕ roo-muh-nee-ya *Romania*

ка ⓕ ruh-ka *arm (body)* • *hand*

кавици ⓕ pl ruh-ka-vee-tse
gloves (clothing)

чна изработка ⓕ
uhch-na eez-ra-bot-ka *handicraft*

чно изработен
uhch-no eez-ra-bo-ten *handmade*

дък rya-duhk *rare • uncommon*

фетка ⓕ sal-fet-ka *napkin*

/сама ⓜ/ⓕ sam/sa-ma *alone*

обръсначка ⓕ sa-mo-bruhs-nach-ka
azor

олет ⓜ sa-mo-let *airplane*

самолетна компания ⓕ
sa-mo-let-na kom-pa-nee-ya *airline*

сантиметър ⓜ san-tee-me-tuhr *centimetre*

сапун ⓜ sa-poon *soap*

САЩ sasht *USA*

свекър ⓜ sve-kuhr
father-in-law (husband's father)

свекърва ⓕ sve-kuhr-va
mother-in-law (husband's mother)

светлина ⓕ svet-lee-na *light* n

светломер ⓜ svet-lo-mer *light meter*

светъл sve-tuhl *light (colour)* a

свободен svo-bo-den
free (available) • *vacant*

свободни стаи ⓕ pl
svo-bod-nee sta-yee *vacancy*

свръхбагаж ⓜ svuhrh-ba-gazh
excess baggage

сгоден sgo-den *engaged (to be married)*

сграда ⓕ sgra-da *building*

север ⓜ se-ver *north* n

Северна Македония ⓕ se-ver-na
ma-ke-do-nee-ya *North Macedonia*

сега se-ga *now*

седалка ⓕ se-dal-ka *seat (chair, etc)*

седалков лифт ⓜ se-dal-kov leeft
chairlift (skiing)

седмица ⓕ sed-mee-tsa *week*

сезон ⓜ se-zon *season* n

сейф ⓜ seyf *safe* n

секс ⓜ seks *sex (intercourse)*

семейство ⓝ se-meyst-vo *family*

сенна хрема ⓕ sen-na hre-ma *hay fever*

сервитьор/сервитьорка ⓜ/ⓕ
ser-veet-yor/ser-veet-yor-ka *waiter*

сестра ⓕ ses-tra *sister*

сив seev *grey*

сиди ⓝ see-dee *CD*

сим-карта ⓕ seem-kar-ta *SIM card*

син ⓜ seen *son*

син seen *blue*

сироп за кашлица ⓜ
see-rop za kash-lee-tsa *cough medicine*

с климатик s klee-ma-teek *air-conditioned*

скоро sko-ro *soon*

скоростна кутия ⓕ
sko-rost-na koo-tee-ya *gearbox*

скулптура ⓕ skoolp-too-ra *sculpture*

скъп skuhp *expensive*

скъпоценен skuh-po-tse-nen *valuable*

сладкарница ① slad-*kar*-nee-tsa
cake shop
сладък *sla*-duhk *sweet*
след sled *after*
следващ sled-vasht *next (following)*
следобед ⑩ sle-*do*-bed *afternoon*
слушам *sloo*-sham *listen*
слънце ⑩ *sluhn*-tse *sun*
слънцезащитен крем ⑩
sluhn-tse-zash-*tee*-ten krem *sunblock*
слънчеви очила ⑩ pl
sluhn-che-vee o-chee-*la* *sunglasses*
слънчево изгаряне ⑩
sluhn-che-vo eez-*gar*-ya-ne *sunburn*
сляза/слизам *slya*-zuh/*slee*-zam
get off (train, etc)
смазочно масло ⑩ *sma*-zoch-no *mas*-lo
lubricant
сменям *smen*-yam *change (money)* v
сметка ① *smet*-ka *account · bill · check* n
смешен sme-*shen* *funny*
снимам snee-mam *take a photo*
снимка ① *sneem*-ka *photo*
сняг ⑩ snyag *snow* n
собствено име ⑩ *sobst*-ve-no *ee*-me
first name
София ① so-*fee*-ya *Sofia*
соча so-chuh *point* v
спален вагон ⑩ *spa*-len va-*gon*
sleeping car
спален чувал ⑩ *spa*-len choo-*val*
sleeping bag
спално бельо ⑩ *spal*-no bel-*yo*
linen (sheets)
спално място ⑩ *spal*-no *myas*-to *berth*
спалня ① *spal*-nya *bedroom*
спасителна жилетка ① spa-*see*-tel-na
zhee-*let*-ka *life jacket*
спешен spe-shen *urgent*
спешен случай ⑩ spe-shen *sloo*-chai
emergency
спирачки ① pl spee-*rach*-kee *brakes*
споделя/споделям spo-*del*-yuh/
spo-*del*-yam *share (a room, etc)* v
спортен магазин ⑩
spor-ten ma-ga-*zeen* *sports store*
сребро ⑩ sreb-*ro* *silver* n
стар star *old*
стачка ① *stach*-ka *strike* n
стая ① *sta*-ya *room*

стая с две легла ① *sta*-ya s dve leg-*la*
double room
стол ⑩ stol *chair*
стомах ⑩ sto-*mah* *stomach*
струвам *stroo*-vam *cost* v
студен stoo-*den* *cold* a
студент/студентка ⑩/①
stoo-*dent*/stoo-*dent*-ka *student*
стълбище ⑩ *stuhl*-beesh-te *stairway*
субтитри ⑩ pl soob-*teet*-ree *subtitles*
сувенир ⑩ soo-ve-*neer* *souvenir*
супермаркет ⑩ soo-per-*mar*-ket
supermarket
сутиен ⑩ soo-tee-*en* *bra*
сух sooh *dry* a
събрание ⑩ suh-*bra*-nee-e
small conference
събуда/събуждам suh-*bood*-yuh/
suh-*boozh*-dam *wake (someone) up*
съвременен suh-*vre*-me-nen *modern*
сън ⑩ suhn *sleep* n
съобщение ⑩ suh-ob-*shte*-nee-e
message
сърбеж ⑩ suhr-*bezh* *itch* n
Сърбия *suhr*-bee-ya *Serbia*
сърдечно заболяване ⑩ suhr-*dech*-no
za-bo-*lya*-va-ne *heart condition*
сърце ⑩ suhr-*tse* *heart*
сянка ① *syan*-ka *shade · shadow*

Т

таблетка ① tab-*let*-ka *pill*
такси ⑩ tak-*see* *taxi*
таксиметрова стоянка ①
tak-*see*-*me*-tro-va sto-*yan*-ka *taxi stan*
там tam *there*
тампон ⑩ tam-*pon* *tampon*
танц ⑩ tants *dance* n
танцувам tan-*tsoo*-vam *dance* v
танцуване ⑩ tan-*tsoo*-va-ne *dancing*
твой tvoy *your* inf sg
твърд tvuhrd *hard (not soft)*
театър ⑩ te-*a*-tuhr *theatre*
тежък *te*-zhuhk *heavy*
телевизия ① te-le-*vee*-zee-ya *televisi*
телевизор ⑩ te-le-*vee*-zor *TV (set)*
телеграма ① te-le-*gra*-ma *telegram*
телефон ⑩ te-le-*fon* *telephone* n

елефонен сигнал ⓜ
te-le-fo-nen seeg-nal dial tone

елефонен указател ⓜ
te-le-fo-nen oo-ka-za-tel phone book

елефонна кабина ⓕ
te-le-fon-na ka-bee-na phone box

емпература ⓕ tem-pe-ra-too-ra
temperature

енджера ⓕ tend-zhe-ra pot (cooking)

енис ⓜ te-nees tennis

ениска ⓕ te-nees-ka T-shirt

енискорт ⓜ te-nees-kort tennis court

етрадка ⓕ tet-rad-ka notebook

и tee you inf sg

иган ⓜ tee-gan frying pan

ирбушон ⓜ teer-boo-shon corkscrew

их teeh quiet

ъст tluhst fat a

оалетна ⓕ to-a-let-na toilet

оалетна хартия ⓕ to-a-let-na har-tee-ya
toilet paper

ой toy he

ок ⓜ tok current (electricity)

опъл to-puhl warm a

остер ⓜ tos-ter toaster

очно toch-no exactly

ока too-ka here

рибуна ⓕ tree-boo-na platform

ролейбус ⓜ tro-ley-boos trolley

ористическа класа ⓕ
too-rees-tee-ches-ka kla-sa
economy class

ористическа спалня ⓕ
too-rees-tee-ches-ka spal-nya
youth hostel

ористическо бюро ⓝ
too-rees-tee-ches-ko byoo-ro
tourist office

оция ⓕ toor-tsee-ya Turkey

мен tuh-men dark

рговия ⓕ tuhr-go-vee-ya business

рговски център ⓜ
tuhr-gov-skee tsen-tuhr shopping centre

ст ⓜ tuhst father-in-law (wife's father)

ща ⓕ tuhsh-ta
mother-in-law (wife's mother)

оворена среща ⓕ
o-go-vo-re-na sresh-ta appointment

удобен oo-do-ben comfortable

ужасен oo-zha-sen awful

уикенд ⓜ oo-ee-kend weekend

улица ⓕ oo-lee-tsa street

уличен пазар ⓜ oo-lee-chen pa-zar
street market

уличен телефон ⓜ oo-lee-chen te-le-fon
public phone

уморен oo-mo-ren tired

универсален магазин ⓜ
oo-nee-ver-sa-len ma-ga-zeen
department store

университет ⓜ oo-nee-ver-see-tet
university

уста ⓕ oos-ta mouth

утре oo-tre tomorrow

утро ⓝ oo-tro morning

ухо ⓝ oo-ho ear

учен oo-chen scientist

учител/учителка ⓜ/ⓕ
oo-chee-tel/oo-chee-tel-ka teacher

Ф

факс ⓜ faks fax

фамилно име ⓝ fa-meel-no ee-me
surname

фар ⓜ far headlight

фенерче ⓝ fe-ner-che flashlight • torch

ферибот ⓜ fe-ree-bot ferry n

филия ⓕ fee-lee-ya slice n

филм ⓜ feelm (cinema/for camera)

фонокарта ⓕ fo-no-kar-ta phonecard

фотоапарат ⓜ fo-to-a-pa-rat camera

фотограф ⓜ fo-to-graf photographer

фотография ⓕ fo-to-gra-fee-ya
photography

фризьор/фризьорка ⓜ/ⓕ
freez-yor/freez-yor-ka hairdresser

футбол ⓜ foot-bol football (soccer)

Х

харесам/харесвам
ha-re-sam/ha-res-vam like v

хартиени кърпички ⓕ pl
har-tee-e-nee kuhr-peech-kee tissues

хартия ⓕ har-tee-ya paper n

хладилник ⓜ hla-deel-neek refrigerator

хлебарница ① hle-*bar*-nee-tsa *bakery*
хотел ⑩ ho-*tel* *hotel*
храна ① hra-*na* *food*
хранителни стоки ① pl
hra-*nee*-tel-nee *sto*-kee *groceries*

Ц

цветарски магазин ⑩
tsve-*tar*-skee ma-ga-*zeen* *florist (shop)*
цвят ⑩ tsvyat *colour* n
цена ① tse-*na* *price* n
цена на билет ① tse-*na* na bee-*let* *fare*
център ⑩ *tsen*-tuhr *centre* n
центърът на града ⑩
tsen-tuh-ruht na gra-*duh* *city centre*
цигара ① tsee-*ga*-ra *cigarette*
цип ⑩ tseep *zip/zipper*
цирк ⑩ tseerk *circus*
църква ① *tsuhr*-kva *church*

Ч

чадър ⑩ cha-*duhr* *umbrella*
чаена лъжичка ①
cha-*e*-na luh-*zheech*-ka *teaspoon*
чакалня ① cha-*kal*-nya *waiting room*
чакам *cha*-kam *wait*
чанта ① *chan*-ta *bag* • *handbag*
чаршаф ⑩ char-*shaf* *bed sheet*
час ⑩ chas *hour*
часова разлика ① cha-*so*-va *raz*-lee-ka *time difference*
частен *chas*-ten *private* a
чаша ① *cha*-sha *cup* • *glass*
чек ⑩ chek *cheque (banking)*
червен cher-*ven* *red*
черен *che*-ren *black*
черно-бял cher-no-*byal* *B&W (film)*
Черно море ⑩ *cher*-no mo-*re* *Black Sea*
четка ① *chet*-ka *brush* n
четка за зъби ① *chet*-ka za *zuh*-bee *toothbrush*
чиния ① chee-*nee*-ya *plate*

число ⑩ chees-*lo* *number* n
чист cheest *clean* a
чистене ① *chees*-te-ne *cleaning*
чист памук ⑩ cheest pa-*mook* *cotton balls*
чистя *cheest*-yuh *clean* v
човек ⑩ cho-*vek* *man*
чорапи ⑩ pl cho-*ra*-pee *socks* • *stocking*
чорапогащник ⑩ cho-ra-po-*gasht*-neel *pantyhose*
чувствам choovst-*vam* *feel (emotions)*
чувство ⑩ choovst-*vo* *feeling (physical)*
чудесен choo-*de*-sen *fantastic* • *great*
чуждестранен choozh-*de*-*stra*-nen *foreign*
чуплив choop-*leev* *fragile*

Ш

шал ⑩ shal *scarf*
шапка ① *shap*-ka *hat*
шивач/шивачка ⑩/①
shee-*vach*/shee-*vach*-ka *tailor* n
шия ① *shee*-ya *neck*
шорти ① pl *shor*-tee *shorts*
шофьорска книжка ①
sho-*fyor*-ska *kneesh*-ka *drivers licence*
шумен *shoo*-men *loud* • *noisy*

Щ

щастлив shtast-*leev* *happy*
щепсел ⑩ *shtep*-sel *plug (electricity)*

Ю

юг ⑩ yoog *south* n
ютия ① yoo-*tee*-ya *iron (for clothes)* n

Я

ядене ⑩ *ya*-de-ne *dish* • *meal*
яке ⑩ *ya*-ke *jacket*
ям yam *eat*

A

abbreviations 10, 44, 56
accidents 60, 189
accommodation 69
addresses 57, 65, 66, 70, 102, 120
addressing people 113, 135, 138, 193
adjectives (grammar) 17
admission (sightseeing) 98
adverbs (grammar) 17
age 109, 110, 116
airports 53, 57
alcoholic drinks 171
allergies 180, 190, 195, 200
alphabet (Cyrillic) 10, 13
alternative treatments 202
ambulance 189
amounts 40, 176
animals 106, 161
apologising 146, 192
appointments (business) 101
arranging to meet 137
art 147
articles (grammar) 18
asking someone out 139
assault 190, 191
automated teller machine 48, 95

B

babies 107, 108, 110, 190
baggage 52, 75, 88, 191
bank accounts 104
banking 47, 95
bargaining 82
bars 134, 164, 172
basic phrases (general) 111, 163, 189
be (verb) 56
beach 56, 159
beliefs 145
bicycle 50, 62
bills (restaurant) 165, 168
blind travellers 105
boat 49, 56, 99, 156
body language 36, 40

body parts (diagram) 201
booking accommodation 70
books 83
border crossing 63
bus 49, 54, 66
business 101

C

cafés 134, 164
calendar 42
cameras 86
camping 69, 76, 158
car (diagram) 61
car (general) 58
cardinal numbers 37
cell phones 90
changing money 48, 73, 95
check (banking) 48, 95
check (restaurant) 165, 168
checking in 52, 70
checking out 75
children (discounts) 51, 98, 107
children (general) 63, 107
children (health) 109, 194, 196
children's menu 107, 166
cinema 121, 122, 124, 133, 134
civilities 111
clothes 84
coach (transport) 54
communications 89
complaints (accommodation) 74
complimenting people 103, 151, 168
computer facilities 87, 89, 102
concerts 122, 134, 135
conditions (health) 196
conferences (business) 101, 102
consonant sounds 11
contact details 102, 120
contraception 142, 199, 203
cooking utensils 178
cost (general) 47, 51, 80, 173, 194
countries 116
credit cards 47, 72, 81, 96, 191

cultural differences......................................146
currency (Bulgarian).....................................47
customs (immigration)...................................64
cycling..50, 62
Cyrillic alphabet......................................10, 13

D

dancing..................121, 122, 134, 139, 140
dates (calendar)..43
days of the week..42
deaf travellers...105
debit cards...47, 81
decimals...39
declaring items (customs).............................64
delays (transport)....................................49, 52
demonstratives (grammar)............................19
dentist...109, 193, 204
deposits..75, 77
digital photography.......................................86
diminutives (grammar)................................178
directions...65
disabled travellers......................................105
discounts.............................51, 73, 98, 107
doctor (children).....................109, 194, 196
doctor (general)...................................189, 193
doctor (women)....................................193, 198
drinks (alcoholic)..171
drinks (nonalcoholic)..................................171
drugs (illegal)...........................138, 191, 195
duty-free shopping.................................53, 64

E

eating in...175
eating out...163
email..89, 102, 120
embassies...192
emergencies......................................189, 193
English (use of)......59, 64, 83, 89, 97, 102,
............................108, 124, 166, 192, 193
entertainment................................83, 108, 121, 133
environment...131
etiquette tips............40, 78, 112, 114, 172
exhibitions...147

F

family (discounts)................................98, 107
family (general)..118
farewells.............................113, 120, 144
fauna...106, 161

feelings..127, 197
film (cinema).........121, 122, 124, 133, 134
film (photographic)..86
fines (punishment)..............................191, 192
fishing..153
flora...161
food (preparation)...............170, 175, 179
food & drink...163
football (soccer)..155
foreign exchange office.........................48, 95
formalities..111
fractions..39
future (grammar)...31
future (time)..45

G

galleries..147
gas (petrol)..59, 61
gas/petrol station...59
gay travellers..133
gender (grammar)...20
gifts...78, 110
going out..133
goodbyes................111, 112, 120, 144
grammar..15
greetings...111, 112
guarantees..81
guide dogs...105
guides......................................59, 97, 99, 153

H

hairdressing...83
have (verb)..26
health..193
helping people.....................78, 131, 189
hiking..153
hire (car & motorbike)...................................59
hire (sports equipment)......152, 154, 155
hobbies...121
holidays...45
homestays...73
hospital...193, 196
hotel...63, 69, 100
hotel room (diagram)....................................72

I

illnesses..193
immigration..64
injuries..151, 193

insurance 59, 104, 190, 195
interests 121
internet 73, 89, 102, 121, 122
interpreters 64, 102
intonation (pronunciation) 12
introductions 112
invitations 103, 134, 151

K

keys 61, 74
kinship terms 119

L

language difficulties 35
language history 9
language map 8
lawyers 192
leaving 75, 113, 120, 144
life jackets 56, 156
local drinks 172
local expressions 43, 47, 83,
.... 115, 136, 140, 143
local food 164, 166, 169, 175
lost 53, 100, 190, 191
love 143
luggage 52, 75, 88, 191

M

mail 94
making conversation 114
map (language) 8
maps 59, 62, 65, 97, 157
markets 65, 79
marriage 118, 143
meals 163, 173
measures (amounts) 40, 176
mechanic 60
medicine 192, 194, 198
meeting people 111
meetings (business) 101, 102
menu decoder 167, 181
menus 166
messages (accommodation) 73, 74
minibus 49, 50, 54
mobile phones 90
money 47, 95, 191
months 42
motorbike 58
movies 121, 122, 124, 133, 134

museums 147
music 85, 121, 122, 133

N

names (Bulgarian) 135, 162
nationalities 116
negatives (grammar) 21
nonalcoholic drinks 171
nouns (grammar) 22, 135
numbers 37

O

occupations 117
older people 98, 122
opinions 125, 128
optometrist 193
ordinal numbers 38
outdoors 157

P

paperwork (border crossing) 68
parking (car) 59, 60, 76, 191
parking (disabled) 105
parts of the body 201
party (entertainment) 134, 135
party (politics) 129
passport 63, 75, 88, 191
past (grammar) 30
past (time) 44
payment (methods of) 47, 72, 81
personal pronouns (grammar) 22, 138
petrol 59, 61
petrol station 59
pharmacist 193, 202
phones 73, 91, 102, 120, 189, 192
photography 86, 121
pick-up lines 139
place names 58
plane 53
plants 161
plurals (grammar) 25
police 189, 190
politics 129
possessives (grammar) 25
post (mail) 94
post office 94
preparing food 170, 175, 179
prepositions (grammar) 27, 192
prescriptions (medical) 192, 194, 202

present (grammar) 29
present (time) 43
pronunciation 11
proverbs 126
public transport 50

Q

quantities 40, 176
questions (grammar) 27

R

rape 190
reading (books) 83, 121, 122
receipts 47, 74, 81, 195
refunds 47, 82
rejections 140, 151
religion 145
renting (accommodation) 77
repairs (car & motorbike) 60
repairs (general) 88
reservations (accommodation) 70
restaurant 134, 135, 164, 165
robbery 53, 189, 190, 191
romance 139
room (diagram) 71
room (hotel) 72

S

safe sex .... s, 195, 199, 203
school 109, 110
script (Cyrillic) 10, 13
seasons 43
seating 49, 51, 106, 124
self-catering 175
senior travellers 98, 105
sex 142
shopping (food) 121, 122, 175
shopping (general) 79
sightseeing 97
signs 55, 59, 64, 72, 100, 158, 189
sizes (clothes) 84
skiing 154
smoking 51, 55, 138, 166, 195
soccer 155
social issues 129
souvenirs 79, 88, 94
special diets 179
sport 121, 149
staying with locals 78

street (diagram) 67
students (discounts) 51, 98
studies 117
symptoms (health) 196

T

table setting (diagram) 169
taking photos 88, 98, 115
taxi (disabled) 106
taxi (general) 57, 66, 75
telephones 73, 91, 102, 120, 189, 192
telling the time 41
thanking people 76, 78, 103, 151
theatre 108, 124, 134
theft 53, 189, 190, 191
tickets 51, 124
tipping 165
titles (addressing people) 113, 193
toasts (drinking) 172
toilets (disabled) 106
toilets (general) 51, 74, 158, 174, 190
tours 73, 99
train 49, 55, 66
transport 49
travellers cheques 47, 72, 81, 95, 19

V

vaccinations 19
valuables 73, 75, 19
vegan food 18
vegetarian food 17
verbs (grammar) 2
visas (immigration) 63, 104, 19
visiting people 7
vowel sounds 1

W

washing (clothes) 73, 7
water (drinkable) 76, 158, 15
water sports 15
weather 16
weights 40, 12
well-wishing 81, 111, 13
wheelchairs 16
women's health 19
women travellers 152, 190, 19
word order (grammar) ....
word stress (pronunciation) ....
work 101, 1

topics covered in this book are listed below in Bulgarian. If you're having trouble
erstanding Bulgarian, show this page to whoever you're talking to so they can
up the relevant section.

обусите 54	музика 85, 122
ргии 200	наемане 77
охолни напитки 171	настаняване 69
ернативна медицина 202	националности 116
аж 52	на плажа 159
алкохолни напитки 171	облекло 84
ети 51	обръщения 113
етарианска ястия 179	обществени проблеми 129
ео и фотография 86	общуване 111
кът 55	околната среда 131
мето 160	отхвърляне 140
ме и дати 41	пазарлък 82
фризьорския салон 84	пазаруване 79
раст 116	пари 47
растни пътници 105	поздрави 112
вания 145	покани 134
тпеката 202	полиция 190
анката 95	поправки 88
ара 172	пощата 94
есторанта 165	при зъболекаря 204
ничен пункт 63	при лекаря 193
ца 107	професия и образование 117
курзии 99	пътници инвалиди 105
ски здравни проблеми 198	разговор 114
ележителности 97	растения и животни 161
ознаване 140	религия 145
уство 147	самолет 53
изане 133	сбогуване 120
ереси 121	семейство 118
ендарът 42	специални диети и алергии 180
о и театър 124	спешни случаи 189
ги и четене 83	спорт 149
яло 62	такси 57
ите и мотопедите 58	телефон 91
ичества 40	транспорт 49
аб 56	туризъм 157
турни различия 146	търговия 101
уване 80	търсене на работа 103
уване на храна 175	упътване 65
мпинг 76	часът 41
бов 139	числа 37
ения 128	чувства 127

KEY PATTERNS

When's (the next bus)?	Кога тръгва (следващият автобус)?	ko·ga truhg·va (sled·vash·tee·yuht av·to·boos)
Where's (the station)?	Къде се намира (гара)?	kuh·de se na·mee·ra (ga·ra)
Where do I buy (a ticket)?	Къде мога да си купя (билет)?	kuh·de mo·guh da see koop·yuh (bee·l...)
How much is (a room)?	Колко струва (стая)?	kol·ko stroo·va (sta·ya)
I'm looking for (a hotel).	Търся (хотел).	tuhr·sya (ho·tel)
Do you have (a map)?	Имате ли (карта)?	ee·ma·te lee (kar·ta)
Is there (a toilet)?	Има ли (тоалетна)?	ee·ma lee (to·a·let·na)
I'd like (the menu), please.	Дайте ми (меню), моля	dai·te mee (me·yoo) mol·yuh
I'd like to hire (a car).	Искам да взема под наем (кола).	ees·kam da vze·muh pod na·em (ko·la)
Can I (park here)?	Мога ли да (паркирам тук)?	mo·guh lee da (par·kee·ram took)
Could you please (help)?	Моля ви/те за (помощ). pol/inf	mo·lyuh vee/te za (po·mosht)
Do I have to (pay)?	Трябва ли да (платя)?	tryab·va lee da (plat·yuh)